Why Do You Need this New Edition?

If you're wondering why you should buy this new edition of *The Curious Researcher,* here are 5 good reasons!

1. New *story of a research essay* **feature** lets you track the progress of a single student researcher all the way from brainstorming to the final essay. Follow along as Amanda Stewart, a real college student, shares the results of her own experience with many of the exercises in each chapter.

2. **A new section on Google vs. the Library** explores the practical advantages and disadvantages of electronic and print sources and helps you develop a complementary research strategy that combines the best of both.

3. **Learn to navigate cutting-edge sources**—rarely mined for academic research—like Web blogs, podcasts, and streaming video in a new section on the freshest sources available online.

4. **More sample citations** and extra guidance for using MLA and APA formats give you the tools you need to cite both traditional and the latest electronic sources with confidence.

5. **New coverage of Wikipedia** tackles tough questions about the virtues and drawbacks of the popular site scorned by some academics.

PEARSON
Longman

About the Author

Bruce Ballenger, a professor of English at Boise State University, teaches courses in composition, composition theory, the essay tradition, and creative nonfiction. He's the author of seven books, including the three texts in the Curious series: *The Curious Researcher, The Curious Reader,* and *The Curious Writer,* all from Longman Publishers. He lives with his wife and two children in Boise, Idaho.

SIXTH EDITION

The Curious Researcher

A Guide to Writing Research Papers

Bruce Ballenger
Boise State University

Longman

New York   San Francisco   Boston
London   Toronto   Sydney   Tokyo   Singapore   Madrid
Mexico City   Munich   Paris   Cape Town   Hong Kong   Montreal

For Rebecca, who reminds me to ask,
Why?

Publisher: Joseph Opiela
Executive Editor: Suzanne Phelps Chambers
Editorial Assistant: Erica Schweitzer
Senior Supplements Editor: Donna Campion
Senior Marketing Manager: Susan Stoudt
Production Manager: Eric Jorgensen
Project Coordination, Text Design, and Electronic Page Makeup:
   Elm Street Publishing Services
Cover Design Manager: John Callahan
Cover Designer: Nancy Saks
Cover Image: Michael Saul/Band X Pictures/Jupiter Images
Visual Researcher: Rona Tuccillo
Senior Manufacturing Buyer: Dennis J. Para
Printer and Binder: Edwards Brothers, Inc.
Cover Printer: Coral Graphic Services

The author and publisher are grateful to the many students who allowed their work to be reprinted here. We would also like to acknowledge the following copyright holders for permission to use their materials in this book:

p.63—Gabe Palmer/Corbis
p.145—Oliver Lassen/Zefa/Corbis
p.169—Jim Cornfield/Corbis

Library of Congress Cataloging-in-Publication Data
Ballenger, Bruce P.
   The curious researcher: a guide to writing research papers/
   Bruce Ballenger.—6th ed.
       p. cm.
   Includes index.
   ISBN 978-0-205-74526-5
       1. Report writing—Handbooks, manuals, etc.   2. Research—Handbooks, manuals, etc.   I. Title.
   LB2369.B246 2009
   808'.02—dc22

                                                                2008028929

This book includes 2009 MLA guidelines.

3 4 5 6 7 8 9 10—V069—12 11 10

Longman
is an imprint of

www.pearsonhighered.com   ISBN 13: 978-0-205-74526-5
   ISBN 10:   0-205-74526-1

Contents

Chapter 1
The First Week   27

Chapter 2
The Second Week 61

Chapter 3
The Third Week   **115**

Chapter 4
The Fourth Week   169

Chapter 5
The Fifth Week   221

Appendix B
Guide to APA Style   319

Preface

Placing Inquiry at the Heart of the Course

Several years ago, the Boyer Commission offered a national report on the state of undergraduate education in America's research universities. The report was sobering. Among other things, the commission complained that undergraduates, particularly first- and second-year students, experience a curriculum dominated by knowledge transmission—large lectures rather than seminars—and rarely get the chance to "enter a world of discovery in which they are active participants, not passive receivers." Commission members called for a "radical reconstruction" of undergraduate education. "The ecology of the university," they wrote, "depends on a deep and abiding understanding that inquiry, investigation, and discovery are the heart of the enterprise. . . . Everyone at a university should be a discoverer, a learner." The freshman year, in particular, should provide "new stimulation for intellectual growth and a firm grounding in inquiry-based learning."

The Curious Researcher answers that call. It is a sad fact that most students misunderstand formal academic research. Because it often reports conclusions—the *results* of the process of inquiry—students naturally assume that the research writer didn't engage in an act of inquiry in the first place. They assume that the academic writer always sets out *to prove* rather than *to find out,* that she scrupulously avoids ambiguity and is more concerned with answers than questions. The conventional research paper in the composition course—often students' first introduction to academic research—reinforces all of these mistaken assumptions about the nature of inquiry.

Teaching the Spirit of Inquiry

While *The Curious Researcher* features plenty of material on the conventions of research writing—citation methods, approaches to organization, evaluating sources, how to avoid plagiarism, and so on—a major emphasis of the book is introducing students to *the spirit of inquiry.* The habits of mind that good research writers develop is something we can teach that is truly multidisciplinary. That spirit is charged with curiosity, of course—the itch to know and learn and discover. But it also involves the ability to ask researchable questions, the instinct to look in the right places for answers, a willingness to suspend judgment, and an openness to changing one's mind. Embracing the spirit of inquiry must begin with the belief that one *can* be an inquirer, a knower, an active agent in making knowledge.

I think this affective dimension of critical thinking is underrated, especially when it comes to writing research papers. That's why this book promotes the research *essay,* a potentially more subjective, less formal, often more exploratory mode than the formal argumentative research paper. The research essay is, I think, a much better *introduction* to research and research writing and excellent preparation for more conventional academic research because it places the writer in the center of the discourse. As a result, he cannot avoid his role as the main agent of the inquiry nor can he escape the question of his own authority in the conversation about what might be true. When it's a good experience, the writer of the research essay often adopts a new identity as a *knower.*

I am often amazed at what students do with this new freedom. I believe little is lost in not prescribing a formal research paper, particularly in an introductory composition course. As students move on from here to their declared majors, they will learn the scholarly conventions of their disciplines from those best equipped to teach them. In the meantime, students will master valuable library skills and learn many of the technical elements of the research paper, such as citation methods and evaluating sources. But most important, students will discover, often for the first time, what college research is really about: *using the ideas of others to shape ideas of their own.*

Ways of Using This Book

Since procrastination ails many student researchers, this book is uniquely designed to move them through the research process, step-by-step and week-by-week, for five weeks, the typical period allotted for the assignment. The structure of the book is flexible, however; students should be encouraged to compress the sequence if their research assignment will take less time or ignore it altogether and use the book to help them solve specific problems as they arise.

Students who follow the five-week sequence usually find that they like the way *The Curious Researcher* doesn't deluge them with information, as do so many other research paper texts. Instead, *The Curious Researcher* doles information out week-by-week, when it is most needed.

The Introduction, "Rethinking the Research Paper," challenges students to reconceive the research paper assignment. For many of them, this will amount to a "declaration of independence." During "The First Week," students are encouraged to discover topics they're genuinely curious about and to learn to develop a "working knowledge" of their topics through library and Web research. This working knowledge will guide them as they decide on a tentative focus for their investigations. In "The Second Week," students develop a research strategy, hone their skills in evaluating sources, and then begin working to develop a "focused knowledge" of their topics by systematically searching for information in the library and on the Web. In "The Third Week," students learn notetaking techniques, the dangers of plagiarism, and tips on how to conduct a search that challenges them to dig more deeply for information. During "The Fourth Week," students begin writing their drafts; this chapter also gives tips on integrating sources, structure, voice, and beginnings. In "The Fifth Week," students are guided through the final revision.

In this edition of *The Curious Researcher,* the details about citation conventions and formats for both the Modern Language Association (MLA) and the American Psychological Association (APA) are in Appendixes A and B, respectively. This organization makes the information easier for students to find and use. Sample student papers—one in MLA format and one in APA format—are included as well.

Unlike other textbooks, which relegate exercises to the ends of chapters, *The Curious Researcher* makes them integral to the process of researching and writing the paper. Though techniques such as fastwriting and brainstorming—featured in some of the writing exercises—are now commonplace in many composition classes, they have rarely been applied to research writing and certainly not as extensively as they have been here. Fastwriting is an especially useful tool, not just for prewriting but for open-ended thinking throughout the process of researching and writing the paper. The exercises are also another antidote to procrastination, challenging students to stay involved in the process as well as providing instructors with a number of short assignments throughout the five weeks that will help them monitor students' progress.

Features of the New Edition

Writing a textbook is like discovering an aunt you never knew you had. She arrives unexpectedly one summer and stands at your door beaming and expectant. Naturally, you welcome her in. How charming she is, and as you get to know your aunt you get to know yourself. This is her gift to you. At some point, many months later, you see her luggage by the door, and with a certain sadness you send her off. "Come again," you yell as she ambles off. "Come again any-time. I'll miss you!" And you do. Your fondness for this newly discovered relative grows as you learn that others, people who aren't even blood related, like her too.

Two years later, your aunt appears at your door again, and of course you're glad to see her. She inhabits your house for the summer, and, while she does get a bit demanding, that doesn't diminish your fondness for the old girl, at least not much. You've grown to know her well, and while familiarity doesn't breed contempt you do develop a slight weariness. You've heard all the same stories a few times, and her voice, well, her voice can get a bit irritating at times. This time when she leaves you confess that you're just a little bit relieved, happy to move on to other things.

But, bless her heart, your aunt has got something of a following and this has given her a new lease on life. It also seems she got a lease on *your* life, and once more she appears one summer day at the door expecting to stay until September or October. You do love her, but you wish she wouldn't visit so often, and though her stay is often pleasant, you feel compelled to remind her that she's getting older and maybe a bit out of fashion. You do what you can to remake her into someone you don't mind spending the summer with.

This sixth time around, I think I've made substantial improvements in *The Curious Researcher* that make it current with the latest advances in information literacy, more streamlined, and more relevant to the actual practices of student writers. Here are a few of the highlights of the sixth edition:

- *Google vs. the library.* Not so long ago, students really needed to walk through the doors of the university library to write academic papers. Now, with the explosion of online databases, full-text documents, Google Scholar, and digital texts, most students are quite confident that they don't have to leave their rooms to get the work done. Is the library irrelevant? Hardly. But in this edition of *The Curious Researcher* I take time to explore the practical advantages and disadvantages of online research and research at the library. More than ever, a complementary research strategy, one that combines the best of both, will strengthen student work.

■ *New sources for information.* One of the exciting developments since the last edition is the growth of Web blogs, podcasts, streaming video, and other sources of information that, until recently, were rarely mined for academic research. The sixth edition provides a fresh look at what new sources are available online.

■ *Expanded treatment of citations.* Along with discussion of new electronic sources is more guidance on how to cite them using both MLA and APA formats. I've also increased the number of sample citations to provide more comprehensive coverage.

■ *The story of a research essay.* For the first time, *The Curious Researcher* follows the progress of a single student researcher, Amanda Stewart, from the beginning of her project to the end. In each chapter, she shares the results of her own experience with many of the exercises, a process that culminates with her final essay, the featured MLA student paper in Appendix A.

■ *What about Wikipedia?* Viewed with scorn by some academics, the free online encyclopedia Wikipedia is a student favorite. The sixth edition tackles questions about the virtues and drawbacks of the popular site.

■ *The NEW MyCompLab website.* The new MyCompLab integrates the market-leading instruction, multimedia tutorials, and exercises for writing, grammar and research that users have come to identify with the program with a new online composing space and new assessment tools. The result is a revolutionary application that offers a seamless and flexible teaching and learning environment built specifically for writers. Created after years of extensive research and in partnership with composition faculty and students across the country, the new MyCompLab provides help for writers in the context of their writing, with instructor and peer commenting functionality, proven tutorials and exercises for writing, grammar and research, an e-portfolio, an assignmentbuilder, a bibliography tool, tutoring services, and a gradebook and course management organization created specifically for writing classes. Visit www.mycomplab.com for more information.

A few weeks ago, I fell off of a ladder and broke my wrist. This was the second time in three years I've done this. This time, when I hit the concrete and noticed that my right wrist was contorted, my first thought was that I wouldn't play the guitar again. My second thought was that I wouldn't be able to type and meet the deadline for this revision of *The Curious Researcher*. My third thought was ouch. That thought pretty much stayed with me for the next few days.

Finally, it settled in that I was a very lucky man. I hadn't fallen on my head, my wife Karen was a tremendous comfort, my friends rallied, and somehow I would find a way to get the writing done. I was lucky, too, that before that ladder collapsed beneath me I had asked one of my former students, Amanda Stewart, to help me with this new edition. This bright young woman was a huge help, offering feedback on the manuscript from a student's perspective, doing the exercises in the book and sharing her journal work, researching new online information sources, and writing an essay that is featured in the back of the book as a memorable example of what a curious researcher can do.

It also helped that I had an understanding editor at Pearson/Longman, Suzanne Phelps Chambers, who never asked me after I took that spill when I'd be able to send more manuscript, though that must have been on her mind. Her subsequent attention to this book, and the attention of her assistant Erica Schweitzer, made things go much more smoothly as I began typing first with one hand, and then, awkwardly, with both. Suzanne is a new editor for me, and I look forward to working with her on other projects without the handicap of broken bones. Suzanne's colleague and my former editor, Joseph Opiela, is a lion in the field of educational publishing, and I'm grateful that he took a chance on a young writer who wanted to write a different kind of composition textbook.

The Curious Researcher began in 1991 when I began to feel that the conventional research paper, a fixture in most composition courses, was largely a failed assignment. Students hated it, and while instructors thought that teaching research was an important obligation, many dreaded the assignment, too. Professor Thomas Newkirk, a colleague at the University of New Hampshire, encouraged me to re-imagine instruction in college research, and it was largely his encouragement that led to this text's first edition. Since then, I've collaborated with legions of colleagues and students on how this book evolved, and they have helped me make it better. I'd like to mention a few.

Dr. Michelle Payne is a colleague who has been an inspiration and help to me for decades on this book and others. She has had a tremendous impact on helping me understand rhetoric, argument, and writing pedagogy. Barry Lane, now an internationally known consultant and teacher to teachers, was once my office mate at University of New Hampshire, and over the years his enthusiastic support of my approach in *The Curious Researcher* motivated me to return to the book again and again. Dr. Brock Dethier, Utah State University, is also a long-time friend and intellectual companion who has always challenged me to think more deeply even as my lungs burn while trying to keep up with him on hikes up Northern Rockies peaks. Finally, Dr. Deborah Coxwell-Teague, Florida State University, has been an unflagging supporter of the book and offered advice from her experience using the text with the hundred or so teaching assistants she leads in their program every year.

My students are always the most important reason I keep returning to *The Curious Researcher*. Since the book first appeared in 1994, I've benefited from the writing, experience, advice, and enthusiasm of students who have been willing to give this approach a try. I still see their faces when I rewrite this text, including those who were in my classes 25 years ago. The success of this book has much to do with them. When I open any page of *The Curious Researcher* these students flutter out, like feathers pressed between its pages that were left there long ago, as reminders of my debt to them.

I would like to thank those individuals who have reviewed my book. Reviewers for the fifth edition included the following: Patricia P. Buckler–Purdue University North Central; Deborah Coxwell Teague–Florida State University; Chris Frick–Colorado College; Don Jones–University of Hartford; Nadene Keene–Indiana University Kokomo; Jennifer Morrison–Niagara University; and Lois Sampson–Cowley College. I would also like to extend my thanks to the reviewers of this edition: Marilyn Annucci–University of Wisconsin-Whitewater; Garnet Branch–University of Louisiana at Lafayette; George Clark–University of Southern Mississippi; Denise Coulter–Atlantic Cape Community College; Deborah Coxwell Teague–Florida State University; Tamara Harvey–George Mason University; Lisa R. Neilson–Marist College; Paula Priamos–California State University, San Bernardino; and Amy Randolph–Waynesburg University.

And finally, I am most indebted to my wife, Karen Kelley, who in the beginning helped me see this project through during a difficult time in our lives.

BRUCE BALLENGER

Rethinking the Research Paper

Unlike most textbooks, this one begins with your writing, not mine. Find a fresh page in your notebook, grab a pen, and spend ten minutes doing the following exercise.

EXERCISE 1

Collecting Golf Balls on Driving Ranges and Other Reflections

Most of us were taught to think before we write, to have it all figured out in our heads before we pick up our pens. This exercise asks you to think *through* writing rather than *before,* letting the words on the page lead you to what you want to say. With practice, that's surprisingly easy using a technique called *fastwriting.* Basically, you just write down whatever comes into your head, not worrying about whether you're being eloquent, grammatical, or even very smart. It's remarkably like talking to a good friend, not trying to be brilliant and even blithering a bit, but along the way discovering what you think. If the writing stalls, write about that, or write about what you've already written until you find a new trail to follow. Just keep your pen moving.

STEP 1: Following is a series of sixteen statements about the research paper assignment. Check the five statements you think most students believe about the assignment. Then, in your notebook, write fast for five minutes about whether you think the statements you checked are true. Speculate about where these ideas about research papers come from and why they might make sense. If you disagree with any of the statements you checked, explore why wrongheaded ideas about the assignment have endured. Whenever you feel moved to do so, tell a story.

- It's okay to say things the instructor might disagree with.
- You need to follow a formal structure.
- You have to know your thesis before you start.
- You have to be objective.
- You can't use the pronoun *I*.
- You can use your own experiences and observations as evidence.
- The information should come mostly from books.
- You have to say something original.
- You're always supposed to make an argument.
- You can use your own writing voice.
- Summarizing what's known about the topic is most important.
- You're writing mostly for the instructor.
- You're supposed to use your own opinions.
- The paper won't be revised substantially.
- Form matters more than content.

STEP 2: Now, consider the truth of some other statements, listed below. These statements have less to do with research papers than with how you see facts, information, and knowledge and how they're created. Choose one of these statements* to launch a five-minute fastwrite. Don't worry if you end up thinking about more than one statement in your writing. Start by writing about whether you agree or disagree with the statement, and then explore why. Continually look for concrete connections between what you think about these statements and what you've seen or experienced in your own life.

There is a big difference between facts and opinions.

Pretty much everything you read in textbooks is true.

People are entitled to their own opinions, and no one opinion is better than another.

There's a big difference between a *fact* in the sciences and a *fact* in the humanities.

When two experts disagree, one of them has to be wrong.

No matter how difficult they are, most problems have one solution that is better than the others.

---

*Source for part of this list is Marlene Schommer, "Effects of Beliefs about the Nature of Knowledge," *Journal of Educational Psychology* 82 (1990): 498–504.

Very few of us recall the research papers we wrote in high school, and if we do, what we remember is not what we learned about our topics but what a bad experience writing them was. Joe was an exception. "I remember one assignment was to write a research paper on a problem in the world, such as acid rain, and then come up with your own solutions and discuss moral and ethical aspects of your solution, as well. It involved not just research but creativity and problem solving and other stuff."

For the life of me, I can't recall a single research paper I wrote in high school, but like Joe, I remember the one that I finally enjoyed doing a few years later in college. It was a paper on the whaling industry, and what I remember best was the introduction. I spent a lot of time on it, describing in great detail exactly what it was like to stand at the bow of a Japanese whaler, straddling an explosive harpoon gun, taking aim, and blowing a bloody hole in a humpback whale.

I obviously felt pretty strongly about the topic.

Unfortunately, many students feel most strongly about getting their research papers over with. So it's not surprising that when I tell my Freshman English students that one of their writing assignments will be an eight- to ten-page research paper, there is a collective sigh. They knew it was coming. For years, their high school teachers prepared them for the College Research Paper, and it loomed ahead of them as one of the torturous things you must do, a five-week sentence of hard labor in the library, or countless hours adrift in the Internet. Not surprisingly, students' eyes roll in disbelief when I add that many of them will end up liking their research papers better than anything they've written before.

I can understand why Joe was among the few in the class inclined to believe me. For many students, the library is an alien place, a wilderness to get lost in, a place to go only when forced. Others carry memories of research paper assignments that mostly involved taking copious notes on index cards, only to transfer pieces of information into the paper, sewn together like patches of a quilt. There seemed little purpose to it. "You weren't expected to learn anything about yourself with the high school research paper," wrote Jenn, now a college freshman. "The best ones seemed to be those with the most information. I always tried to find the most sources, as if somehow that would automatically make my paper better than the rest." For Jenn and others like her, research was a mechanical process and the researcher a lot like those machines that collect golf balls at driving ranges. You venture out to pick up information here and there, and then deposit it between the title page and the bibliography for your teacher to take a whack at.

Learning and Unlearning

I have been playing the guitar ever since the Beatles' 1964 American tour. In those days, *everyone* had a guitar and played in a group. Unfortunately, I never took guitar lessons and have learned in recent years that I have much "unlearning" to do. Not long ago, I finally unlearned how to do something as simple as tying my strings to the tuning keys. I'd been doing it wrong (thinking I was doing it right) for about forty years.

Recent theories suggest that people who have developed a great deal of prior knowledge about a subject learn more about it when they reexamine the truth of those beliefs, many of which may no longer be valid or may simply be misconceptions. The research paper, perhaps more than any other school assignment, is laden with largely unexamined assumptions and beliefs. Perhaps some of the statements in the first part of Exercise 1 got you thinking about any assumptions you might have about writing academic research papers. Maybe you had a discussion in class about it. You may be interested to know that I presented that same list of statements to 250 first-year writing students, and the statements are listed in the order they were most often checked by students. In that case, however, students checked the statements they *agreed* with. For example, 85 percent of the students surveyed agreed that "it's okay to say things the instructor might disagree with," something I find encouraging. However, 60 percent believed that they had to know their thesis before they began their papers, an attitude that implies discovery is not the point of research.

The second part of Exercise 1 might have got you thinking about some beliefs and attitudes you haven't thought much about— what a "fact" is, the nature and value of "opinions," and how you view experts and authorities.

I hope that these beliefs about the assignment you are about to undertake and your perspectives on how knowledge is made and evaluated are views that you return to again and again as you work through this book. You may find that some of your existing beliefs are further reinforced, but I'd wager that you might find *you* have some unlearning to do, too.

Using This Book

The Exercises

Throughout *The Curious Researcher,* you'll be asked to do exercises that either help you prepare your research paper or actually help you write it. You'll need a research notebook in which you'll do the exercises and perhaps compile your notes for the paper. Any notebook will do, as long as there are sufficient pages and left margins. Your instructor may ask you to hand in the work you do in response to the exercises, so it might be useful to use a notebook with detachable pages.

Several of the exercises in this book ask that you use techniques such as fastwriting and brainstorming. This chapter began with one, so you've already had a little practice with the two methods. Both fastwriting and brainstorming ask that you suspend judgment until you see what you come up with. That's pretty hard for most of us because we are so quick to criticize ourselves, particularly about writing. But if you can learn to get comfortable with the sloppiness that comes with writing almost as fast as you think, not bothering about grammar or punctuation, then you will be rewarded with a new way to think, letting your own words lead you in sometimes surprising directions. Though these so-called creative techniques seem to have little to do with the serious business of research writing, they can actually be an enormous help throughout the process. Try to ignore that voice in your head that wants to convince you that you're wasting your time using fastwriting or brainstorming. When you do, they'll start to work for you.

The Five-Week Plan

But more about creative techniques later. You have a research paper assignment to do. If you're excited about writing a research paper, that's great. You probably already know that it can be interesting work. But if you're dreading the work ahead of you, then your instinct might be to procrastinate, to put it off until the week it's due. That would be a mistake, of course. If you try to rush through the research and the writing, you're absolutely guaranteed to hate the experience and add this assignment to the many research papers in the garbage dump of your memory. It's also much more likely that the paper won't be very good. Because procrastination is the enemy, this book was designed to help you budget your time and move through the research and writing process in five weeks. (See the box, "Steps to Writing Your Research Essay.") It may take you a little longer, or you may be able to finish your paper a little more quickly. But at least initially, use the book sequentially, unless your instructor gives you other advice.

This book can also be used as a reference to solve problems as they arise. For example, suppose you're having a hard time finding enough information on your topic or you want to know how to plan for an interview. Use the Table of Contents by Subject

Steps to Writing Your Research Essay

Week One

- Discover your subject
- Develop "working knowledge" of your subject
- Narrow your subject by finding your focusing question

Week Two

- Plan a research strategy that balances library and Internet sources
- Fine-tune search terms
- Begin developing "focused knowledge" of your subject
- Plan interviews or surveys

Week Three

- Write about your find
- Try advanced searching techniques
- Conduct interviews and surveys

Week Four

- Write the first draft

Week Five

- Clarify your purpose, and hone your thesis
- Revise draft
- Edit, proofread, and finalize citations

as a key to typical problems and where in the book you can find some practical help with them.

Alternatives to the Five-Week Plan

Though *The Curious Researcher* is structured by weeks, you can easily ignore that plan and use the book to solve problems as they arise. The Contents by Subject in the front of the text is keyed to a range of typical problems that arise for researchers: how to find a topic, how to focus a paper, how to handle a thesis, how to search the Internet, how to organize the material, how to take useful notes, and so on. The overviews of Modern Language Association (MLA) and American Psychological Association (APA) research paper conventions in Appendixes A and B, respectively, provide complete guides to both formats and make it easier to find answers to your specific technical questions at any point in the process of writing your paper.

The Research Paper and the Research Report

In high school, I wrote a research "paper" on existentialism for my philosophy class. I understood the task as skimming a book or two on the topic, reading the entry on "existentialism" in the *Encyclopaedia Britannica,* making some note cards, and writing down everything I learned. That took about six pages. Was I expressing an opinion of some kind about existentialism? Not really. Did I organize the information with some idea about existentialism I wanted to relay to readers? Nope. Was I motivated by a question about that philosophy I hoped to explore? Certainly not. What I wrote was a research *report,* and that is a quite different assignment than most any research paper you'll be asked to write in college.

Discovering Your Purpose

For the paper you're about to write, the information you collect must be used much more *purposefully* than simply reporting what's known about a particular topic. Most likely, you will define what that purpose is. For example, you may end up writing a paper whose purpose is to argue a point—say, eating meat is morally suspect because of the way stock animals are treated at slaughterhouses. Or your paper's purpose may be to reveal some less-known or surprising aspect of a topic—say, how the common housefly's eating habits are not unlike our own. Or your paper may set out to explore a thesis, or idea, that you have about your topic—for example, your topic is the cultural differences between men and women, and you suspect the way girls and boys play as children reflects the social differences evident between the genders in adults.

Whatever the purpose of your paper turns out to be, the process usually begins with something you've wondered about, some itchy question about an aspect of the world you'd love to know the answer to. It's the writer's curiosity—not the teacher's—that is at the heart of the college research paper.

In some ways, frankly, *research reports* are easier. You just go out and collect as much stuff as you can, write it down, organize it, and write it down again in the paper. Your job is largely mechanical and often deadening. In the *research paper,* you take a much more active role in *shaping and being shaped by* the information you encounter. That's harder because you must evaluate, judge, interpret, and analyze. But it's also much more satisfying because what you end up with says something about who you are and how you see things.

Where Did the Research Paper Come From?

Do you want to know whom to blame or whom to thank? The undergraduate assignment first arose in the first decade of the 20th century, a development related to two things: the rapid growth of the size of university library collections and the transformation of American colleges into places that privileged research rather than cultivating character and eloquence.

It's hard to underestimate this revolution in the goal of American universities. Until after the Civil War, going to college meant preparing for a "gentlemanly" profession like religion or law, and the purpose of college was to make sure that graduates were well-spoken, well-read, and virtuous. In just a few decades, this goal was abandoned in favor of the idea that universities should advance human knowledge.

Documented research papers were the method for accomplishing this new mission. Professors wrote research papers, and then, naturally, they assigned them to their graduate students. As graduate students assumed undergraduate teaching roles, they started to assign research papers to their students.

The very first research papers were often called "source themes," expository essays that were casually written rather than formal. By the 1920s, however, the research paper hardened into a relatively rigid form—one that owed its existence less to genuine inquiry than to the worship of the qualities of scientific method: objectivity, impersonality, originality, and documentation. Most research paper assignments today are still captive to this history. They seem to focus more on formal requirements than to the larger purpose of the endeavor: discovery.

How Formal Should It Be?

When I got a research paper assignment, it often felt as if I were being asked to change out of blue jeans and a wrinkled Oxford shirt and get into a stiff tuxedo. Tuxedos have their place, such as at the junior prom or the Grammy Awards, but they're just not me. When I first started writing research papers, I used to think that I *had* to be formal, that I needed to use big words like *myriad* and *ameliorate* and to use the pronoun *one* instead of *I*. I thought the paper absolutely needed to have an introduction, body, and conclusion—say what I was going to say, say it, and say what I said. It's no wonder that the first college research paper I had to write— on Plato's *Republic* for another philosophy class—seemed to me as though it were written by someone else. I felt at arm's length from the topic I was writing about.

You may be relieved to know that not all research papers are necessarily rigidly formal or dispassionate. Some are. Research papers in the sciences, for example, often have very formal structures, and the writer seems more a reporter of results than someone who is passionately engaged in making sense of them. This *formal stance* puts the emphasis where it belongs: on the validity of the data in proving or disproving something, rather than on the writer's individual way of seeing something. Some papers in the social sciences, particularly scholarly papers, take a similarly formal stance, where the writer not only seems invisible but also seems to have little relation to the subject. There are many reasons for this approach. One is that *objectivity*—or as one philosopher put it, "the separation of the perceiver from the thing perceived"—is traditionally a highly valued principle among some scholars and researchers. For example, if I'm writing a paper on the effectiveness of Alcoholics Anonymous (AA), and I confess that my father—who attended AA—drank himself to death, can I be trusted to see things clearly?

Yes, *if* my investigation of the topic seems thorough, balanced, and informative. And I think it may be an even better paper because my passion for the topic will encourage me to look at it more closely. However, many scholars these days are openly skeptical about claims of objectivity. Is it really possible to separate the perceiver from the thing perceived? If nothing else, aren't our accounts of reality always mediated by the words we use to describe it? Can language ever be objective? Though the apparent impersonality of their papers may suggest otherwise, most scholars are not nearly as dispassionate about their topics as they seem. They are driven by the same thing that will send you to the library or the Web over the next few weeks—their own curiosity—and most recognize that good research often involves both objectivity and subjectivity. As the son of an alcoholic, I am motivated to explore my own perceptions of his experience in AA, yet I recognize the need to verify those against the perceptions of others with perhaps more knowledge.

When "Bad" Writing Is Good

You might find it tempting to simply dismiss formal academic writing as "bad" writing, particularly after writing the less formal research essay. But that would be a mistake. Some academic writing only *seems* bad to you because you're not familiar with its conventions—the typical moves writers in that discipline make—nor are you aware of the ongoing conversation in that field to which a particular academic article contributes. It's a little like stumbling into the electricians' convention at the Hyatt while they're discussing new regulations on properly grounding outlets. Unless you're an electrician, not a whole lot will make sense to you.

In a way, *The Curious Researcher* represents an apprenticeship in academic writing much like an apprenticeship to a master electrician. Among other things, you'll learn how to ground an outlet—learn some of the technical moves academic writers use, such as citation, incorporating source material, and using indexes—but even more important I hope you'll learn to *think* like an academic writer. Ironically, I think this is easier to practice by not necessarily writing formal academic research papers because they so often *conceal* the open-ended, even messy, process of inquiry. Less formal exploratory essays seem to make the process of inquiry more apparent.

Thinking Like an Academic Writer

What does it mean to *think* like an academic writer? Quite a few different things, of course, some of which vary from discipline to discipline. But there are a few habits of mind or perspectives that I think often shape academic inquiry no matter what the field.

1. Inquiry, especially initially, is driven by questions, not answers.
2. It is normal and often necessary to suspend judgment and to tolerate ambiguity.
3. New knowledge or perspectives are made through the back and forth of conversation in which the writer assumes at least two seemingly contrary roles: believer and doubter, generator and judge.

4. Writers take responsibility for their ideas, accepting both the credit for and the consequences of putting forth those ideas for dialogue and debate.

Your instructor may want you to write a formal research paper. You should determine if a formal paper is required when you get the assignment. (See the box, "Questions to Ask Your Instructor about the Research Assignment.") Also make sure that you understand what the word *formal* means. Your instructor may have a specific format you should follow or tone you should keep. But more likely, she is much more interested in your writing a paper that reflects some original thinking on your part and that is also lively and interesting to read. Though this book will help you write a formal research paper, it encourages what might be called a *research essay,* a paper that does not have a prescribed form though it is as carefully researched and documented as a more formal paper.

"Essaying" or Arguing?

Essay is a term that is used so widely to describe school writing that it often doesn't seem to carry much particular meaning. But I have something particular in mind.

The term *essai* was coined by Michel Montaigne, a sixteenth-century Frenchman; in French, it means "to attempt" or "to try." For Montaigne and the essayists who follow his tradition, the essay is less an opportunity *to prove* something than an attempt *to find out.* An essay is often exploratory rather than argumentative, testing the truth of an idea or attempting to discover what might be true. (Montaigne even once had coins minted that said *Que sais-je?*—"What do I know?") The essay is often openly subjective and frequently takes a conversational, even intimate, form.

Now, this probably sounds nothing like any research paper you've ever written. Certainly, the dominant mode of the academic research paper is impersonal and argumentative. But if you consider writing a *research essay* instead of the usual *research paper,* four things might happen:

1. *You'll discover your choice of possible topics suddenly expands.* If you're not limited to arguing a position on a topic, then you can explore any topic that you find puzzling in interesting ways and you can risk asking questions that might complicate your point of view.

Questions to Ask Your Instructor About the Research Assignment

It's easy to make assumptions about what your instructor expects for the research paper assignment. After all, you've probably written such a paper before and may have had the sense that the "rules" for doing so were handed down from above. Unfortunately, those assumptions may get in the way of writing a good paper, and sometimes they're dead wrong. If you got a handout describing the assignment, it may answer the questions below, but if not, make sure you raise them with your instructor when he gives the assignment.

- How would you describe the audience for this paper?
- Do you expect the paper to be in a particular form or organized in a special way? Or can I develop a form that suits the purpose of my paper?
- Do you have guidelines about format (margins, title page, outline, bibliography, citation method, etc.)?
- Can I use other visual devices (illustrations, subheadings, bulleted lists, etc.) to make my paper more readable?
- Can I use the pronoun *I* when appropriate?
- Can my own observations or experiences be included in the paper if relevant?
- Can I include people I interview as sources in my paper? Would you encourage me to use "live" sources as well as published ones?
- Should the paper *sound* a certain way (have a particular tone), or am I free to use a writing voice that suits my subject and purpose?

2. *You'll find that you'll approach your topics differently.* You'll be more open to conflicting points of view and perhaps more willing to change your mind about what you think. As one of my students once told me, this is a more honest kind of objectivity.
3. *You'll see a stronger connection between this assignment and the writing you've done all semester.* Research is something all writers do, not a separate activity or genre that exists only upon demand. You may discover that research can be a revision strategy for improving essays you wrote earlier in the semester.

4. *You'll find that you can't hide.* The research report often encourages the writer to play a passive role; the research essay doesn't easily tolerate passivity. You'll probably find this both liberating and frustrating. While you may likely welcome the chance to incorporate your opinions, you may find it difficult to add your voice to those of your sources.

You may very well choose to write a paper that argues a point for this assignment (and, by the way, even an essay has a point). After all, the argumentative paper is the most familiar form of the academic research paper. In fact, a sample research paper that uses argument is featured in Appendix B. It's an interesting, well-researched piece in which the writer registers a strong and lively presence. But I hope you might also consider essaying your topic, an approach that encourages a kind of inquiry that may transform your attitudes about what it means to write research.

The Research Essay and Academic Writing

"If I'm going to have to write formal research papers in my other classes, why should I waste my time writing an informal research essay?" That's a fair question. In fact, the research essay you're about to write *is* different in some ways from the more formal academic scholarship you may be reading as you research your topic (see Figure 1, "Research Essays vs. Research Papers"). And it's also a bit different from research papers you may write in other classes. But the *methods of thought*, what I call the "habits of mind" behind academic inquiry, are fundamentally the same when writing the research essay and the formal research paper.

Because the research essay makes visible what is often invisible in formal academic writing—the process of coming to know what you've discovered about your topic—it's a great introduction to what academic research is all about. And because it removes what is often an artifice of objectivity in research papers, the research essay is like a hound flushing a grouse from the brush—writers can't hide under the cover of invisible authorship, concealing themselves in the safety of "one wonders" or "this paper will argue." *Writers* wonder and argue. *Your* questions, analysis, or assertions take center stage in the research essay as they do just as fundamentally, though less explicitly, in formal academic research. The research essay is good practice for this essential element of all academic inquiry: what you think and how you came to think it.

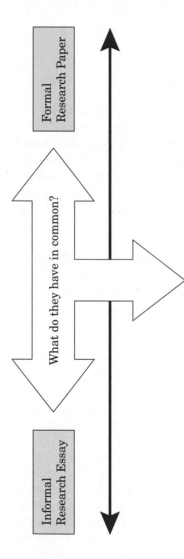

Informal Research Essay

- Often explicitly subjective, using the first person
- Exploratory
- Written for an audience of nonexperts on the topic
- Few rules of evidence
- Thesis may be delayed rather than stated in introduction
- Writer may express tentativeness about conclusions
- Structure determined by purpose and subject
- *Process* of coming to know often included

What do they have in common?

- Motive is to answer a question or solve a problem
- Establish context of what has already been said about the question or problem
- Doubt and ambiguity natural part of process
- Have a thesis or tentative claim
- Use evidence/information to explore or prove claim

Formal Research Paper

- Often avoids the first person
- Argumentative
- Written for other experts on the topic
- Established rules of evidence
- Thesis often stated in introduction
- Conclusions stated authoritatively
- Form usually prescribed
- Story of *how* conclusions were reached limited to methods

FIGURE 1 Research Essays vs. Research Papers

14

Becoming an Authority by Using Authorities

Whether formal or less so, all research papers attempt to be *authoritative*. That is, they rely heavily on a variety of credible sources beyond the writer who helped shape the writer's point of view. Those sources are mostly already published material, but they can also be other people, usually experts in relevant fields whom you interview for their perspectives. Don't underestimate the value of "live" and other nonlibrary sources. Authorities don't just live in books. One might live in the office next door to your class or be easily accessible through the Internet.

Though in research papers the emphasis is on using credible outside sources, that doesn't mean that your own experiences or observations should necessarily be excluded from your paper when they're relevant. In fact, in some papers, they are essential. For example, if you decide to write a paper on Alice Walker's novel *The Color Purple,* your own reading of the book—what strikes you as important—should be at the heart of your essay. Information from literary critics you discover in your research will help you develop and support the assertions you're making about the novel. That support from people who are considered experts—that is, scholars, researchers, critics, and practitioners in the field you're researching—will rub off on you, making your assertions more convincing, or authoritative.

Reading and talking to these people will also change your thinking, which is part of the fun of research. You will actually learn something, rather than remain locked into preconceived notions.

"It's Just My Opinion"

In the end, *you* will become an authority of sorts. I know that's hard to believe. One of the things my students often complain about is their struggle to put their opinions in their papers: "I've got all these facts, and sometimes I don't know what to say other than whether I disagree or agree with them." What these students often *seem* to say is that they don't really trust their own authority enough to do much more than state briefly what they feel: "Facts are facts. How can you argue with them?"

Step 2 of Exercise 1 that began this chapter may have started you thinking about these questions. I hope the research assignment you are about to start keeps you thinking about your beliefs about the nature of knowledge. Are facts unassailable? Or are they simply claims that can be evaluated like any others? Is the struggle to evaluate conflicting

claims an obstacle to doing research, or the point of it? Are experts supposed to know all the answers? What makes one opinion more valid
than another? What makes *your* opinion valid?

I hope you write a great essay in the next five or so weeks. But
I also hope that the process you follow in doing so inspires you to
reflect on how you—and perhaps all of us—come to know what
seems to be true. I hope you find yourself doing something you may
not have done much before: thinking about thinking.

Facts Don't Kill

You probably think the words *research paper* and *interesting*
are mutually exclusive. A prevalent belief among my students is that
the minute you start having to use facts in your writing, then the
prose wilts and dies like an unwatered begonia. It's an understandable attitude. There are many examples of dry and wooden informa-
tional writing, and among them, unfortunately, may be some
textbooks you are asked to read for other classes.

But factual writing doesn't have to be dull. You may not consider
the article "The Bothersome Beauty of Pigeons" (see the following
exercise) a research paper. It may be unlike any research paper you've
imagined. While the piece includes citations and a bibliography—two
features of most research papers—it reads more like a personal essay,
with narrative strands, personal experiences and observations, and a
personal voice. "The Bothersome Beauty of Pigeons" is an essay like
those I encourage you to write—it grows from an experience I had
while traveling in Italy that quickly became a research project on
pigeons. I knew little about them except that a pair insisted on roosting under the eaves of my Boise, Idaho, home, clucking and cooing at
all hours and splattering the bedroom window with droppings. I was
not amused. When in Italy I felt a bit differently about pigeons as
I watched them sweep in and out of the piazzas in great flocks, feeding
at the feet of tourists.

The essay you are about to read explores my ambivalence about
the birds, a question that naturally led me to research their habits
and behaviors, methods of controlling them, and even a bit of philosophy that speculates about animal consciousness. While "The Bothersome Beauty of Pigeons" is not a formal academic research paper
(I write those, too), it does reflect many of the features of academic
writing and especially academic inquiry. For example, the essay is
driven by questions, works toward a controlling idea or thesis,
involves my willingness to suspend judgment, and attempts to build

on the ideas of others to extend my own thinking. While the essay is personal—growing from my experience—it attempts to say something larger; it is an effort to comment on "our" experience, and uses research to help enrich those understandings.

The purpose of research writing is not simply to show readers what you know. It is an effort to *extend a conversation about a topic* that is ongoing, a conversation that includes voices of people who have already spoken, often in different contexts and perhaps never together. The research writer begins with his own questions, and then finds the voices that speak to them. He then writes about what others have helped him to understand. As you read "The Bothersome Beauty of Pigeons," look for the traces of this process of inquiry. It may also inspire you to have a similar adventure.

EXERCISE 2

Reflecting on "The Bothersome Beauty of Pigeons"

Read my research essay first for pleasure, and then reread it with a pen in your hand. Use two opposing pages of your notebook to explore your response to the piece. Begin on the left page by:

- Jotting down, in quotes, your favorite line or passage from the essay.
- Copying a passage—a few lines or paragraph—that uses outside research. Choose one that you particularly liked or didn't like, or both.
- Composing, in your own words, what you think is the main idea or thesis of the essay. Begin by speculating about exactly what central question seemed to be behind the essay. What do you think I was trying to understand? What is it that I *came* to understand by the end of the essay?

Shift across to the opposing, or right, page of your notebook. Looking to the left at the notes you just took, begin a seven-minute fastwrite that explores your thinking in response to one or more of the following questions:

- When *you* write your research essay, what techniques or methods could you use to keep the essay interesting to readers even if it is fact-based?
- In what ways was "The Bothersome Beauty of Pigeons" *unlike* what you understood to be a research paper? Does it challenge those assumptions in ways that make you more interested in

research? What questions does the essay raise about what
you're supposed to do in your research assignment?

- Explore your thoughts about the contents of the essay. Did you
find you could relate in some way to what the essay seemed to
say? Did you learn anything about yourself, or about pigeons, or
our relationships to nature that struck you in some way?

The Bothersome Beauty of Pigeons

by Bruce Ballenger

The cardboard display tables of the mostly African vendors in
Florence's largest piazzas are marvels of engineering. They are designed
to be light and portable, and to fold in an instant without disrupting the
orderly display of fashionable sunglasses, silver cigarette lighters, or art
posters. I watch these street entrepreneurs from the steps of the city's
great cathedral, Santa Maria della Fiore, as they work the roving bands
of Italian schoolchildren on school holiday. It is a hard sell. The vendors
line up side by side and though many sell exactly the same kinds of sunglasses or lighters or posters, they don't seem to aggressively compete
with each other; in fact, they borrow money from each other to make
change, and laugh together at quiet comments I can't hear.

For a few moments my attention to the scene strays, and when
I look back the vendors and their cardboard displays have simply
vanished. At first, I can't figure out a reason for the disappearing
act. Nor can I explain the street vendors' sudden return minutes
later, sweeping in like the flocks of pigeons that are everywhere in
these squares. Then I see the small Renault of the Florence polizia
driving slowly down an adjacent street, where two officers sit stiffly
in their crisp blue uniforms and white leather belts; the police seem
bored, indifferent, not even remotely interested in the sudden flight
their slow passage through the square inspires.

The vendors are apparently unlicensed and the police routinely
attempt to flush them out, but this is clearly a half-hearted campaign. Who can blame them? The vendors are everywhere, lingering
at the edge of crowds, a fraternity of friendly bandits clutching their
neatly folded cardboard tables, each equipped with a convenient handle of rope and duct tape. Within seconds of the officers' departure,
the vendors descend on the square again, once again unfolding their
tables to which the merchandise magically adhered.

I watch this flight and return again and again, and along with it
I notice the pigeons, who participate in a similar performance of their

own in these same squares. The birds are also everywhere, in bold flocks that peck at the heels of the sloppy eaters, each bird turning a greedy red eye up at the diner, the other eye fixed on the ground before it. It is impossible to ignore the pigeons, and tourists delight in tossing food and witnessing the free-for-all at their feet. I find myself looking for crumbs from the pannini I have just finished for lunch, wondering at my own impulse to feed a bird against which I had recently waged war.

Pigeons seem to inspire such paradoxical feelings. Pigeon racers in the Bronx tenderly kiss the beaks of their birds, finally home after flying 500 miles to their lofts after a remarkable feat of solar navigation (Blechman). Meanwhile, pigeon haters host Web sites like Pigeonsmakemesick.com and propose plans for ridding cities of the "vermin," including the tactical use of tennis rackets and loaves of bread (Thorne). Most of us, I think, can swing both ways in our feelings towards pigeons, an ambivalence that doesn't seem to apply to other "pests" because pigeons occupy an odd category of creatures that we can both love and hate, animals that are untidy and irritating yet, at times, utterly enchanting.

––––––––––

Florence does not feed a pigeon lover's longings nearly as well as Venice. In Florence's Piazza San Giovanni, where I sat, there were no seed sales, a business that thrives in Venice's St. Mark's square. For one euro, tourists there can buy a small bag of seeds to feed the pigeons, who respond to the encouragement by gathering in great flocks around the seed thrower. The birds lose their grace and shamelessly stumble over each other with eagerness, pecking wildly at the stone street and even eating out of the tourist's hand or perching on his head. This becomes a photographic occasion as tourists stand, arms outstretched before the great church, covered with pigeons.

One guidebook recommends that this feeding should be followed by throwing an article of clothing in the air, which like the police and the sunglass vendors, makes the pigeons take flight in a sudden pulse of wings, only to circle back in their greed and quickly land again at the tourists' feet (Steve 91). The same guidebook offers advice on dealing with pigeon droppings in one's hair—an obvious hazard for the pigeon lover and hater alike—suggesting that it's far better to wait until the stuff dries because it's easier to remove (85).

Such a thing goes completely against instinct. Among my most chilling childhood memories is politely heeding the patrol boy who commanded me to stop before I crossed the street in front of my home. He towered above me, no doubt growing some in memory, and I didn't see him gather the spit in his mouth to deposit on the top of my head. I ran home, heedless of traffic, my vision blurred by tears and my fingers wildly clawing at my fouled hair.

It is also, I think, instinctual for human beings to respond warmly to many other animals, particularly those that we find attractive. Pigeons would seem to qualify. They are, after all, close relatives to doves—the lovely white birds of peace—and despite the unsettling red eyes, brown in the youngsters, most *Columbia livia* have smoothly sculpted bodies of blue-gray, and a certain grace when they're not pecking at the stale remnants of someone's lunch. While people rant online about the pestilence of pigeons, it's easy to find organizations of pigeon lovers all over the Web, including the many pigeon fanciers who race them from the rooftops of New York City and other urban areas around the world. Apparently, the fighter George Foreman and actor Paul Newman are among them. Others admire the pigeons' intelligence, something that has been demonstrated by behaviorists like B. F. Skinner who selected pigeons as their primary study subjects. "Pound for pound," gushes Pigeons.com, citing a University of Montana study, "[the pigeon] is one of the smartest, most physically adept creatures in the animal kingdom" ("Resources"). One recent study even demonstrated that pigeons could learn to distinguish between a Van Gogh and a Chagall (Watanabe 147).

It takes special skills to thrive in the world's cities, and pigeons, also called rock doves, are endowed with several ecological advantages that allow them to indulge in "high risk" behavior and escape unscathed. The birds, introduced to North America from Europe in the 1600s, possibly find in urban canyons the high cliffs of their wild ancestors ("FAQs"), and from their high perches they can live and breed and look down on the rest of us.

But they have other evolutionary advantages as well, some of which save them from the well-placed kicks of pigeon-haters or the tires of speeding taxis. For one thing, they "suck" puddle water rather than take it in their beaks and throw their heads back to swallow it, something like the difference between drinking a juice box and slinging back a shot of tequila. Sucking is quicker, apparently, and in very short order they get the water they need, 10 to 15 percent of their body weight daily. In addition, because they can store food in a crop, a pouch in the throat, pigeons can quickly gorge on bread crumbs and seed as the birds weave between the shuffling feet of busy urbanites and then fly to a safe roost to digest what they gathered (Wells and Wells 324).

It's hard not to admire these traits that give the birds such biological success, and yet somehow these evolutionary gifts seem unfair and unearned. I'm disappointed that, say, bluebirds weren't given these advantages, birds that would use them more graciously, judiciously. Pigeons are punks. Looking them in the eye, I'm sure they know this but they just don't care. Yet looking at pigeons also reminds me of my own arrogance, and I both hate them and love them for it.

———————

"The problem with pigeons," said Lia Bartolomei, an Italian who led me through the churches of Lucca one day, "is that they turn marble to dust" (Bartolomei). She then pointed to the small statues and marble carving on the church that were pocked and disfigured. The blame seemed clear. Apparently marble is particularly vulnerable to the acid in pigeon droppings, an unintended consequence of the birds' passion to roost on high places as their ancestors did on cliffs.

This is made worse by the pigeon's social nature. Unlike most other birds, they apparently are not particularly territorial, something that is obvious watching pigeons stumble over each other pursuing breadcrumbs. In great concentrations, the birds produce especially damaging piles of droppings, stuff that not only turns marble to dust but can be an ideal medium for fungus that can cause histoplasmosis and cryptococcossis, both lung infections in humans ("Health Hazards"). It costs the city of London $150,000 a year to clean up pigeon poop in Trafalgar Square alone ("Proposed").

It's the decay of marble monuments, the caked pigeon poop on city bridges, the messy nests on office buildings, and the health threats of dung fungus that long ago thrust the pigeon into the category of "pest." This is an undesirable label if you happen to be the plant or animal that earned it because life for such things can suddenly become complicated. The rock dove—cousin to the bird of peace, messenger for the Romans, brave racer for the homing pigeon enthusiast—also earned the unlovely name of "skyrat." Pigeon-haters find comrades on the Web and confer on the most effective poisons. Their anthem is folksinger Tom Lehrer's song "Poisoning Pigeons in the Park," a macabre tune noting that *When they see us coming, the birdies all try an' hide / But they still go for peanuts when coated with cyanide* (Lehrer). But despite the rants of pigeon-haters, (some of which are tongue-in-cheek) pigeons are not rats because among other things they aren't ugly. "Pests" like these make things complicated for us, too.

———————

Like every urban area in the U.S., the pigeon thrives in Boise, Idaho, where I live, and recently I went to war with a pair determined to roost in the eaves of our turn-of-the century craftsman home. Let me be clear about one thing: I am a lover of wild birds, even hooligan crows who moodily gather in the neighborhood trees in late afternoon muttering curses. I never disliked pigeons, and even admired their success and intelligence. But the white and green streaks on my windows, and the pile of droppings at my back door turned me against them. The pigeons' indifference to my shouts and shirt waving whenever I found them on the eaves began to infuriate me.

It is human to rail against nature from time to time, and it may even be human nature. It's true that one of the ecological lessons of our time is that our determined efforts to dominate the natural world are not, generally, successful or wise. Ecologically speaking, then, the belief that we're apart from nature, that it can be easily "managed," doesn't help ensure our survival as a species; in fact, our grand engineering efforts often endanger our survival. But aren't these often matters of scale? Pigeon wars, like the battle against dandelions in a suburban lawn, may not matter as much in the ecological scheme of things, or at least this is what we tell ourselves. Still, these campaigns against the wild things that threaten our tidy world—bugs and weeds, rats and pigeons—can say a great deal about the ecology of emotion that shapes our response to nature.

Pigeons, unlike rats, aren't very good enemies. They *are* attractive, and the sweep of their flocks in and out of the squares and streets in Europe or America, expanding and contracting against the bright sky, can almost seem like breathing. Virginia Woolf compared the movement of the great flocks of starlings in the fall to the throwing of a net with "thousands of black knots" expanding and then contracting as the birds settle on the tops of trees (Woolf 5). From a distance, flocks of pigeons can seem like that, and unless you've imprinted images from Hitchcock's film *The Birds,* even the throbbing wings of dozens of the birds landing at your feet can be a little thrill.

Years ago, when I lived on the New England coast, I went on several whale watches to Stellwaggen Bank, an offshore area where there is an unusual concentration of the animals, including some of the rarest like the Right Whale. On every one of these trips, I noticed that there was a longing not only to see these great animals but to *get close* to them. I sensed this desire had as much to do with the longing to make contact—to look in the eye of a whale, to feel a mutual presence between watcher and animal—as it did the desire to simply get a good look at something that large. I wonder if it's that same longing that feeds the pigeon watchers in St. Mark's square as they feed the pigeons. This might explain why there could be such an outcry when, several years ago, London's mayor proposed to end the long history of pigeon feeding in London's Trafalgar Square.

⅄ "People come from abroad just to do it," said one critic of the proposal. "For many children the pigeons are the first contact they have with animals. If a pigeon lands on a child's shoulder, it will paint a good picture in their mind and who then know that animals are worth caring for" ("Proposed"). I'm not sure what is behind this longing to get close. But perhaps it appeals to the biological memory, buried deep, that we are indeed a part of nature, not apart from it. Eye contact is the closest thing we get to a language of intimacy with wild things, though we won't look a rat in the eye. We don't want to get close to just anybody.

Yet these two feelings, our separation and connection to the natural world, are always in conflict, even among those who have tutored themselves to believe in one rather than the other. This seems especially true when confronted with creatures like pigeons, who aren't easy to hate and aren't easy to love, who both foul the nest and yet possess the beauty of a gray river stone, smoothed by the timeless movement of current. All of this was on my mind as I pounded small nails into my pigeons' favorite perches under the eaves and cut the tops off of them to make them sharp, one of the many methods recommended by experts for "controlling" pigeons. Another popular method that uses something called Avitrol, corn bait laced with toxic chemicals, might even mean killing them. The language of "pest control," like the language of warfare, is not immune to euphemism.

Most of the tactics recommended against pigeons, however, are intended to simply make life uncomfortable for them, methods that are more likely, as one combatant put it, to create "a good public relations image" (Loven 3): a perception problem, by the way, that campaigns against rats don't have. These more benign methods of pigeon combat include "porcupine wire," electric wires on roosting places, or chemical pastes that the birds find distasteful. Several cities are experimenting with pigeon contraceptives. Shouting, water pistols, and twirling T-shirts provide momentary satisfaction but are not considered effective. It was a plastic long-eared owl with a head that moves in the wind that finally scared my pigeons away. I moved the owl every two days, and found a strange satisfaction in bullying the birds with what I imagine is their worst nightmare. A big owl with a twirling head would scare the devil out of me if I were a pigeon.

My pigeons moved next door where an elderly couple feed them bird seed and have the time and the willingness to clean up after their new charges; so it seems, in this case, things worked out for everyone. But the large flocks still haunt the piazzas in Florence and Venice, the squares in London, and similar places in nearly every city across the globe. Despite their ability to distinguish between a

Van Gogh and a Chagall, pigeons still deposit droppings that deface the great marble statues and facades—the works of art and architecture that are part of our human heritage—and yet people still buy bags of seed for about a dollar and pose for photographs, drenched in doves. Meanwhile, officials in these cities continue, sometimes quietly, to wage war against the birds.

Some historians believe that another war, this one in Viet Nam more than thirty years ago, was one that we could never win because politicians were unable to convince Americans to fully commit to it. That was a hard sell, too, because most Americans were smart enough to eventually realize that even with a full commitment the rewards of "winning" would not be worth the cost. We battle the birds with the same lack of conviction. Like Viet Nam, "pigeon control" is a war that we will never win because we also battle our own conflicting desires: the feeling that it is our obligation to protect and preserve humankind's great works and our hunger to coexist with at least the more appealing creatures with which we share space in our cities. We struggle, as we always have, with the sense that we are both a part of and apart from other species on the planet.

I've managed to scare the pigeons away from the eaves of my house. But it's not so easy to flush them from where they roost now in the back of my mind, cooing and clucking defiantly, daring me to hate them. I can't. This aggravates me because I know that part of the reason is, quite simply, that pigeons are not rats. It seems unlikely that pigeons know this, though certain philosophers believe that some animals know what it's like to *be* that animal (Nagel 435–50). If this is true, I imagine pigeons may be aware that they're fouling the head of a human being when they roost on the copy of Michelangelo's *David* in Florence's Piazza della Signoria. It is part of the pigeon "experience" to sit confidently on marble heads, knowing that the unthinking stone beneath their feet is neither a source of food nor threat, just a benign roost from which they can turn their red eyes to the humans on the ground below. We look back at them with amusement and disgust, curiosity and contempt—the conflicting feelings and desires that bothersome beauty in nature often arouses. Meanwhile, pigeons hasten the mortality of marble, turning a dream to dust.

Works Cited

Bartolomei, Lia. Personal Interview. 15 April 2002.
Blechman, Andrew. "Flights of Fancy." *Smithsonian Magazine* March 2002: 44–50.

"Frequently Asked Questions." Project Pigeon Watch. 5 May 2002 <http:// birds.cornell.edu/ppw/faq.htm>.

"Health Hazards Associated with Bird and Bat Droppings." Illinois Department of Public Health-Health Beat. 2 May 2002 <http://www.idph.state.il.us/ public/hb/hbb&bdrp.htm>.

Lehrer, Tom. "Poisoning Pigeons in the Park." 7 May 2002 <http://www. hyperborea.org/writing/pigeons.html>.

Loven, Judy. "Pigeons." Animal Damage Management: Purdue Cooperative Extension Service. April 2000. 4 pgs. 7 May 2002 <http://www.entm.purdue. edu/Entomology/ext/targets/ADM/index.htm>.

Nagel, Thomas. "What Is It Like to Be a Bat?" *Philosophical Review* 83 (1974): 435–50.

"Proposed Trafalgar Square Changes Ruffle Feathers." CNN.com. 15 November 2000. 2 May 2002 <www.cnn.com/2000/travel/news/11/15/Britain. trafalgar.ap/>.

"Resources: Interesting and Amazing Facts about Pigeons." Pigeons.com Resources. 2 May 2002 <http://www.pigeons.com/resources/facts.html>.

Steve, Rick. *Rick Steve's Italy, 2001.* Emeryville, CA: Avalon, 2001.

Thorne, Jacob. "Jacob Rants Semicoherently about Pigeons." 18 November 2002 <http://www.angelfire.com/art/glorious/pigeons.html>.

Watanabe, Shigeru. "Van Gogh, Chagall, and Pigeons: Picture Discrimination in Pigeons and Humans." *Animal Cognition* 4 (2001): 147–151.

Wells, Jeffrey V. and Allison Childs Wells. "Pigeons and Doves." *The Sibley Guide to Bird Life and Behavior.* Illust. David Allen Sibley. New York: Knopf, 2001, 319–325.

Woolf, Virginia. "Death of a Moth." *Eight Modern Essayists.* 6th ed. William Smart. New York: St. Martin's, 1995, 5–7.

The Question Habit

The most uninspired research writing lumbers along from fact to fact and quote to quote, saying "Look at what I know!" *Demonstrating* knowledge is not nearly as impressive as *using* it toward some end. And the best uses of research are to answer questions the writer is really interested in. In the next few days, your challenge is to find those questions.

The First Week

The Importance of Getting Curious

A few years back, I wrote a book about lobsters. At first, I didn't intend it to be a book. I didn't think there was that much to say about lobsters. But the more I researched the subject, the more questions I had and the more places I found to look for answers. Pretty soon, I had 300 pages of manuscript.

My curiosity about lobsters began one year when the local newspaper printed an article about what terrible shape the New England lobster fishery was in. The catch was down 30 percent, and the old-timers were saying it was the worst year they'd seen since the thirties. Even though I grew up in landlocked Chicago, I'd always loved eating lobsters after being introduced to them at age eight at my family's annual Christmas party. Many years later, when I read the article in my local newspaper about the vanishing lobsters, I was alarmed. I wondered, Will lobster go the way of caviar and become too expensive for people like me?

That was the question that triggered my research, and it soon led to more questions. What kept me going was my own curiosity. If your research assignment is going to be successful, you need to get curious, too. If you're bored by your research topic, your paper will almost certainly be boring as well, and you'll end up hating writing research papers as much as ever.

Learning to Wonder Again

Maybe you're naturally curious, a holdover from childhood when you were always asking, Why? Or maybe your curiosity paled as you got older, and you forgot that being curious is the best reason for wanting to learn things. Whatever condition it's in, your curiosity must be the driving force behind your research paper. It's the most essential ingredient. The important thing, then, is this: *Choose your research topic carefully. If you lose interest in it, change your topic to one that does interest you, or find a different angle.*

In most cases, instructors give students great latitude in choosing their research topics. (Some instructors narrow the field, asking students to find a focus within some broad, assigned subject. When the subject has been assigned, it may be harder for you to discover what you are curious about, but it won't be impossible, as you'll see.) Some of the best research topics grow out of your own experience (though they certainly don't have to), as mine did when writing about lobster overfishing or pigeons. Begin searching for a topic by asking yourself this question: *What have I seen or experienced that raises questions that research can help answer?*

Getting the Pot Boiling

A subject might bubble up immediately. For example, I had a student who was having a terrible time adjusting to her parents' divorce. Janabeth started out wanting to know about the impact of divorce on children and later focused her paper on how divorce affects father-daughter relationships.

Kim remembered spending a rainy week on Cape Cod with her father, wandering through old graveyards, looking for the family's ancestors. She noticed patterns on the stones and wondered what they meant. She found her ancestors as well as a great research topic.

Manuel was a divorced father of two, and both of his sons had recently been diagnosed with attention deficit disorder (ADD). The boys' teachers strongly urged Manuel and his wife to arrange drug therapy for their sons, but they wondered whether there might be any alternatives. Manuel wrote a moving and informative research essay about his gradual acceptance of drug treatment as the best solution for his sons.

For years, Wendy loved J. D. Salinger's work but never had the chance to read some of his short stories. She jumped at the opportunity to spend five weeks reading and thinking about her favorite author. She later decided to focus her research paper on Salinger's notion of the misfit hero.

Accidental topics, ideas that you seem to stumble on when you aren't looking, are often successful topics. For example, Amy spent some time in an America Online chat room one night, and the conversation took an interesting turn. Participants began to discuss the theory that suggests a correlation between depression and heavy computer use. Could that be true? She wondered. She decided to write a paper to find out.

Sometimes, one topic triggers another. Chris, ambling by Thompson Hall, one of the oldest buildings on his campus, wondered about its history. After a little initial digging, he found some 1970s newsclips from the student newspaper describing a student strike that paralyzed the school. The controversy fascinated him more than the building did, and he pursued the topic. He wrote a great paper.

If you're still drawing a blank, try the following exercise in your notebook.

EXERCISE 1.1

Building an Interest Inventory

STEP 1: From time to time I'll hear a student say, "I'm just not interested in *anything* enough to write a paper about it." I don't believe it. Not for a second. The real problem is that the student simply hasn't taken the time to think about everything he knows and everything he might want to know. Try coaxing those things out of your head and onto paper by creating an "interest inventory."

Start with a blank journal page, or if you're using a word processor, define columns—say, three per page. Title each column with one of the words below:

PLACES, TRENDS, THINGS, TECHNOLOGIES,
PEOPLE, CONTROVERSIES, HISTORY,
JOBS, HABITS, HOBBIES

Under each title, brainstorm a list of words (or phrases) that come to mind when you think about *what you know and what you might want to know* about the category. For example, under TRENDS you might be aware of the use of magnets for healing sore muscles, or you might know a lot about extreme sports. Put both down on the list. Don't censor yourself. Just write down whatever comes to mind, even if it makes sense only to you. This list is for your use only. You'll probably find that ideas come to you in waves—you'll jot down a few things and then draw a blank. Wait for the next wave to come and ride it. But if you're seriously becalmed, start a new column with a new word from the list above and brainstorm ideas in that category. Do this at least four times with different words. Feel free to return to any column to add new ideas as they come to you, and don't worry about repeated items. Some things simply straddle more than one category. For an idea of what this might look like, see what I did with this exercise (Figure 1.1).

CONTROVERSIES

Guantanamo bay
Iraq war
Palestine vs. Israel
Beijing Olympics
Steroids in baseball
Racism/sexism in politics
Gender identity
Homosexual marriage
Death penalty
When is a person created?
Right to euthanasia
Vegetative states
Drinking bottled water
Is organic stuff better?
Does the glass ceiling
    still exist?
Why are people poor?
Religion in the U.S.
    government
Sex lives of elected officials
What makes people fat?
Evolution in the school
    system
Gas vs. ethanol
Sales tax on groceries

JOBS

Prison guard
Garbage man
Sewer cleaners
Undertakers
TV anchor
Hotel housekeepers
Rap stars
Child stars
Interior decorators
Manicurists
Tailors
Cobblers
Tour guides

HABITS

Using a toothpick
Fingernail biting
Bouncing a leg
Verbal ticks, "so
    anyway . . . "
Wringing hands
Eating with mouth open
Chewing gum loudly
Laughing to oneself
Checking locks
Leaving cell phone on
Talking too loud
Nose picking
Hair twirling
Habits vs. superstitions
"God bless you"

TRENDS

Bluetooth headsets
Ipods
Drinking coffee
Crocs shoes
Giant purses
Designer everything
Organic products
Green/eco consciousness
"Some disease" awareness
Celebrity spokespeople
Internet television
Pets as children
Going to prison
Adult-oriented cartoons
Model/actress/singer
    combo
High-stakes kindergarten

HISTORY

The Holocaust
The Vietnam War
Ancient China
Who built the
    pyramids?
Why did the Aztecs
    die?
When did man leave
    Africa?
What was Pres.
    Washington like?
The Underground
    Railroad
Feudal Japan
Human sacrifices
Spanish Inquisition
Napoleonic wars

FIGURE 1.1   Amanda's Interest Inventory

TRENDS	HISTORY
Myspace	Stonecutter's guilds
Blogs	Nostradamus
Cohabitating	The Gold Rush
White teeth	Immigrants to the
Specialized TV channels	U.S. in the 1900s
Hardwood floors	The Triangle
Locavores	Shirtwaist fire
Wikipedia	The importance of the
Pink shirts for men	printing press
Heated car seats	Hygiene habits in
Splenda	ancient Greece
Energy drinks	Gender roles in
	ancient Egypt
	Torture chambers
	Footbinding
	Pre-Christian
	religions
	Canada's freedom
	from Europe.

Allot a total of twenty minutes to do this step: ten minutes to generate lists in four or more categories, a few minutes to walk away from it and think about something else, and the remaining time to return and add items to any column as they occur to you. (The exercise will also work well if you work on it over several days. You'll be amazed at how much information you can generate.)

STEP 2: Review your lists. Look for a single item in any column that seems promising. Ask yourself these questions: Is this something that raises questions that research can help answer? Are they potentially interesting questions? Does this item get at something you've always wondered about? Might it open doors to knowledge you think is important, fascinating, or relevant to your own life?

Circle the item.

Many interesting things surfaced on my lists. My TRENDS list seemed the richest. For example, when I finished Jon Krakauer's book *Into Thin Air,* a nonfiction account of a doomed Mt. Everest expedition, I was left wondering about the range of motivations that might account for the increasing popularity of that dangerous climb. On the same list I also wrote "decline of songbirds." I'm aware from personal experience and some limited reading that there has been a steady decline in songbird populations in North America during the last few decades. I spent many happy days watching warblers in the treetops behind my suburban Chicago home as a kid, and it makes me sad that those trees in some future month of May might be more silent. What's going on?

STEP 3: For the item you circled, generate a list of questions—as many as you can—that you'd love to explore about the subject. Here's what Amanda, one of my students, did with her topic on teeth whitening:

> Are tooth whiteners safe?
>
> What makes teeth turn browner over time?
>
> How has society's definition of a perfect smile changed over time?
>
> Are whiter teeth necessarily healthier than darker teeth?
>
> Is it true that drinking coffee stains your teeth?
>
> How much money is spent on advertising tooth whitening products each year?
>
> What percentage of Americans feel bad about the shade of their teeth?
>
> Do dentists ever recommend that people whiten their teeth?
>
> Is there any way to keep your teeth from getting darker over time?
>
> Can teeth get too white?
>
> Why do I feel bad that my teeth aren't perfect?
>
> Do other cultures have the same emphasis on perfectly white teeth as Americans do?
>
> Are there the same standards for men's teeth and women's teeth?
>
> What judgments do we make about people based simply on the color of their teeth?
>
> How does America's dental hygiene compare with other countries? Is the "Austin Powers" myth really true?

The kinds of questions I came up with on my tentative topic seem encouraging. Several already seem "researchable," and several remind me that I *feel* something about those missing warblers. I may not have developed a hunger to know more yet, but it has piqued my interest. Do you have an appetite for anything yet?

Other Ways to Find a Topic

If you're still stumped about a tentative topic for your paper, consider the following:

■ *Surf the Net.* The Internet is like a crowded fair on the medieval village commons. It's filled with a range of characters—from the carnivalesque to the scholarly—all participating in a democratic exchange of ideas and information. There are promising research topics everywhere. Maybe begin with a site such as The Virtual Library (http://www.vlib.org), which tries to organize Internet resources by subject. Choose a subject that interests you, say autos or cognitive science, and follow any number of trails that lead from there into cyberspace.

■ *Search an index.* Visit your library's Web site and check an online index or database in a subject area that interests you. For example, suppose you're a psychology major and would like to find a topic in the field. Try searching PyschINFO, a popular database of psychology articles. Most databases can be searched by author, subject, keyword, and so on. Think of a general area you're interested in—say, bipolar disorder—and do a subject or keyword search. That will produce a long list of articles, some of which may have abstracts of summaries that will pique your interest. Notice the "related subjects" button? Click that and see a long list of other areas in which you might branch off and find a great topic.

■ *Browse Wikipedia.* While the online "free content" encyclopedia isn't a great source for an academic paper (see page 41), Wikipedia is a warehouse of potential research topic ideas. Start with the main page and take a look at the featured or newest articles. You can also browse articles by subject or category.

■ *Consider essays you've already written.* Could the topics of any of these essays be further developed as research topics? For example, Diane wrote a personal essay about how she found the funeral of a classmate alienating—especially the wake. Her essay asked what purpose such a ritual could serve, a question, she decided, that would best be answered by research. Other students wrote essays on the difficulty of living with a depressed brother or an alcoholic parent, topics that yielded wonderful research papers. A class assignment to read Ken Kesey's *One Flew Over the Cuckoo's Nest* inspired Li to research the author.

■ *Pay attention to what you've read recently.* What newspaper articles have sparked your curiosity and raised interesting questions?

Rob, a hunter, encountered an article that reported the number of hunters was steadily declining in the United States. He wondered why. Karen read an account of a particularly violent professional hockey game. She decided to research the Boston Bruins, a team with a history of violent play, and examine how violence has affected the sport. Don't limit yourself to the newspaper. What else have you read recently—perhaps magazines or books—or seen on TV that has made you wonder?

■ *Consider practical topics.* Perhaps some questions about your career choice might lead to a promising topic. Maybe you're thinking about teaching but wonder about current trends in teachers' salaries. One student, Anthony, was being recruited by a college to play basketball and researched the tactics coaches use to lure players. What he learned helped prepare him to make a good choice.

■ *Think about issues, ideas, or materials you've encountered in other classes.* Have you come across anything that intrigued you, that you'd like to learn more about?

■ *Look close to home.* An interesting research topic may be right under your nose. Does your hometown (or your campus community) suffer from a particular problem or have an intriguing history that would be worth exploring? Jackson, tired of dragging himself from his dorm room at 3:00 A.M. for fire alarms that always proved false, researched the readiness of the local fire department to respond to such calls. Ellen, whose grandfather worked in the aging woolen mills in her hometown, researched a crippling strike that took place there sixty years ago. Her grandfather was an obvious source for an interview.

■ *Collaborate.* Work together in groups to come up with interesting topics. Try this idea: Organize the class into small groups of five. Give each group ten minutes to come up with specific questions about one general subject—for example, American families, recreation, media, race or gender, health, food, history of the local area, environment of the local area, education, and so forth. Post these questions on newsprint as each group comes up with them. Then rotate the groups so that each has a shot at generating questions for every subject. At the end of forty minutes, the class will have generated perhaps a hundred questions, some uninspired and some really interesting. You can also try this exercise on the class website using the discussion board or group features.

What Is a Good Topic?

A few minutes browsing the Internet convinces most of my students that the universe of good research topics is pretty limited: global warming, abortion rights, legalization of pot, same sex marriage, and the like. These are usually the topics of the papers you can buy with your Visa card at sites like "freeessays.com" (yea, right). These are also often topics with the potential to bore both reader and writer to death because they inspire essays that are so predictable.

But beginning with a good question, rather than a convenient answer, changes everything. Suddenly subjects are everywhere: What is with our cultural obsession about good teeth? Is it true that lawnmowers are among the most polluting engines around? What's the deal with the devastation of banana crops and how will that affect prices at Albertson's down the street? Even the old tired topics get new life when you find the right question to ask. For example, what impact will the availability of medical marijuana vending machines in California have on the legal debate in that state?

What's a good topic? Initially, it's all about finding the right question, and especially one that you are really interested in. (See the box on page 37.) Later, the challenge will be limiting the number of questions your paper tries to answer. For now, look for a topic that makes you at least a little hungry to learn more.

Checking Out Your Tentative Topic

Consider the potential of the tentative topic you've chosen by using this checklist:

- Does it raise questions I'd love to learn the answers to? Does it raise a lot of them?
- Do I feel strongly about it? Do I already have some ideas about the topic that I'd like to explore?
- Can I find authoritative information to answer my questions? Does the topic offer the possibility of interviews? An informal survey? Internet research?
- Will it be an intellectual challenge? Will it force me to reflect on what *I* think?
- Are a lot of people researching this topic or a similar one? Will I struggle to find sources in the library because other students have them?

Don't worry if you can't answer yes to all of these questions or if you can't answer any at all just yet. Being genuinely curious about your topic is the most important consideration.

Five Research Essays I'd Like to Read

- **The rise of reality shows.** I'm embarrassed to admit this but my daughter's got me watching what some critics call the penultimate TV reality show—Project Runway. The show annoys me. A lot. But if it's on, I'll sit down and watch with enjoyment and hate myself for doing it. What might explain both the appeal and the repugnance of this particular show, and perhaps reality shows generally?
- **Cell phones on airplanes.** Legislation was introduced in Congress recently to ban cell phones on American airlines while many European air carriers now allow them. Is this a good thing? Just because technology enables us to do something, should we do it?
- **The sociology of Mount Everest.** The first human successfully climbed the world's tallest mountain more than fifty years ago. On one day in 1993, forty people made it to the top. Climbing the mountain is now big business. What are people's motives for spending tens of thousands of dollars to be led to the summit? Have these motives changed? And what does it say about the changing definition of "adventure?"
- **The history of toothpaste.** People have brushed their teeth for ages but Crest has only been around for a half century or so. What did people use as toothpaste in medieval times? Was it effective? And what might the evolution of toothpaste say about human vanity or inventiveness or even ignorance?
- **The floating continent of plastic.** In a region of the North Pacific that few ever see, there is reportedly a huge island of litter, twice the size of Texas, composed mostly of plastic. The debris accumulates there because of a quirk in ocean currents. What danger does this pose to marine mammals or even to phytoplankton on which the ecosystem relies? What kinds of plastic is this island made of and what does this say about our appetite for convenience?

Making the Most of an Assigned Topic

If your instructor limits your choice of topics, then it might be a little harder to find one that piques your curiosity, but it will not be nearly as hard as it seems. It is possible to find an interesting angle on almost any subject, if you're open to the possibilities. If you're not convinced, try this exercise in class.

EXERCISE 1 . 2

The Myth of the Boring Topic

This exercise requires in-class collaboration. Your instructor will organize you into four or five small groups and give each group a commonplace object; it might be something as simple as a nail, an orange, a pencil, a can of dog food, or a piece of plywood. Whatever the object, it will not strike you as particularly interesting, at least not at first.

STEP 1: Each group's first task is to brainstorm a list of potentially interesting questions about its commonplace object. Choose a recorder who will post the questions as you think of them on a large piece of newsprint taped to the wall. Inevitably, some of these questions will be pretty goofy ("Is it true that no word rhymes with orange?"), but work toward questions that might address the *history* of the object, its *uses,* its possible *impact on people,* or *the processes* that led to its creation in the form in which you now see it.

STEP 2: After twenty minutes, each group will shift to the adjacent group's newsprint and study the object that inspired that group's questions. Spend five minutes thinking up more interesting questions about the object that didn't occur to the group before you. Add these to the list on the wall.

What Makes a Question "Researchable"?

- It's not too big or too small.
- It focuses on some aspect of a topic about which something has been said.
- It interests the researcher.
- Some people have a stake in the answer. It has something to do with how we live or might live, what we care about, or what might be important for people to know.
- It implies an approach, or various means of answering it.
- It raises more questions. The answer might not be simple.

STEP 3: Stay where you are or return to your group's original object and questions. Review the list of questions, and choose *one* you find both interesting and most "researchable" (see previous box). In other words, if you were an editorial team assigned to propose a researched article for a general interest magazine that focuses on this object, what might be the starting question for the investigation? The most interesting question and the most researchable question may or may not be the same.

In Idaho where I live there are stones called geodes. These are remarkably plain looking rocks on the outside, but with the rap of a hammer they easily break open to reveal glittering crystals in white and purple hues. The most commonplace subjects and objects are easy to ignore because we suspect there is nothing new to see or know about them. Sometimes it takes the sharp rap of a really good question to crack open even the most familiar subjects, and then suddenly we see that subject in a new light. What I'm saying is this: A good question is the tool that makes the world yield to wonder, and knowing this is the key to being a curious researcher. Any research topic—even if it's assigned by the instructor—can glitter for you if you discover the questions that make you wonder.

If all else fails, examine your assigned topic through the following "lenses." One might give you a view of your topic that seems interesting.

- *People.* Who has been influential in shaping the ideas in your topic area? Do any have views that are particularly intriguing to you? Could you profile that person and her contributions?

- *Trends.* What are the recent developments in this topic? Are any significant? Why?

- *Controversies.* What do experts in the field argue about? What aspect of the topic seems to generate the most heat? Which is most interesting to you? Why?

- *Impact.* What about your topic currently has the most effect on the most people? What may in the future? How? Why?

- *Relationships.* Can you put one thing in relationship to another? If the required subject is Renaissance art, might you ask, "What is the relationship between Renaissance art and the plague?"

Admittedly, it is harder to make an assigned topic your own. But you can still get curious if you approach the topic openly, willing to see the possibilities by finding the questions that bring it to life for you.

Developing a Working Knowledge

If you have a tentative topic that makes you curious, then you're ready to do some preliminary research. At this stage in the process, it's fine to change your mind. As you begin to gently probe your subject, you may discover that there's another topic that interests you more—or perhaps a question that hadn't occurred to you. One of the advantages of developing a "working knowledge" of your topic at this stage is that these other possibilities may present themselves.

What's a working knowledge? William Badke, in his great book *Research Strategies*, calls a "working knowledge" of a topic the ability "to talk about it for one minute without repeating yourself." The advantage of developing a working knowledge of your tentative topic at this point is that it will help you find a focus, the problem that vexes more research writers than any other. Aside from giving you something new to talk about when conversation lags at Thanksgiving dinner, a working knowledge helps you to understand the following:

1. How your topic fits into the *context* of other subjects.
2. Some of the areas of controversy, debate, questions, or unresolved problems that ripple through expert conversation about your topic.

Knowing both of these things really helps when you want to stake out your own small piece of the larger landscape, and it helps you find the question that will mark your location and drive your investigation.

Working Together

In small groups, plan one-minute presentations of "working knowledge" you've developed on your topic doing Exercise 1.3. Following each presentation, ask group members to brainstorm a list of questions they have about your topic based on what you've said.

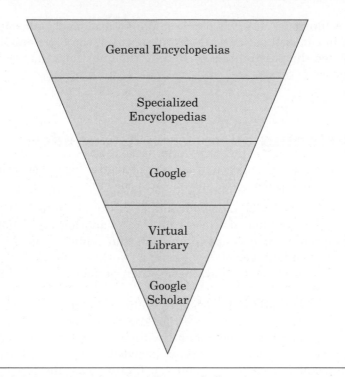

FIGURE 1.2   Working Knowledge Research Strategy

Research Strategies

There are many ways to develop a working knowledge of your topic, but generally the research strategy is like many others: Work from more general information to more specialized information (see Figure 1.2). That means, in this case, that you start with that old standby, the encyclopedia. That will not be your impulse, of course. You'll want to fire up Google and do a quick search, gather some online documents, and call it good. If at all possible, you'll want to avoid the library. But should you, even at this early stage in your investigation?

EXERCISE   1 . 3

Seeing the Broad View

Fortunately, one of the Web's strengths is subject coverage, and an online search will give you a good initial vantage point on your research topic. A logical starting point is an Internet version of the encyclopedia—the age-old reference for surveying a topic's landscape—and for most of us that means one thing: Wikipedia.

Wikipedia: Right or Wrong?

When you say "Wikipedia" to some academics, it's the equivalent of fingernails on a blackboard. Why do they cringe so? Because they see more and more students citing Wikipedia in their essays, and since articles on the site are authored by anyone, no matter his or her credentials on a topic, Wikipedia potentially violates one of the most important criteria for using any source in an academic paper: accuracy and reliability. There is some evidence, however, that the site compares fairly well with its more credible cousin, *Encyclopedia Britannica*. When they compared science articles in the two encyclopedias, researchers found that Wikipedia had an average of four inaccuracies while *Britannica* had three, and these were all relatively minor.* Still, in most cases, Wikipedia should not be a citation in your final paper, but it can be a useful starting point for your research when used cautiously.

WIKIPEDIA GOOD	WIKIPEDIA BAD
■ On some topics, it has more current information on a subject than the conventional encyclopedia.	■ Reliability is always suspect because authors may lack credentials.
■ Because articles are authored by people around the world, some topics have a multicultural perspective.	■ There is no attempt to be comprehensive, to give appropriate treatment to important subjects.
■ Articles frequently include helpful hyperlinks.	■ Many articles don't cite sources, so reliability and accuracy is difficult to check.
■ Stable articles—those that have undergone substantial revision so that they represent consensus— approach the standard of a conventional encyclopedia.	■ Some articles, particularly young ones on new topics, may reflect a strong bias because of their limited number of authors.

STEP ONE: Consult an online encyclopedia like Wikipedia, *Encyclopedia Britannica*, or one of the more scholarly wikis currently in development like Scholarpedia (www.scholarpedia.org) or Citizendium

*Jim Giles, "Special Report: Internet Encyclopedias Go Head to Head," *Nature* 438 (2005): 900–901.

(en.citizendium.org/wiki/Main_Page). You can also find a good list of the Web encyclopedias at the site www.refdesk.com. Try out several search terms on these sites until you find information relevant to your topic. Then, on the left page of your open notebook, jot at least three or four facts, interesting ideas, or quotations from the encyclopedias you consulted. Make sure you bookmark the pages so you can consult them later!

STEP TWO: Consult a specialized encyclopedia on your topic. These are more subject-focused works, obviously, that often have a wealth of information on a topic lacking in a more general work.

SPECIALIZED ENCYCLOPEDIAS

HUMANITIES	SOCIAL SCIENCES
Dictionary of Art	African-American Encyclopedia
International Dictionary of Films and Filmmakers	Dictionary of Psychology
Encyclopedia of World Art	Encyclopedia of Marriage and the Family
Encyclopedia of Religion	Encyclopedia of Psychology
Encyclopedia of Philosophy	The Blackwell Encyclopedia of Social Pyschology
Encyclopedia of African American Culture and History	Encyclopedia of Educational Research
Encyclopedia of America	Encyclopedia of Social Work
Encyclopedia of Sociology	Encyclopedia of World Cultures
Social History	Encyclopedia of the Third World
	Encyclopedia of Democracy
	Guide to American Law: Everyone's Legal Encyclopedia

SCIENCE	OTHER
Dictionary of the History of Science	Encyclopedia of the Modern Islamic World
Dictionary of the History of Medicine	The Baseball Encyclopedia
Encyclopedia of the Environment	Encyclopedia of Women and Sports
Concise Encyclopedia of Biology	Encyclopedia of World Sport
Encyclopedia of Bioethics	The World Encyclopedia of Soccer
Encyclopedia of Science and Technology	Worldmark Encyclopedia of the Nations
Macmillan Encyclopedias of Chemistry and Physics	
Food and Nutrition Encyclopedia	

These specialized references abound. (My personal favorite is the *Encyclopedia of Hell*). The accompanying list provides a sampling of specialized encyclopedias. To find these and other focused references relevant to your topic, you'll probably have to go to your academic library. Few are online. To find specific titles, ask your reference librarian or search your campus library's online book index. Try searching using the subject area with the word "encyclopedia" or "dictionary" (e.g., Internet and encyclopedia).

STEP THREE: Go ahead and Google your topic (or use another general search engine). Typically, Google users do keyword rather than subject searches, trying out a few (usually two) search terms rather than working down through subject categories. Both strategies are useful, but for now choose some keywords that you think might produce good results. Try combining three or more words to narrow your search. Instead of *plastic pollution* (a half million hits) try *plastic pollution ocean seabirds* (seventy thousand hits). Don't forget the quotation convention on Google that allows you to search for a specific phrase. For instance, *"plastic continent" Pacific*. Bookmark useful documents.

STEP FOUR: As you probably know, information on the Web is horribly disorganized; it's a librarian's worst nightmare. But there are librarians and others who are knowledgeable about organizing information who have worked quietly for years trying to impose some order on the chaos. What they've done is created *subject directories* on the Web. Perhaps the most famous subject directory is Yahoo! (yahoo.com), but there are several other sites that feature directories that were specifically developed by library experts and educators, people who are concerned both with order and the value of information in cyberspace One of the best subject directories is The Virtual Library. It's not the largest, but it is managed by people—mostly volunteers—all over the world who are experts in the library's various subject areas, contributing and evaluating the best sites.

Visit The Virtual Library (vlib.org) and drill down into your subject, starting with the broadest category and then refining and narrowing as you go. (See Figure 1.3 and Figure 1.4). Again, bookmark particularly relevant documents.

STEP FIVE: One of the great innovations for academic researchers is specialized search engines that focus on scholarly sources. The best of these is Google Scholar, though there are others (see the

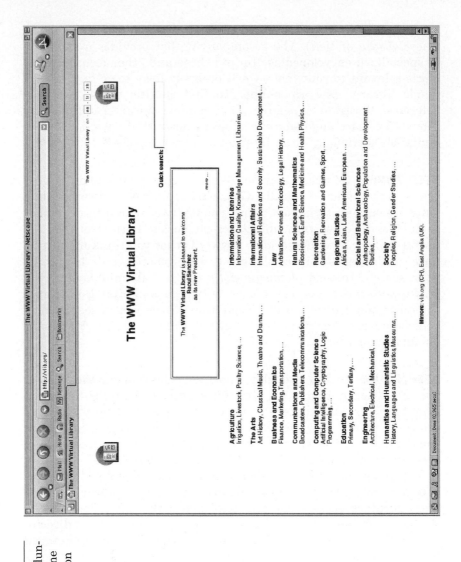

FIGURE 1.3 Managed by volunteers, The Virtual Library is one of the best subject directories on the Internet.

44

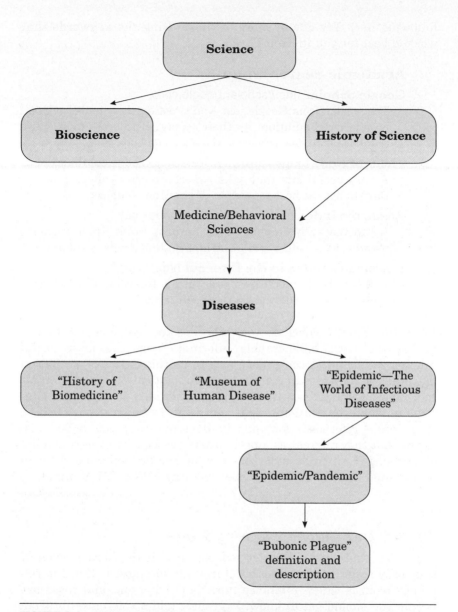

FIGURE 1.4 Navigation Map of Subject Search. A student interested in the bubonic plague, a pandemic that wiped out nearly a third of Europe's population in the fourteenth century, began in the "Science" category at the Virtual Library. She followed the most promising trail down through the subject hierarchy (using the "back" button on her browser to get out of dead ends when necessary), and ended finally at a Museum of Natural History site with an interesting definition and description of the plague. On the way, she began to think about AIDs and the plague. Might she explore the connection between the two?

following list). Try one or more of these using the keywords that worked best for you in Step Three.

Academic Search Engines

Google Scholar http://scholar.google.com/
> Those folks from Google just won't rest on their laurels. This is a recent addition to their array of search tools. Its database includes articles and even some books.

Fields of Knowledge http://www.fieldsofknowledge.com/index.html
> A very useful site that asks experts (mostly college professors) to list the best sources they know on a subject.

Academic Index http://www.academicindex.net
> A "metasearch" engine that returns Web sites recommended by scholars and librarians on thousands of subjects.

Librarian's Index to the Internet http://lii.org/
> Indexes about 16,000 Web sites on the Internet, all of which, they pledge, is "information you can trust."

STEP SIX: Finally, conclude your working knowledge search by collecting the basic bibliographic information on the most useful sources you found. A convenient way to do this is to use a "citation machine," a Web-based program that automatically prompts you for the bibliographic information and then magically turns it into citations in whatever citation format you want. Don't trust one of these to generate references for your final essay—they can make mistakes—but they're great as a preliminary method for collecting a list of citations. Visit citationmachine.net (or another site) and enter in information about your best sources choosing APA or MLA format.

The Reference Librarian: A Living Source

Alas, there are still other reasons to visit the library, even at this early stage in your research. First and foremost is that the reference room is where reference librarians hang out, and these are people you should get to know. I recently told a reference librarian that I was having a hard time keeping up with the changes in library technology, and she said, "Things are changing so fast it even makes my head spin." Even blurred, the eyesight of reference librarians—people who know where to look and what to look for—is far better than ours. Reference specialists are invaluable to college researchers; without a doubt, they're the most important resource in the library.

Narrowing the Subject

It never occurred to me that photography and writing had anything in common until I found myself wandering around a lonely beach one March afternoon with a camera around my neck. I had a fresh roll of film and, full of ambition, I set out to take beautiful pictures. Three hours later, I had taken only three shots, and I was definitely not having fun. Before quitting in disgust, I spent twenty minutes trying to take a single picture of a lighthouse. I stood there, feet planted in the sand, repeatedly bringing the camera to my face, but each time I looked through the viewfinder, I saw a picture I was sure I'd seen before, immortalized on a postcard in the gift shop down the road. Suddenly, photography lost its appeal.

A few months later, a student sat in my office complaining that he didn't have anything to write about. "I thought about writing an essay on what it was like going home for the first time last weekend," he said. "But I thought that everyone probably writes about that in freshman English." I looked at him and thought about lighthouse pictures.

Circling the Lighthouse

Almost every subject you will choose to write about for this class and for this research paper has been written about before. The challenge is not to find a unique topic (save that for your doctoral dissertation) but to find an angle on a familiar topic that helps readers to see what they probably haven't noticed before. In "The Bothersome Beauty of Pigeons," I took the most common of subjects—the urban pigeon—and took a close look at its habits and behaviors, finding in them an explanation for my conflicted feelings about "pests" that are inconveniently attractive.

I now know that it was a mistake to give up on the lighthouse. The problem with my lighthouse picture, as well as with my student's proposed essay on going home, was not the subject. It was that neither of us had yet found our own angle. I needed to keep looking, walking around the lighthouse, taking lots of shots until I found one that surprised me, that helped me see the lighthouse in a new way, in *my* way. Instead, I stayed put, stuck on the long shot and the belief that I couldn't do better than a postcard photograph.

It is generally true that when we first look at something, we mostly see its obvious features. That became apparent when I asked my freshman English class one year to go out and take pictures of anything they wanted. Several students came back with single photographs of Thompson Hall, a beautiful brick building on campus. Coincidentally, all were taken from the same angle and distance—straight on and across the street—which is the same shot that appears in the college recruiting catalog. For the next assignment, I asked my students to take multiple shots of a single subject, varying angle and distance. Several students went back to Thompson Hall and discovered a building they'd never seen before, though they walk by it every day. Students took abstract shots of the pattern of brickwork, unsettling shots of the clock tower looming above, and arresting shots of wrought iron fire escapes, clinging in a tangle to the wall.

The closer students got to their subjects, the more they began to see what they had never noticed before. The same is true in writing. As you move in for a closer look at some aspect of a larger subject, you will begin to uncover information that you—and ultimately your readers—are likely to find less familiar and more interesting. One writing term for this is *focusing.* (The photographic equivalent would be *distance from the subject.*)

From Landscape Shots to Close-Ups

The research reports many of us wrote in high school typically involved landscape photography. We tried to cram into one picture as much information as we could. A research report is a long shot. The college research essay is much more of a close-up, which means narrowing the boundaries of a topic as much as you can, always working for a more detailed look at some smaller part of the landscape.

You are probably not a photographer, and finding a narrow focus and fresh angle on your research topic is not nearly as simple as it might be if this were a photography exercise. But the idea is the same. You need to see your topic in as many ways as you can, hunting for the angle that most interests you; then go in for a closer look. One way to find your *focus* is to find your *questions.*

EXERCISE 1.4

Finding the Questions

Although you can do this exercise on your own, your instructor will likely ask that you do it in class this week. That way, students can help each other. (If you do try this on your own, only do Steps 3 and 4 in your research notebook.)

STEP 1: Take a piece of paper or a large piece of newsprint, and post it on the wall. At the very top of the paper, write the title of your tentative topic (e.g., *Plastics in the Ocean*).

STEP 2: Take a few minutes to briefly describe why you chose the topic.

STEP 3: Spend five minutes or so briefly listing what you know about your topic already (e.g., any surprising facts or statistics, the extent of the problem, important people or institutions involved, key schools of thought, common misconceptions, observations you've made, important trends, major controversies, etc.).

STEP 4: Now spend fifteen or twenty minutes brainstorming a list of questions *about your topic* that you'd like to answer through your research. Make this list as long as you can; try to see your topic in as many ways as possible. Push yourself on this; it's the most important step.

STEP 5: As you look around the room, you'll see a gallery of topics and questions on the walls. At this point in the research process, almost everyone will be struggling to find her focus. You can help each other. Move around the room, reviewing the topics and questions other students have generated. For each topic posted on the wall, do two things: Add a question *you* would like answered about that topic that's not on the list, and check the *one* question on the list you find most interesting. (It may or may not be the one you added.)

If you do this exercise in class, when you return to your newsprint, note the question about your topic that garnered the most interest. This may not be the one that interests you the most, and you may choose to ignore it altogether. But it is helpful to get some idea of what typical readers might want most to know about your topic.

You also might be surprised by the rich variety of topics other students have tentatively chosen for their research projects. The last time I did this exercise, I had students propose papers on controversial issues such as the use of dolphins in warfare, homelessness, the controversy over abolishment of fraternities, legalization of marijuana, and censorship of music. Other students proposed somewhat more personal issues, such as growing up with an alcoholic father, date rape, women in abusive relationships, and the effects of divorce on children. Still other students wanted to learn about more historical subjects, including the role of Emperor Hirohito in World War II, the student movement in the 1960s, and the Lizzie Borden murder case. A few students chose topics that were local. For example, one student recently researched the plight of 19th-century Chinese miners digging for gold in the mountains just outside of Boise. Another did an investigation of skateboard culture in town, a project that involved field observation, interviews, as well as library research.

EXERCISE 1.5

Finding the Focusing Question

Review the questions you or the rest of the class generated in Exercise 1.4, Steps 4 and 5, and ask yourself, Which questions on the list am I most interested in that could be the focus of my paper? Remember, you're not committing yourself yet.

STEP 1: Write the *one* question that you think would be the most interesting focus for your paper on the top of a fresh piece of newsprint or paper: This is your *focusing question.*

STEP 2: Now build a new list of questions under the first one. What else do you need to know to answer your focusing question? For example, suppose your focusing question is, *Why do some colleges use unethical means to recruit athletes?* To explore that focus, you might need to find out:

> Which colleges or universities have the worst records of unethical activities in recruiting?
>
> In which sports do these recruiting practices occur most often? Why?
>
> What are the NCAA rules about recruiting?
>
> What is considered an *unethical practice?*
>
> What efforts have been undertaken to curb bad practices?

Many of these questions may already appear on the lists you and the class generated, so keep them close at hand and mine them for ideas. Examine your tentative focusing question carefully for clues about what you might need to know. See also the box "Methods for Focusing Your Paper: An Example," which describes how one student completed this exercise.

EXERCISE 1.6

Finding the Relationship

One of the best ways to frame a research question is to use it to describe the relationship between your topic and something else. This is something researchers do all the time. For instance, suppose you're interested in anorexia, an eating disorder that afflicts a friend of yours. One way to get a handle on this big subject is to ask the following question: *What is the relationship between anorexia and* _____*?* How might you fill in the blank? Brainstorm some ideas that you think might show some interesting—and researchable—relationships. A "concept map" is one way to do this. Begin by writing your topic in capital letters in the middle of an unlined piece of paper, and then draw nodes with double-ended arrows that lead back to your topic. Write words and phrases in the nodes that suggest a possible relationship with your topic.

In this example, the map shows four possible relationships:

1. What is the relationship between anorexia and the anorexic's relationship with her father?
2. What is the relationship between anorexia and the anorexic's age? How young is she?
3. What is the relationship between anorexia and advertising?
4. What is the relationship between anorexia and the anorexic's history of sexual abuse?

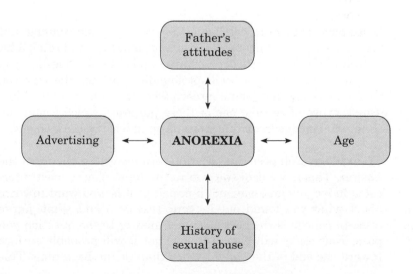

Other Ways to Narrow Your Subject

1. **Time.** Limit the time frame of your project. Instead of re-searching the entire Civil War, limit your search to the month or year when the most decisive battles occurred.
2. **Place.** Anchor a larger subject to a particular location. Instead of exploring "senioritis" at American high schools, research the phenomenon at the local high school.
3. **Person.** Use the particulars of a person to reveal generalities about the group. Instead of writing about the homeless problem, write about a homeless man.
4. **Story.** Ground a larger story in the specifics of a "smaller" one. Don't write about dream interpretation, write about a dream *you* had and use the theories to analyze it.

By marrying your topic to something else, and seeking to explore the relationship between them, you succeed in narrowing your focus. Now, instead of simply looking for information on anorexia—watch out for the avalanche!—you will be looking only for information that connects that topic with, say, anorexics' relationships with their fathers.

Possible Purposes for a Research Assignment

If you have a decent research question, you're off and running. But your first step should be to pause, look at your question, and think a bit about which of the following purposes are implied by the question you chose. Each of these purposes will profoundly influence the way you read your sources and how you approach writing the first draft. While any essay can use more than one of these purposes, which would you say is your *main* motive in writing your paper, at least at the moment?

1. **To explore.** You pose the question *because* you're unsure of the answer. This is what draws you to the topic. You're most interested in writing an essay, not a paper; that is, you want to write about what you found out in your research, and what you've come to believe is the best or truest answer to the question you pose. Your essay will have a thesis, but it will probably surface toward the end of the paper rather than at the beginning. This

is what I would call a *research essay* rather than a research paper, and it's the most open-ended form for academic inquiry.

2. **To argue.** You know you have a lot to learn about your topic, but you have a very strong hunch—or maybe even a strong conviction—about what the answer to your research question might be. Your initial purpose in writing the paper embraces your readers as well as yourself. You want to affect what they think, and even how they behave. Your thesis is a statement—*Muslim religious schools in Pakistan are not to blame for Islamic extremism*—that you can probably roughly articulate at the beginning of your project. It may very well change as you learn more, but when you write your paper, your purpose is to state a central claim and make it convincing. Frequently that claim is stated near the beginning of the paper.

3. **To analyze.** Some researchers collect data, examine it closely, and see how closely it conforms to what they initially thought to be true. They begin with a theory. Maybe you have a theory, too, and you want to test it by collecting information to see if you're right. For instance, you're doing field research on the culture of 15-year-old girls at a local school, focusing particularly on those on the social margins. Your theory is that a lot of these girls suffer from depression, and your interviews will provide information that you can analyze to discover if that's true. While you may not consider yourself much of a theorist, you are developing theories all the time about the way things are. This paper is a chance to test one of them using information you collect from your sources.

EXERCISE 1.7

Research Proposal

This is an important moment in the research process. How well you've crafted your research question will significantly influence the success of your project. You can change your mind later, but for now, jot down a brief proposal that outlines your research plan in your research notebook or to turn in to your instructor. It should include the following:

1. Focusing question
2. Primary purpose
   - *Explore:* What are additional questions that most interest you and might help you discover the answers to your research question?

Methods for Focusing Your Paper:
An Example

A clear, narrow research question is the one thing that will give you the most traction when trying to get your research project moving. It's also one of the hardest steps in the process. Like gulping air after a dive into the deep end of a pool, our natural instinct at the beginning of a research project is to inhale too much of our subject. We go after the big question— why is poverty a problem?—and quickly wonder why we are submerged in information, struggling to find a direction. That's why I've spent so much time on a range of methods to craft a workable research question.

Here's an example of how one student used some of these approaches to satisfy both her general curiosity about the origins of terrorism and her need to write an essay about it that would be interesting, specific, and manageable over a five-week period. Helen used the *time, person, place*, and *story* methods as a means of refining her research question (see "Other Ways to Narrow Your Subject" on page 52). Any one of these questions would be a good starting place for her inquiry into terrorism.

Topic: Terrorism

Opening Question: What is the cause of terrorism by Islamic extremists?

1. Time as a Focusing Device—What might be the historical roots of Islamic extremism during the first jihad in the 7th century?

2. Person as a Focusing Device—Did President Jimmy Carter's policies in the Middle East contribute to the radicalization of some Islamic groups?

3. Place as a Focusing Device—Have Islamic religious schools in Pakistan contributed to the extremist thought and the radicalization of Muslim activists?

4. Story as a Focusing Device—What might the story of Shehzad Tanweer, one of the men who allegedly participated in the 2005 London bombings, reveal about how young men are radicalized?

■ *Argue:* What is your tentative main claim or thesis?
■ *Analyze:* What theory about your topic are you testing?

3. What, if any, prior beliefs, assumptions, preconceptions, ideas, or prejudices do you bring to this project? What personal experiences may have shaped the way you feel?

Reading for Research

EXERCISE 1.8

Ways of Reading to Write

1. Complete the following sentence in your journal or notebook:
   *The most important thing about **reading** for a research paper is*

   _____.

2. The following passage is from the opening chapter of John Yount's wonderful novel, *Trapper's Last Shot*. It's a pretty startling scene, powerfully narrated. Read the excerpt, and then in your journal compose an explanation of how you interpret the purpose of this scene as an opening to the novel. What themes and feelings does it seem to introduce that you predict might be central to the rest of the story? Don't forget to use specific passages from the excerpt to support your assertions.

Chapter One

The summer of 1960 was hot and dry in Cocke County, Georgia. No rain fell from the second week in June through the entire month of July. The loblolly pines turned yellow in the drought. The grass scorched and withered in the fields, and bare patches of red clay earth began to appear and to crack and cake in the sun like the bottoms of dried up lakes. The first day of August some clouds drifted in from the mountains in Tennessee and the Carolinas, and the air grew still and heavy, and for a while a thin rain fell as warm as sweat. But before the rain had quite stopped, the sun came out again, and steam began to rise from the fields and woods, from the dirt roads and concrete slab highways, and the countryside cooked like so many vegetables in a pot.

The next day five boys started out to go swimming in the south fork of the Harpeth River. Except for a thin crust like a pastry shell over the pink dust, there was no evidence of the rain. As they walked toward the river, the heat droned and shimmered in the fields, and locusts sprang up before them to chitter away and drop down and then spring up again as they came on. When they got among the trees on the river bank, the oldest of them, who was fourteen, shucked quickly out of his britches and ran down the bank and out on a low sycamore limb and, without breaking stride, tucked up his legs and did a cannonball into the water. The surface all around, even to the farthest edge, roiled when he hit as if the pool were alive, but they didn't see the snakes at first. The boy's face was white as bleached bone when he came up. "God," he said to them, "don't come in!" And though it was no more than a whisper, they all heard. He seemed to struggle and wallow and make pitifully small headway though he was a strong swimmer. When he got in waist deep water, they could see the snakes hanging on him, dozens of them, biting and holding on. He was already staggering and crying in a thin, wheezy voice, and he brushed and slapped at the snakes trying to knock them off. He got almost to the bank before he fell, and though they wanted to help him, they couldn't keep from backing away. But he didn't need them then. He tried only a little while to get up before the movement of his arms and legs lost purpose, and he began to shudder and then to stiffen and settle out. One moccasin, pinned under his chest, struck his cheek again and again, but they could see he didn't know it, for there was only the unresponsive bounce of flesh.

From the novel *Trapper's Last Shot* by John Yount.

3. The following is an excerpt from an academic article on how college students think about their own masculinity. Obviously, this differs in many ways from the piece you just read. Your aim here is to carefully read the passage and write a summary of the author's main idea(s) based on your understanding of the text. A summary, you'll recall, is a brief capsulation of the important ideas in a much longer text. Write this summary in your journal and be prepared to share it with others in the class.

   Researchers' understanding of identity formation is commonly attributed to Erikson's (1968) developmental theory. According to Erikson, individuals gain a sense of who they are by confronting a universal sequence of challenges or crises (e.g., trust, intimacy, etc.) throughout their lives. Marcia (1966) operationalized Erikson's original theory and similarly suggested that identity formation is the most important goal of adolescence. Marcia viewed identity development as a process of experiencing a series of crises with one's ascribed childhood identity and subsequently emerging with new commitments. That is, as individuals consider new ideas that are in conflict with earlier conceptions, they weigh possibilities, potentially experiment with alternatives, and eventually choose commitments that become the core of a newly wrought identity. Individuals avoiding the process altogether, neither experiencing crises nor making commitments, are in a state of identity diffusion. Individuals may also be somewhere between these two possibilities by either simply maintaining a parentally derived ideology (foreclosed) or actively by experimenting with and resolving identity-related questions prior to commitment (moratorium).*

4. After you've completed the preceding three steps, spend some time fastwriting in your journal your responses to some of the following questions. These will also be discussed in class.

   ■ Did your approach to reading the two excerpts differ? How?
   ■ What are your "typical" reading strategies. Did you use them here?
   ■ What are your typical reading "behaviors," things such as underlining, highlighting, marginal notes, rereading, and so on? Would they vary with each excerpt?
   ■ To what extent did you take your own advice in your answer to Step 1 of this exercise;

   The most important thing about reading for a research paper is
   _____?

   ■ The two excerpts are clearly different kinds of writing—one is literary and the other academic. They're also different *forms* of writing. What are the key differences between them?
   ■ What problems did you encounter when you read these excerpts? How did you solve them?

Reading Rhetorically

We all learned to read in school, but we probably never really learned how to read *rhetorically*. Reading rhetorically means selecting particular reading strategies that are most effective in certain situations and for certain purposes and applying them. In high school, much of the writing about reading you may have done was in English class, writing critical essays about novels, poems, or short stories. In many ways, reading to write about a novel or a short story is quite different from reading to write research essays, something you may have discovered in

*T. L. Davis, "Voices of Gender Role Conflict: The Social Construction of College Men's Masculinity," *Journal of College Student Development* 43: 508–521.

Exercise 1.8. For one thing, there are very basic differences between a literary text and a research article. In a short story, the author's purpose may be *implicit*; you have to "read into" the evidence provided in a narrative to make some interpretation about its meaning. An academic article, on the other hand, is *explicit*. The author states his or her conclusions rather than inviting the reader to make a reasoned interpretation. In addition, academic writing, like the second excerpt in Exercise 1.8, uses specialized language and conventions—terms, references, evidence, and organizing principles that the people for whom the article was intended (usually other experts in the field) can understand. Stories have their own internal logic and language, but these are usually accessible to most readers even if the meaning is not.

Finally, we usually enjoy the *experience* of reading a story, or at least feel something in response to a good one, but we usually read articles with a much more practical purpose in mind: to acquire information.

Shouldn't the fundamental differences between these types of texts mean that the *way* we read them is also different? I think so. But we rarely think about our reading strategies, pretty much resorting to reading the way we always have in school. Maybe you never highlight, or maybe the pages you read are fields plowed with yellow rows. Maybe you make marginal notes when you read, or maybe you never write a thing. Maybe you always read everything just once, or maybe you read a text many times to make sure you understand it. Maybe you always read every word, or maybe you skim like a flat rock on smooth water. Whatever your reading practices, becoming aware of them is a first step to reading strategically.

Reading Like an Outsider

Why spend precious time thinking about your reading process? For the same reason this course focuses on the writing process: By becoming aware of *how* you do things that have become habits, you exercise more control over them. In many ways, this book is about challenging old habits and assumptions about research, and this includes approaches to reading when you have to write a research essay. For example, consider what's unique about this situation:

▪ In a general sense, you're just reading to collect information. But researchers use what they read in some particular ways: to provide support for their ideas, to create a context for the questions they're asking, and to complicate or extend their thinking.

▪ College research often requires students to read the specialized discourses of fields they're not familiar with. That means they must struggle with jargon and conventions that make reading particularly difficult.

■ Typically, the purpose of the research paper is not to report, but to explore, argue, or analyze. Information is in the service of the writer's own ideas about a topic.

■ In some classes (though probably not this one), the main audience for the research essay is an expert in the subject the writer is exploring.

In a way, the student researcher has to read like an outsider—or as essayist Scott Russell Sanders put it, "an amateur's raid in a world of specialists." What does this suggest about your reading strategy? First, it makes sense to develop a working knowledge of your topic *before* you tackle the more scholarly stuff. Research in reading suggests that knowledge of a subject makes a big difference in comprehension and retention of information. Second, your own purposes should firmly guide what you read and how you read it. Mentally juggle at least the three purposes I mentioned earlier—reading for example, for context, and for challenge. Third, anticipate your own resistance to the scholarly writing that seems "boring." It's boring because you're an outsider and haven't broken the code. The more you read in your subject area, the more you'll understand; the learning curve is steep. Fourth, in scholarly writing especially, quickly learn the organizing principles of the articles. For example, in the social sciences, articles often have *abstracts, introductions, methods*, and *discussion* sections. Each provides particular kinds of information that might be useful to you. It often isn't necessary to read an academic article from beginning to end. And finally, the most important thing: Read with a pen in your hand. In the next chapter, I'll introduce you to some notetaking strategies that encourage you to use writing to think about what you're reading *as* you're reading it. Write-to-learn activities such as fastwriting can help you take possession of information and help you write a stronger paper.

Reading Strategies for Research Writers

■ First develop a working knowledge.
■ Let your own purposes guide: example, context, challenge.
■ Anticipate your own resistance.
■ Learn the organizing principles of articles.
■ Read with a pen in your hand.

CHAPTER 2

The Second Week

Developing a Research Strategy

A few years ago, I wanted a pair of good birding binoculars for my birthday. I thought of the local store that seemed to carry the largest selection of binoculars, went down there, and within twenty minutes or so spent about $300 on some Swift binoculars, a brand that is highly regarded by wildlife watchers. Did you ever notice that is often *after* your purchase when you're most motivated to seek out information that reinforces your decision to buy something? Within days of buying the Swifts, I searched the Internet just to make certain that the model I bought was the one recommended by most birders. Sure enough, that seemed to be the case. Then I casually checked the prices on the binoculars, quite certain that I made a fairly good deal on them. To my horror I discovered that I had paid about $100 more than I had to.

Sometimes having no research strategy costs more than time.

A research essay is time consuming and, although you aren't risking money, the quality of your paper may make a big difference in your final grade. Your time and your grade are two reasons that it pays to be thoughtful about *how* you approach gathering and using information. A typical "strategy" is something like this: (1) get the assignment, (2) choose a topic, (3) wait until a few days before the paper is due, (4) madly search the Internet, (5) write the paper the night before you have to hand it in, (5) pray.

In fact, you've already approached this paper more strategically. In the last chapter, you spent time exploring possible topics, narrowing your focus, and developing research questions that will help guide your search for information. This will make a big difference in the efficiency of your research in the library and the Web. But what do experienced researchers know that will help you find

what you're looking for fast, and use what you find effectively?
Here's what you will learn this week:

1. A chronology for the search
2. How to control the language of your searches to get the best
   results
3. Advanced searching techniques for the library and the Web, and
   other sources of information including surveys and interviews
4. Evaluating what you find
5. Notetaking methods that will help you to begin writing your
   essay even before you begin the draft

Google vs. the Library

Despite all the fat, the carbs, and the empty calories, the convenience
of a Big Mac is hard to ignore. Similarly, a few minutes feasting on
the information served up by Google is far more convenient than
searching an online database at the university library. Actually *going*
there seems, well, out of the question. As one analyst put it recently,
"Googling has become synonymous with research." Another called the
relentless feast of online information "infobesity."

Should we be wringing our hands about this? The answer is
yes, and no. The power and accessibility of Google and other Internet search tools has turned virtually everyone into a researcher. No
question is too arcane, no quest completely hopeless when typing
a few words into a search window allows you to lurch through
millions of documents in a second. It's really hard to understate the
wonder of this. Along with the junk, the results of Internet
searches often turn up something useful, even for an academic
paper. In fact, at least one study* suggests that when Google
searches are matched with searches on library databases, the
popular search engine doesn't do too badly. When researchers
looked for relevant documents on four test topics, they found a total
of 723 relevant sources. Google produced 237 of these, and the
library databases turned up 163. Predictably, however, the documents from the library were generally a much higher quality—they
were from more qualified sources, more up-to-date, more balanced,

---

*Jan Brophy and David Bawden. "Is Google Enough? Comparison of an Internet
Search Engine with Academic Library Sources," *Aslib Proceedings: New Information Perspectives* 57 (2005): 498–512.

and more accurate. Still, while Google produced more stinkers, researchers concluded that 52 percent of its results were actually pretty good.

Undoubtedly, it's Google's accessibility that makes it so irresistible. In addition to avoiding a hike to the library or sorting through academic databases online, Google gives you results you can often find and use immediately. In the Google matchup with the library, 90 percent of the documents produced by the popular search engine were instantly accessible, full-text articles, while the library fared less well—only 65 percent of those results were full-text. In some cases, getting an article on a library database required interlibrary loan or a microfilm search.

Yet for all Google's appeal, in academic writing *quality matters.* A lot. You must always try to use accurate sources that are written by people who know what they're talking about. For those kinds of sources, your library is indispensable. The dilemma here is this: Do you value the accessibility of an Internet search above the quality of the library sources? At first, not many of my students struggle with this. Google wins, hands down. But savvy researchers know that's like juggling with one hand—you're making it much harder than it needs to be. In academic research, you need as much relevant, accurate information as you can get. The answer, obviously, is to learn how you can *complement* your Google searches with library searches.

A Complementary Research Strategy

Writers are always better off when they work from abundance. It is far better to have more information than you can use since this allows you to understand your subject more deeply and focus your investigation more narrowly. Attack your research question on multiple fronts—the Internet, the library, and interviews or surveys—and you're much more likely to succeed in finding out what you want to know (see Figure 2.1). This inclusive approach will help you accomplish the three things that make up a sound search strategy.

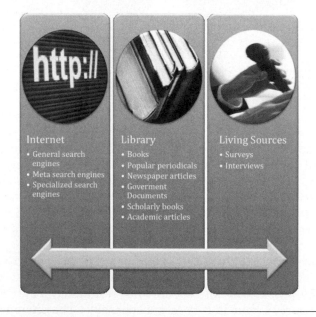

Internet
- General search engines
- Meta search engines
- Specialized search engines

Library
- Books
- Popular periodicals
- Newspaper articles
- Goverment Documents
- Scholarly books
- Academic articles

Living Sources
- Surveys
- Interviews

FIGURE 2.1   Maximize coverage of quality sources by investigating on three fronts.

1. Find *sufficient* information to fully explore a narrowly focused topic.
2. Find *varied* sources.
3. Find *quality* information.

Find Sufficient Information by Using the Best Search Terms

Around our house a few years back, the Harry Potter phenomenon had everyone muttering magic words. "Flipendo," said Julia, trying to turn the dog into a gerbil. "Wingardium leviosa," said Becca, who was determined to elevate her little sister six feet off the ground. Chopsticks substituted for magic wands. I knew this because we suddenly had too few when the take-out Chinese meal arrived; that was the only part of this magical revival that swept the household that I didn't much like.

Some writers foolishly think that there's magic involved in getting good words to the page when it's really much more simple and not at all mysterious: You have to have your seat in the chair and your fingers on the keyboard or curled around a pen. But there is a kind of magic you can perform as a researcher, and it also involves the right words uttered in the right order. *How* you phrase your search of a library database or the World Wide Web makes an enormous difference in the results. I've come to believe that this ability, almost more than any other, is the researcher's most important skill.

Controlled Language Searches Using Library of Congress Subject Headings

One of the things that is so good about libraries compared to the Web is that information there is organized. That's the good news. The bad news is that there is so much information to organize that librarians had to develop a special language for searching it. It's not alien language—the words are familiar—but it is a language that requires that certain words be used in the combinations that librarians use to organize information. These are *controlled language searches,* and they are much more common in the library than on the Web.

Skilled researchers who want to know what words to use in a library search turn to the *Library of Congress Subject Headings.* This five-volume book is in your library's reference room. The *LSCH,* also known as "the big red books," is a little-appreciated but incredibly useful catalog of the standard headings used by most librarians to index information (see Figure 2.2).

Subject heading in boldface. The notation "(May Subd Geog)" indicates that a subject may also be subdivided according to geographic location (e.g., Animal Rights—United States).

UF *stands for "used for." It lists less suitable terms for the same subject.*

Animal rights *(May Subd Geog)*
[HV4701-HV4959]
Here are entered works on the inherent rights attributed to animals. Works on the protection and treatment of animals are entered under Animal welfare.
UF Animal liberation
   Animals' rights
   Rights of animals

When subjects correspond to Library of Congress (LC) class numbers (i.e., number classifications by subject areas), they are included here. These numbers can be very helpful if you just want to browse the shelves for books. Scope notes are sometimes added to explain headings.

BT *means "broader term," NT means "narrower term."*

BT Animal welfare—
   Moral and ethical aspects
—Law and legislation
   USE Animal welfare—
   Law and legislation

USE *is a code that lists the standard LC term under one that is not standard.*

—**Religious aspects**
——**Baptists,**
   [Catholic Church, etc.]
——**Buddhism,**
   [Christianity, etc.]
Animal running
   USE Animal locomotion
Animal sculptors
   (May Subd Geog)
   UF Animaliers
   BT Sculptors
   Zoological artists

Subdivisions of the main subject heading, also in boldface.

FIGURE 2.2   There's no need to guess what subject headings to use when searching on your topic. The *Library of Congress Subject Headings* will get you off to the right start. Here a student looking for sources on animal liberation will discover that "Animal rights" is the heading to use.

Locate your topic in the book. You might begin by imagining a subject within which your topic probably falls, looking up that subject in the *LSCH,* and then finding a good match among the many subheadings listed. Look for the abbreviation BT, or "broader term," to see if you might be redirected to a more appropriate subject heading. Look especially at the NT, or "narrower term" listing. That may lead you to an appropriate description of the topic you've chosen.

As you're perusing the *Library of Congress Subject Headings*, get a sense of how your subject area is broken down. What are some other topics or subtopics within the area of knowledge you're considering? Do any sound more interesting? Are there other trails you might want to follow?

You want to save these *LSCH* terms for your topic for later. These will help you know the words to use when you search the library's online book index and many of the library's periodical databases. Essentially, you've just had a language lesson that allows you to speak "libraryese"—the words that will help you find information more directly and quickly.

Boolean Searching

Frequently, you'll be searching using a *combination* of keywords. For example, searching for books using the word "Wildfires" will produce an avalanche that will quickly bury you. Efficient research requires that you maximize the number of relevant results and minimize the number of irrelevant ones. That's where searches that use careful combinations of keywords are so important. Many libraries and some Internet search engines use something called "Boolean" connectors to help you do this when you search databases. George Boole, a British logician, invented the system more than a hundred years ago, and it still dominates library searching (it's somewhat less widespread on the Web).

The system essentially requires the use of the words AND, OR, and NOT between the search terms or keywords. The word AND, say, between the "Animal" and "Rights" will search a database for documents that include *both* of those terms.

The use of the connector OR between search terms, obviously, will produce a list of documents that contain either of the terms. That can be a lot of results. Sometimes by simply putting two words together, "Animal Rights," the OR is implied and you'll get the same results as if you used the word. This is often true when using a Web search engine.

The NOT connector is less frequently used but really can be quite helpful if you want to *exclude* certain documents. Suppose, for example, you were interested in researching the problem of homelessness in Washington State, where you live. To avoid getting information on Washington D.C., where it's also a problem, use the connector NOT.

Homeless AND Washington NOT D.C.

As you can see from the example above, it's possible to use the connectors between a number of terms, not just two. In fact, the art of creating keyword searches is using both the right words (those used by librarians) in the right combination (those that in combination sufficiently narrow your search and give you the best results).

One final search technique that can be very useful, especially in library searches, is something called "nesting." This involves the use of parentheses around two or more terms in a phrase. This prompts the computer to look for those terms first. For example, suppose you were searching for articles on the ethics of animal rights, but you were particularly interested in information in two states, Idaho and Montana. You might construct a search phrase like this one:

(Montana OR Idaho) AND animal AND rights AND ethics

Magic Words on the World Wide Web

In the last chapter, you did a subject search on the Web, using popular sites such as The Virtual Library that specialize in those kinds of searches. Far more common are searches that use so-called search engines such as Google. As you probably know, these are really quite remarkable software programs that in a split second "crawl" the Web, searching for documents that contain the keywords you type in. Lately, the magic of these search engines has been tarnished a bit by commercialism, allowing advertisers to purchase priority listings in search engine results and not always making that fact obvious to the searcher. But these search engines are still essential and getting better all the time.

Keyword searches are the most common methods of searching the Web. Unfortunately, there isn't consistency in search languages used by the many search engines available for scouring the Web. Some permit Boolean searching. Some use a variation on Boolean that involves symbols rather than words. But Google, the giant of search engines, has made all of this a bit simpler by providing a search form in which you simply enter the words or phrases that define your search (see Figure 2.3). You can find this when you click on the "Advanced Search" link, something that most student researchers rarely do.

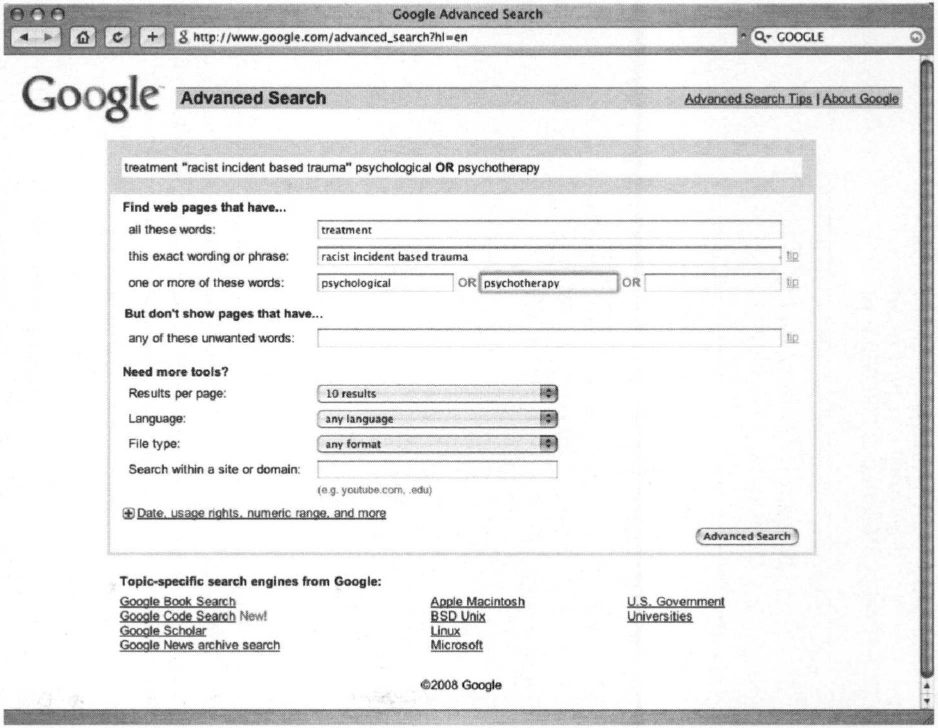

FIGURE 2.3 Google's Advanced Search page makes it easy to take advantage of multiple search terms that will focus your query and produce better results.

Google Advanced Search

8 http://www.google.com/advanced_search?hl=en

Q▾ GOOGLE

Google Advanced Search

Advanced Search Tips | About Google

treatment "racist incident based trauma" psychological OR psychotherapy

Find web pages that have...

all these words: treatment

this exact wording or phrase: racist incident based trauma

one or more of these words: psychological OR psychotherapy

But don't show pages that have...

any of these unwanted words:

Need more tools?

Results per page: 10 results

Language: any language

File type: any format

Search within a site or domain:

(e.g. youtube.com, edu)

⊕ Date, usage rights, numeric range, and more

Advanced Search

Topic-specific search engines from Google:

Google Book Search
Google Code Search New!
Google Scholar
Google News archive search

Apple Macintosh
BSD Unix
Linux
Microsoft

U.S. Government
Universities

©2008 Google

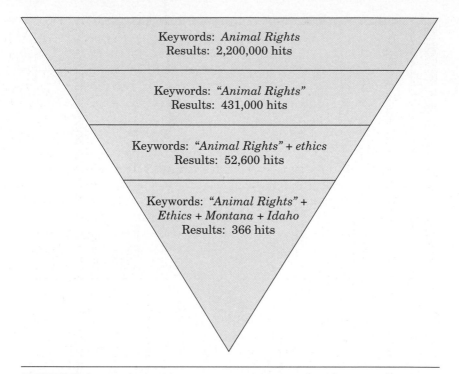

Keywords: *Animal Rights*
Results: 2,200,000 hits

Keywords: *"Animal Rights"*
Results: 431,000 hits

Keywords: *"Animal Rights" + ethics*
Results: 52,600 hits

Keywords: *"Animal Rights" +*
Ethics + Montana + Idaho
Results: 366 hits

FIGURE 2.4   Effects of Keyword Elaboration. A search on Google offers dramatically different numbers of results as the keywords are refined and elaborated on. Whenever possible use three or more terms to narrow your results.

Because of the mind-boggling amount of information on the Web, careful keyword searches are critical. Researchers waste more online time either not finding what they wanted or sifting through layers and layers of irrelevant documents because of thoughtless keyword searches. For example, notice in Figure 2.4 how the search on the ethics of animal rights can be dramatically changed by adding terms. An initial search on Google simply using the broad keywords "animal rights" produced 2.2 million documents. Using quotations marks to search for only documents that include that phrase, along with three additional terms, winnowed those results to 366 hits, many of which will be relevant.

Find Varied Sources

One of the first things I notice when I'm reading research essay drafts is whether the writer leans too heavily on a single source. Does this author or article keep reappearing, again and again on page after page, like a pigeon at a favorite roost? This is not good. It

What Studies Say about How Students Research Online

- Most use a trial-and-error approach to searching.
- They rarely use anything more than basic searches, avoiding advanced searching features.
- Typically, they only use two search terms every session, and these search sessions last an average of 15–19 minutes.
- Only 8 percent use Boolean operators.
- 60 percent admit that they are overwhelmed by the amount of information available to them.
- Nearly three quarters use the Internet rather than the library.

typically means that the writer has too few sources and must keep turning to these few, or one source is especially relevant to the topic or the research question and the writer can't resist repeated invitations for the author to reappear.

Vary your sources. This not only means using a sufficient number so that your essay is informative but using different *kinds* of sources whenever you can.

In part, the kinds of sources you rely on in preparing your paper depend on your topic. Sandra has chosen as her tentative focusing question, *How has the Kosovo conflict influenced the way war crimes are prosecuted?* Because Sandra's topic addresses public policy and current events, she'll likely find a wealth of information in newspapers and magazines but not much in books. She certainly should check the academic indexes on this topic—a database called PAIS, or Public Affairs Information System, would be a good bet—because it's likely that political scientists have something to say on the subject. Pat's working on a piece about the debate over the use of "water-boarding" by U.S. officials when interrogating suspected terrorists. He may rely more heavily on opinion pieces by commentators on the political left and right than on more objective studies, and because it's a current topic he will probably find much of his information on the Internet.

There are several ways to think about how sources can be distinguished from each other.

- Are they primary or secondary sources?
- Are they objective or subjective?
- Are they stable or unstable?

Primary vs. Secondary Sources

One way of looking at information is to determine whether it's a *primary* or a *secondary* source. A primary source presents the original words of a writer—his speech, poem, eyewitness account, letter, interview, autobiography. A secondary source analyzes somebody else's work. Whenever possible, choose a primary source over a secondary one, since the primary source is likely to be more accurate and authoritative.

The subject you research will determine the kinds of primary sources you encounter. For example, if you're writing a paper on a novelist, then his novels, stories, letters, and interviews are primary sources. A topic on the engineering of the Chicago River in 1900, a partly historical subject, might lead to a government report on the project or a firsthand account of its construction in a Chicago newspaper. Primary sources for a paper in the sciences might be findings from an experiment or observations. For a paper in business, marketing information or technical studies might be primary sources. A videotape of a theatrical performance is a primary source, while the reviews in the local newspaper are secondary sources.

Objective vs. Subjective

For now, I'm going to sidestep the debate over whether *any* source can be fully objective and simply point out that, generally speaking, we can divide all sources into those that attempt to report facts that have been gathered systematically, minimizing author bias, and those that don't pretend to be anything more than the author's opinion, perhaps supported by evidence gleaned from objective sources. You can probably guess some examples of objective sources: experiments, survey results, carefully designed studies of many kinds. The best of these are "peer reviewed" (see page 76) to double-check their accuracy. As you know, many academics prize these objective sources as the best evidence. Subjective sources are all over the map. Imagine a continuum in which on one end are advertisements and on the other are research essays like the one you're working on, a project that reflects your own ideas about a topic based on what you discover others have said. Ads, of course, typically have little or no information and often make claims without supporting evidence. In the middle there are blogs, radio essays, newspaper op-ed pieces, popular nonfiction books, and so on.

You might assume that objective sources are always better. But there are many occasions when it makes perfect sense to draw on a subjective source. It depends, as always, on the topic. If your research question is related to a public controversy—say, the accuracy of claims that a certain product will make your teeth whiter—then you will undoubtedly cite these claims in your essay. When you do use subjective sources, however, you must try to make it clear in your work what the nature of the bias might be. Is the author a right-wing commentator, an environmentalist, a spokesperson for a special interest?

Stable or Unstable?

When information went digital, a new phenomenon emerged—sometimes the information would just simply disappear. That Web page that you cited in your draft with the great statistics on scooter fatalities is there one day and gone the next. Since one of the reasons why you cite sources in academic writing is that readers can consult a writer's sources, that missing Web page is a serious problem. Disappearing Web pages, of course, are hard to predict, but you can make some judgments about the stability of an online source. Has it been around for a long time? Is it routinely updated? Are print versions of an online document available? Is the site associated with a reputable institution?

Find Quality Sources

The aim of your research strategy is not only to find interesting information on your topic but also to find it in *authoritative* sources. What are these? The highest quality sources are those types found on the bottom of the pyramid (see Figure 2.5). These are works that are most likely to be written by and then reviewed by experts in their field. You find these "peer-reviewed" articles in scholarly journals, some of which are now available online as well as in the library. The downside of dealing with sources at the bottom of the authoritative pyramid is that they may be written in the *discourse* of the field; to you that will make it seem as if the writing is jargon-filled and hard to follow. Of course, as a nonspecialist you aren't the intended audience for the work. But if you can glean some useful information, facts, or ideas from journal articles—and you usually can—your essay will draw on the best sources available on the topic.

When Was It Published?

If you're researching the treatment of slaves in nineteenth-century New Orleans, then currency is obviously less of an issue

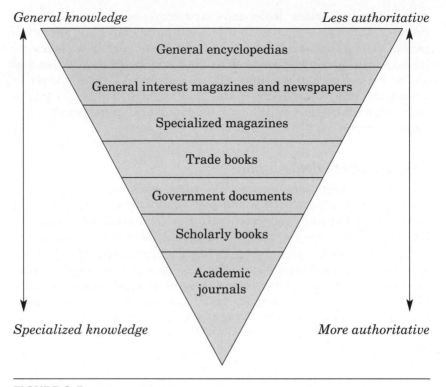

General knowledge   Less authoritative

General encyclopedias

General interest magazines and newspapers

Specialized magazines

Trade books

Government documents

Scholarly books

Academic
journals

Specialized knowledge   More authoritative

FIGURE 2.5   **Pyramid of Library Sources**

than it might be if your project were to explore the impact of the
Toyota Prius on marketing practices for hybrid vehicles. Generally,
in any project related to the social sciences, a recent publication
date carries more weight, which is one reason that the APA citations emphasize date of publication. The currency of Web pages
and online documents can also be important. A site that is regularly
updated is obviously more likely to have the latest information on
the topic.

Why Journal Articles Are Better Than Magazine Articles

If your topic has been covered by academic journal articles,
rely heavily on these sources if you can. An article on, say, suicide
among college students in a magazine like *Time* is less valuable
than one in the *American Journal of Psychology*. Granted, the latter
may be harder to read, but you're much more likely to learn something from a journal article because it's written by an expert and
is usually narrowly focused. Also, because academic articles are

carefully documented, you may be able to mine bibliographies for additional sources. And finally, scholarly work, such as that published in academic journals and books (usually published by university presses), is especially authoritative because it's subject to peer review. That means that every manuscript submitted for publication is reviewed by other authorities in the field, who scrutinize the author's evidence, methods, and arguments. Those articles that end up being published have truly passed muster.

Look for Often-Cited Authors

As you make your way through information on your topic, pay attention to names of authors whose works you often encounter or who are frequently mentioned in bibliographies. These individuals are often the best scholars in the field, and it will be useful to become familiar with their work and use it, if possible, in your paper. If an author's name keeps turning up, use it as another term for searching the card catalog library databases, or Google Scholar. Doing so might yield new sources you wouldn't necessarily encounter in other ways.

Not All Books Are Alike

When writing my high school research reports, I thought that a book was always the best source because, well, books are thick, and anyone who could write that much on any one subject probably knows what she's talking about. Naive, I know.

One of the things college teaches is *critical thinking*—the instinct to pause and consider before rushing to judgment. I've learned not to automatically believe in the validity of what an author is saying (as you shouldn't for this author), even if she did write a thick book about it.

If your topic lends itself to using primarily books as sources, then evaluate the authority of each before deciding to use it in your paper. This is especially important if your paper relies heavily on one particular book. Consider the following:

- Is the book written for a general audience or more knowledgeable readers?
- Is the author an acknowledged expert in the field?
- Is there a bibliography? Is the information carefully documented?
- How was the book received by critics? To find out quickly, search the Web with the author or title of the book using one of the academic search engines listed on page 46 in Chapter 1.

What Does "Peer Reviewed" Mean?

Broadly speaking, periodicals, books, Web sites, and magazines are one of two types: scholarly or popular. Popular publications include magazines like *Newsweek* or online sites like *Slate,* which are staff-written, usually by nonexperts for a more general audience. Scholarly publications are written and edited by experts for others in their fields, and the best of these are "peer reviewed." This means that before an article is published online or in print, a group of fellow experts read and comment on its validity, argument, factual accuracy, and so on. The article doesn't appear in print until this review is completed and the journal editor is satisfied that the other scholars think the work is respectable.

What does this mean to you? It means that you can count on the authoritative muscle of a peer-reviewed source to help you make a strong point in your paper.

Evaluating Online Sources

Librarians are gatekeepers protecting order, stability, and quality of information in the library. By comparison, the Internet is anarchy. Everyone knows that you have to be vigilant about trusting the accuracy, balance, and reliability of Web documents. Unfortunately, there's continuing evidence that student researchers still have a hard time assessing the quality of online sources. While many of the criteria for evaluating sources just mentioned apply equally to Web documents, they deserve special attention.

Here are some general guidelines to follow. Later I'll suggest a more vigorous approach for evaluating online sources:

■ *Always keep your purpose in mind.* For example, if you're exploring the lobbying methods of the National Rifle Association, then you will want to hear, and see, what this organization has to say on its Web site, knowing full well that this is not an unbiased source. The NRA Web pages are, however, both relevant and authoritative in this instance. After all, who knows more about the NRA than the NRA?

■ *Favor governmental and educational sources over commercial ones.* There are plenty of exceptions to this (like the one just mentioned), but in general you're wise to rely more heavily on material sponsored by groups without a commercial stake in your topic. How can you tell the institutional affiliation of sources? Sometimes it's obvious. They tell you. But when it's not obvious, the *domain name* provides a clue. The *.com* that follows a server name signifies a commercial site, while *.edu, .org,* or *.gov* usually signals an educational, nonprofit, or governmental entity. The absence of ads on a Web site also implies a site that is noncommercial.

■ *Favor authored documents over those without authors.* There's a simple reason for this: You can check the credentials of an author. You can do this by sending an e-mail message to him or her, a convenience often available as a link on a Web page, or you can do a quick search with the name on library indexes to see if that author has published other books or articles on your topic. If writers are willing to put their names on a document, they might be more careful about the accuracy and fairness of what they say.

■ *Favor documents that are also available in print over those only available online.* These might be articles that have appeared in magazines or newspapers or even journals. They might be conference reports or studies or even books. Sources that are published in more than one medium may be more credible because they undergo more scrutiny.

■ *Favor Web pages that have been recently updated over those that haven't been changed in a year or more.* Frequently at the bottom of a Web page there is a line indicating when the information was posted to the Internet and/or when it was last updated. Look for it.

■ *Favor Web sources that document their claims over those that don't.* Most Web documents won't feature a bibliography. That doesn't mean that they're useless to you, but be suspicious of a Web author who makes factual assertions without supporting evidence.

A Key to Evaluating Internet Sources.   As an undergraduate, I was a botany major. Among other things, I was drawn to plant taxonomy because the step-by-step taxonomic keys for discovering the names of unfamiliar plants gave the vegetative chaos of a Wisconsin meadow or upland forest a beautiful kind of logic and order. The key that follows is modeled after the ones I used in field taxonomy, but this one is a modest attempt to make some sense of the chaos on the Web for the academic researcher, particularly when the usual approaches for establishing the authority of traditional scholarship and publications fail. For one thing, many Internet documents are anonymous, and the date of publication isn't always clear. In some cases, even if there is an author of an online document, his or her affiliation or credentials may not be apparent.

If you're not sure whether a particular Web document will give your essay credibility, see Figure 2.6 and work through the following steps:

1. Does the document have an author or authors? If *yes,* go to Step 2. If *no,* go to Step 10.

Authored Documents

2. Does the document appear in an online journal or magazine that is "refereed"? In other words, is there any indication that every article submitted must be reviewed by other scholars in the field before it is accepted for publication? If *yes*, you've found a good source. If *no* (or you're unsure), go to Step 3.

3. Is the document from a government source? If *yes,* then it may be a good source. If *no*, go to Step 4.

4. Does the document appear in an online publication affiliated with a reputable educational institution or organization? If *yes*, its likely to be trustworthy. If *no*, go to Step 5.

5. Is *the author* affiliated with a reputable educational institution or organization? (For example, is he or she connected with a large university or a national nonprofit organization? Individuals associated with businesses or special interest groups may be reliable, though researchers should be vigilant about whether they have axes to grind and qualify the information to make that clear.) If *yes*, be encouraged. If *no*, move on to Step 6.

6. If the author isn't clearly affiliated with a reputable institution, does he or she offer any credentials that help establish his or her expertise to write on the topic? (For example, an advanced degree in the relevant discipline is encouraging.) If *no*, go to Step 7.

7. Did you find the document on a Web site that has earned high marks from scholarly reviewers and others interested in the reliability of Internet information? *Yes*? Great. *No*? Move on to Step 8.

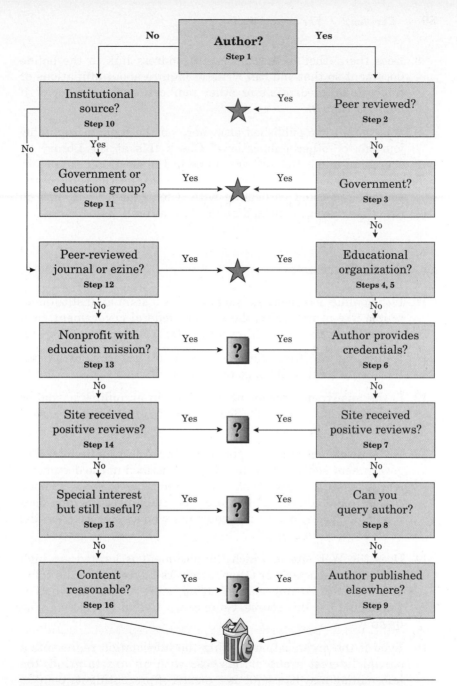

FIGURE 2.6 Follow the flowchart for a rigorous review of a Web document or page, beginning with whether the author is obvious or not. Sites that earn stars are generally more trustworthy. Those with question marks still may be useful, depending on the situation. Be particularly wary of information on commercial or special interest sites.

8. Does the author include an e-mail address link in the online document so that you can write to inquire about affiliations or professional credentials or other publications on the topic? If *no*, go to Step 9.

9. Has the author published elsewhere on the topic in reputable journals or other publications? Check this at the library by searching under the author's name in the electronic catalog or appropriate CD-ROM indexes. If *no*, reconsider the value of the source. You could be dealing with a lone ranger who has no expertise on your topic and no relevant affiliations.

Unauthored Documents

10. If the online document has no author, is it from an institutional source like a university, the state or federal government, or a nonprofit organization? If *yes*, go to Step 11. If *no*, go to Step 14.

11. Is the material from the federal or state government? If *yes*, that's encouraging. If *no*, go to Step 12.

12. Is the anonymous document published in an online journal or magazine? Is it refereed? (See Step 2.) If *yes*, it's likely a good source. If *no*, go to Step 13.

13. Is the document part of a publication or Web page from a non-government source whose mission is described in the document, and does it suggest that the organization's goals include research and education? Is there a board of directors, and does it include professionals and academics who are respected in the field? If *no*, go to Step 14.

14. Does the Web site in which the document is located get high marks from scholarly or other reviewers interested in the reliability of Internet information? If *no*, start to wonder whether you should use this source. Go to Steps 15 and 16 before giving up on it.

15. Even if the organization offering the information represents a special interest group or business with an axe to grind, the information may be useful as a means of presenting its point of view. Make sure, if you use it, that the information is qualified to make that obvious.

16. Do any of the usual criteria for evaluating a source apply to this anonymous document? Does it have a citations page, and do the

citations check out? Was it published on the Internet recently? Does the argument the writer is making seem sound? Do the facts check out? If the answer is *no* to all of the above, then don't trust the document. If you can answer *yes* to more than one of these questions, the material probably has marginal value in a college paper, though there might be exceptions.

A good researcher always takes a skeptical view of claims made in print; she should be even more wary of claims made in Internet documents. And while these approaches for evaluating online sources should help, it still can be pretty tricky deciding whom to take seriously in cyberspace. So to sort it all out, always ask yourself these questions: How important is this Internet document to my research? Do I really need it? Might there be a more reliable print version?

Developing Focused Knowledge

If working knowledge equips you to sustain a one-minute dinner conversation on your topic, then focused knowledge is enough for you to make a fifteen- or twenty-minute presentation to the rest of the class. You'll probably be able to answer all their questions, too. (See suggestions for class presentations on page 84 in the box, "Working Together: 'Could You Clarify, Mr. Ziegler?'"). You'll hardly be an expert, but you'll probably know a lot more about your topic than any of your peers.

Focused knowledge is the product of smart research this week and the next, refining your search terms, knowing where to look for the most useful information, and using your time efficiently. As you'll see later in this section, focused knowledge also depends on what you *do* with what you find. Are you able to not only collect information on your topic but think about its significance to your project? Remember that you'll be reading with at least three questions in mind:

1. Does this information help create a *context* for the question I'm posing?
   - Can it provide background on what has already been said about it, and who has said it?
   - Can it provide background on what is already known and when it was discovered?

- Can it provide background on why this is a question worth asking?
2. Does the information *support* or *develop* an idea or claim I'm making?
   - Is it evidence that what I'm saying might be true?
   - Does it help refine or qualify an idea I have about my topic?
3. Does this information *challenge* or *complicate* what I've been thinking about my topic?
   - Does it raise new questions I hadn't thought of?
   - Is it a point of view that is opposed to mine? If so, what do I think about it?
   - Does this change my thinking in some way?

What About a Thesis?

Ultimately, you must have something to say about your research question. But when should you know what that is?

Suspending Judgment?

Should you have a thesis or claim at this point? That depends on the purpose of your project. If it's exploratory, if your motive is to discover what you think, then it's too early to make any bold statements that answer the question you're researching. It might even be counterproductive. Inquiry-based investigations depend on your willingness to *suspend judgment* long enough to discover what you think.

What Do You Presume?

On the other hand, you might have a theory—some sense of the answer to your research question. We have theories all of the time, but we rarely test them against the evidence. I have a theory that every Labrador retriever I ever owned was a few cards short of a full hand in the intelligence department. Naturally, this prompts me to generalize about the breed. A research question arising from my experience is this: *What is the best way to evaluate canine intelligence?* Or put another way, who is really stupid—me or my dogs? Some theories, or presumptions, grow out of this. Here are a few of them.

1. My dogs' inability to follow simple commands, despite some training, is their fault.
2. Labs are usually pretty dumb.
3. Intelligence in dogs is fairly easy to evaluate.

Now would be an excellent time to make a list of your theories, assumptions, or beliefs about your topic. They will be invaluable guides for your research this week because you can examine these beliefs against the evidence and potentially break through to new understandings about your research question.

What Are You Arguing?

In some cases, you know what you think is the best answer to your research question even before you've done much investigation of the topic, and your motive is to build a convincing argument around that claim. For example, consider this claim: *Lawnmowers make a significant contribution to CO² emissions in the U.S.* Maybe this is something you heard or read somewhere from a reputable source, and it's something you strongly suspect is true. Maybe your instructor asked you to make that argument, or you're writing an opinion piece for an assignment. Conventional research papers are frequently organized from the beginning around a thesis or claim. If that's the kind of project you're working on, now would be a good time to craft a sentence that states your most important assertion or main idea. This may well be refined or even discarded later on as you learn more, but it will help with your research this week.

To generate a *tentative* thesis statement at this point, try finishing one of the following sentences:

1. While most people think _____ about _____, I think _____.
2. The most convincing answer to my research question is __IDC__.
3. The main reason that _____ is a problem is _____, and the best solution is _____.
4. Among the causes of _____, the least understood is _____.
5. Though much has been said about _____, very little attention has been paid to _____.
6. All of the evidence so far about _____ points to _____ as a significant cause/solution/effect/problem/interpretation/factor.

With these three questions in mind—and a number of others that interest you—you'll be implementing your research strategy this week and next, looking at sources in the library and on the Web. The exercises that follow will help guide these searches, making sure that you don't overlook some key source or reference. Your instructor may ask you to hand in a photocopy of the exercise as a record of your journey.

Working Together: "Could You Clarify, Mr. Ziegler?"

By the end of this week, you should be ready to make a presentation to your class on your topic. Imagine that it's a press conference similar to the ones shown on television. You will give a fifteen-minute talk on your topic to your classmates, who will later, like veteran newspaper reporters, follow up with questions. Your presentation will be carefully timed. It shouldn't be any longer than the allotted time limit; any less than the allotted time suggests that you haven't yet developed a deeper knowledge of your topic.

Plan your presentation with the following things in mind:

- *Rather than simply report everything you've learned about your topic, try to give your talk some emphasis.* For example, focus on what you've learned so far that most surprised you and why. Or present the most common misconceptions about your topic and why they miss the mark. Or provide some background about why the question you're exploring is important and share some of the answers you've discovered so far. If your topic has a personal dimension, tell the story, and share how your research has helped you understand your experience differently.
- *Don't read a speech.* It's fine to have notes with you—in fact, it's a good idea—but try to avoid reading them. Make your presentation as interesting as you can. After all, this is a chance to discover what other people think about your topic—what interests them about it and what doesn't. This talk is a great chance to try out some approaches to your topic that you may later use to make your essay more compelling.
- *Consider visuals.* Itching to try out PowerPoint? Here's your chance. Also think about photographs, graphs, charts, and other visual ways to present your information.
- *Begin by stating your focusing question.* Every presentation should start by establishing what question is driving your investigation. You might even put this on the board when you begin.

> While you listen to your peers' presentations, think about what questions they raise that interest you. These might be questions of clarification, questions about an assertion the presenters or one of their sources made, or areas that the speakers didn't cover but that you wonder about. Imagine that you're a hard-nosed reporter anxious to get the story right.

Library Research Techniques

Despite the appeal of the Web, the campus library remains your most important source of information for academic research. Sure, it can be aggravating. There's that missing book that was supposed to be there or that article that isn't available in full-text. You needed that article. Most of all, there's the sense of helplessness you might feel as a relative novice using a reference system that is bigger and more complicated than the library back home.

In the last chapter, you were introduced to basic library search strategies, knowledge that will help give you some mastery over the university library. In the exercise that follows, you'll expand on that knowledge, and at the same time you'll move from a working knowledge of your topic to a deeper understanding, one that will crystallize by reading and writing about what you find.

Finding Books

In the years since I wrote the first edition of *The Curious Researcher*, the old card catalog has completely disappeared. In its place is an electronic Web-based catalog that allows researchers to search for books even from home. This is a wonderful advance, one of the many ways technology has made researching easier, faster, and more efficient. But not everything has changed. Cataloging and indexing books is still done the old-fashioned way, and it helps to know how librarians organize books in the university library.

There are two systems for classifying books: the Dewey Decimal and the Library of Congress systems. Each is quite different. The Dewey system, reportedly conceived in 1873 by an Amherst College undergraduate while daydreaming in church, is numerical, dividing all knowledge into ten broad areas and further subdividing each of these into one hundred additional classifications. Adding decimal points allows librarians to subdivide things even further. Just knowing the *call number* of a book will tell you its subject.

The Library of Congress system, which uses both letters and numbers, is much more common in college libraries. This is the system with which you should become most familiar. Each call number begins with one or two letters, signifying a category of knowledge, which is followed by a whole number between 1 and 9,999. A decimal and one or more Cutter numbers sometimes follow. The Library of Congress system is pretty complex, but it's not hard to use. As you get deeper in your research, you'll begin to recognize call numbers that consistently yield useful books. It is sometimes helpful to simply browse those shelves for other possibilities.

Understanding Call Numbers*

The call number, that strange code on the spine of a library book, is something most of us want to understand just well enough to find that book on the shelf. How much do you need to know? First, you should know that there is more than the alphabet at work in arranging books by their call numbers and that call numbers tell you more than merely where books are shelved.

For example, the call number shown in Figure 2.7 tells you the subject area of the book, a little something about its author, and when the book was published. This is useful to know not only because

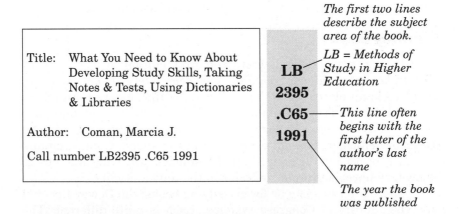

FIGURE 2.7   Deciphering the Call Number Code

*"Understanding Call Numbers" is adapted from the Web site of the Hawaii Community College library and used here with permission.

Read call numbers line by line:

LB

2395

.C65

1991

Read the first line in alphabetical order:

A, B, BF, C, D, . . . L, LA, LB, M, ML . . .

Read the second line as a whole number:

1, 2, 3, 45, 100, 101, 1000, 2000, 2394, 2395

The third line is a combination of letters and numbers.
Read the letter alphabetically.
Read the number as a decimal, e.g., .C65 = .65, .C724.= .724

This is the year the book was published.

FIGURE 2.8   Reading Call Numbers

it will help you find the book, but it might prompt you to find other, possibly more recent books on the same subject on a nearby shelf.

Figure 2.8 shows you how to read call numbers. Read them from top to bottom (or left to right if displayed horizontally). While alphabetical and numerical order are key to understanding the sequencing of books in the library, the third line of a call number is a weird combination of letters and decimals. This always mystifies me.

In Figure 2.9, you can see how Library of Congress call numbers determine the arrangement of books on the shelf. The only tricky part is that odd letter and decimal combination in the third line of the call number. Note that the small decimal number (.B22) precedes a larger one (.B27). The year a book was published also determines its position on the shelf.

It's likely your college library, like mine, has retired its 3" × 5" cards and replaced them with an *online card catalog*. This online system uses a computer to do the same thing that you used to do, thumbing through the card catalog. And of course the computer is much faster.

E X E R C I S E   2 . 1

Library Investigations

STEP 1: It's the rare topic that isn't covered, in some way, in a book or part of one. Subject headings on your topic that you gleaned from *Library of Congress Subject Headings* really pay off when you use the electronic index to launch a search for relevant books. Begin with those, manipulating search terms on the search page of your online

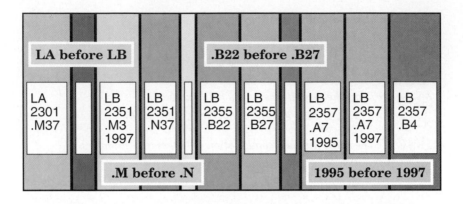

FIGURE 2.9   How Books Are Arranged on the Library Shelf

book index. Try several until you begin to see book titles that look promising. Figure 2.10 shows a sample search page.

Sort your results on a separate piece of paper from most promising to least promising. This is the beginning of your working bibliography and may be part of your progress report to your instructor this week. Use the following format for each entry. (It's based on

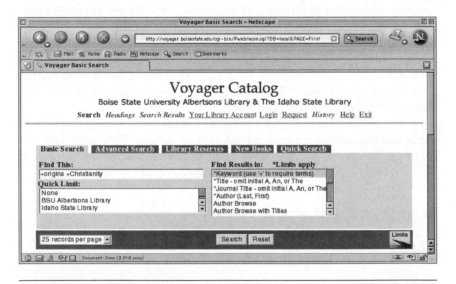

FIGURE 2.10   Online library indexes are now Web-based. The software varies, but nearly all of the search forms feature a range of search options, from basic to advanced, and ways to limit your search to certain databases, libraries, or terms. The terms you discover in the *Library of Congress Subject Headings* will help boost the relevance of the results.

the MLA method of listing citations, something you'll learn more about later.) You can also use an online "citation machine" like citationmachine.net to record the bibliographic information.

Call number: _____

Author(s): _____

Title: _____

Place of publication: _____

Date of publication: _____

Two- or three-sentence summary of what seems relevant about

each text to your project: _____

_____

_____

Coming Up Empty-Handed?

In the unlikely event that you can't find any books by searching directly using the online catalog, there's another reference you can check that will help locate relevant articles and essays that are *a part* of a book whose title may otherwise seem unpromising. Check to see if your library has a database called the Essay and General Literature Index. Search that database with your keywords or subject and see if it produces something useful. List the relevant results as instructed previously.

Checking Bibliographies

One tactic that might lead to a mother lode of sources for your essay is to look at the bibliographies at the back of (mostly) scholarly books (and articles). Don't ever set aside a promising book until you've checked the bibliography! Jot down complete bibliographic information from citations you want to check out later. Keep a running list of these in your research notebook.

Interlibrary Loan

If your library doesn't have the book (or article) you really want, don't despair. Most college libraries have a wonderful low- or no-cost service to students called interlibrary loan. The library will search the collections of other libraries to find what you're looking for and have it sent, sometimes within a week or less. Use the service by checking with the reference desk or your library's Web site.

Finding Magazine and Journal Articles Using Online Databases

It used to be that those green, well-thumbed volumes of the *Readers' Guide to Periodical Literature* were the only game in town if you were after an article published in a general-interest magazine. However, online databases have replaced indexes like the old *Readers' Guide*. Good riddance! While the *Guide* is still invaluable for finding articles published before 1990 (and as early as 1890) that may not be included in the new databases, the online indexes are much easier to use. See Figure 2.11. But perhaps the real weakness of the *Readers' Guide* and its online descendant, particularly for academic research, is that it's mostly an index of nonscholarly sources such as *Time, Redbook*, and *Sports Illustrated*. There's nothing wrong with these publications. In fact, you may end up using a few in your essay. But as you dig more

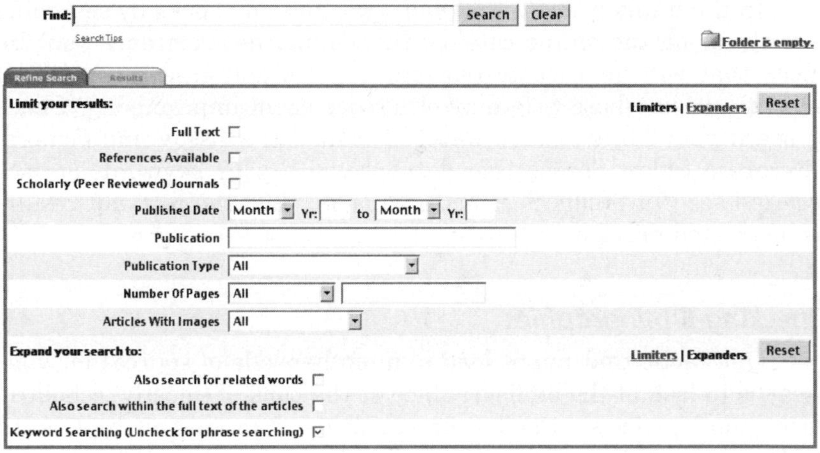

FIGURE 2.11   Since the periodical databases are huge, most search pages invite you to limit results not simply through careful use of search terms but by publication dates, full-text versions, peer-reviewed, and so on. A favorite choice is to ask only for articles that are available online in full text. The reason is obvious—it saves you a trip to the library to find the article in a bound volume. Remember, though, that full-text articles are not necessarily the best articles on your topic. The companies that sell the databases to libraries don't necessarily use quality as a criterion for which articles to offer in full-text.

deeply into your subject, you may find that the information in popular periodicals will often begin to tell you what you already know.

There are two kinds of article databases at your library: general subject databases that cover multiple disciplines and specialized databases that are discipline specific. Of course, I don't know which of these general databases you have at your library, but here are some of the most common:

GENERAL SUBJECT DATABASES

Academic OneFile

Academic Search Premier

ArticleFirst

IgentaConnect

General OneFile

Academic Search

JSTOR

Academic Universe on Lexis Nexis

EBSCO MasterFile

Many of these multidisciplinary databases include popular magazines, but they also index some scholarly journals as well. That's another reason they're so useful. For example, EBSCO MasterFile indexes nearly 3,000 journals and magazines and even provides full-text articles—rather than simply citations—from more than 1,800 periodicals. Increasingly, these databases include full-text articles, an extraordinary convenience for students working from home.

Specialized databases are subject specific. These are usually listed by discipline on your library's Web pages. The advantage of using these databases is that they will produce many more scholarly articles that might be relevant to your research question, though they may not all be full text. For a list of some of these, see the following table.

STEP 2: Visit your library's Web page that lists all of the available periodical databases. Begin your search by trying out one of the general subject databases. As before, if you find articles that seem relevant to your project, collect their bibliographic material or, if you're quite certain you might use the piece and it's available in full text, print out the articles. Most college libraries will allow you to mark citations you want to keep on the search form and later print them out as well. Now try an appropriate specialized database or two on your topic. As before, collect either bibliographic information on promising sources or print out full-text copies.

Your working bibliography for each promising source should include the following information:

Author: _____

Title: _____

Title of periodical: _____

Volume or issue number and date: _____

Pages covered by the article: _____

Two- or three-sentence comment about what information you hope to get from the article or what questions you hope it answers: _____*

_____

_____

COMMON SPECIALIZED DATABASES

HUMANITIES	SCIENCE AND TECHNOLOGY	SOCIAL SCIENCES
America, History and Life	Applied Science & Technology Index	Anthropological Index
Arts and Humanities Search	CINAHL (Nursing)	ComAbstracts (Communication)
Art Index	Biological Abstracts	PsychINFO
MLA Bibliography (Literature and composition)	GeoRef (Geology) Abstracts	Social Work
	MathSciNet	Sociological Abstracts
Historical Abstracts	Medline (Medicine)	Worldwide Political Science Abstracts
Literary Index	Computer Literature Index	PAIS (Public Affairs)
Music Index	Health Reference Center	Criminal Justice Abstracts
Philosopher's Index	AGRICOLA (Agriculture)	Contemporary Women's Issues
Humanities Index	General Science Index	Social Sciences Index
Religion Index		

BUSINESS	EDUCATION
ABI/Inform	ERIC
FreeEDGAR	Education Index
Business Source Elite	Education Full Text

Finding Newspaper Articles with Online Databases

If your topic is local, current, or controversial, then it's likely that newspapers will be an important source of information for your essay. You'll rarely get much in-depth information or analysis from newspapers, but they can often provide good quotes, anecdotes, and case studies as well as the most current printed information on your topic. Newspapers are also sometimes considered primary sources because they provide firsthand accounts of things that have happened.

STEP 3: Guess what? There are databases of newspaper articles, too. See the accompanying list. They don't index the hometown paper, but they do provide citations to the so-called national newspapers such as *The New York Times, Washington Post, Los Angeles Times, The Wall Street Journal,* and *The Christian Science Monitor.* Bound indexes of several of these papers are in your university library, but nobody ever uses them anymore. What's good about the national newspapers is that they're among the most authoritative journalistic sources; in other words, because of their large and experienced staffs, the information they provide is more trustworthy.

NEWSPAPER DATABASES

National Newspaper Index

Proquest National Newspapers

Newspaper Source

Lexis-Nexis Academic Universe

Newspaper Abstracts

Custom Newspapers

Alternative Press Index

The larger papers also have their own Web sites where you may be able to search their archives and retrieve full-text articles. Sometimes they charge for this service. A convenient method for searching some of these sites is to use a news search engine that will consult thousands of papers in a few seconds. Here are several of the best of these search engines:

NEWSPAPER SEARCH ENGINES

Google News (http://news.google.com)

Yahoo News (http://news.yahoo.com)

AlltheWeb News (http://www.alltheweb.com/?cat=news)

You can also configure some of these sites to send you alerts when articles are published on a topic relevant to your project.

Occasionally, the local papers are also indexed online by the university library, and copies are available on microfilm. More and more frequently, however, local papers, like their larger counterparts in major cities, have their own Web sites where you use keyword searches to scour their archives.

Search for newspaper articles on your topic. Begin with one of the larger databases such as the National Newspaper Index, and then, depending on your topic, search the archives or online indexes of your local newspapers. If you find a promising full-text article on the Web, print it out. Also try to find a citation for a promising article on one of the databases and go to the microfilm room of your campus library, find the article, and copy it. If your topic just doesn't lend itself to a newspaper search, then use Google News or another of the newspaper search engines listed above and print an article that was posted today from a foreign newspaper. Choose the country from which your ancestors came.

Advanced Internet Research Techniques

I love the word "portal." It summons images of a little window on some vast space ship that frames the face of an open-mouthed observer looking in wonder at the vast reaches of the universe beyond. Researching on the Internet is a lot like peeping out of that window. There is just so much out there, billions of documents, gazillions of words, each a fragment of electronic data floating in cyberspace like dust motes in some vast sunbeam. Earlier in this chapter, you were reminded that this universe, while tantalizing, is also a librarian's nightmare. There's useful knowledge for academic writing out there, but it's hard to find and it's easy to get lost.

You're already better prepared for the search than most. Earlier you learned how to evaluate Web sources and design keyword searches. This is crucial knowledge. In Exercise 1.3 you also used some of the Web's key subject directories, several of which are maintained by librarians, actual human beings who sift and sort Internet materials and list those that are worthy. However, the more common method of searching the Web doesn't use a human being at all but a piece of software that electronically crawls the Web creating massive indexes of documents that respond to your keyword searches.

Types of Search Engines

The most popular search engine is Google, a search engine with an enormous database that is relatively simple to use. There are many other search engines like Google, including Ask, Yahoo!, AlltheWeb, Live Search, Alta Vista, and others. For current reviews and ratings of each of these, as well as research on what particular search engines do well and not so well, visit Search Engine Watch (http://searchenginewatch.com/) and click on the link for "Search 101." Google and the others are really quite amazing, but they do have limitations. For one thing, they only index pages on the Web that have hyperlinks pointing to them elsewhere, or whose creators have requested they be indexed by a particular search tool. In addition, these databases may not be current.

Search tools such as Yahoo! or Google aren't the only vehicles for scouring the Web. There are also specialized search engines that focus on particular subjects such as education, politics, and psychology, as well as search engines that specialize in going where conventional Web crawlers like Google do not go—the vast invisible Web, containing the types of documents that Google and other search engines cannot find or will not find. No one knows the size of the invisible Web, but it's probably much larger than the visible one.

Finally, there are so-called metasearch tools such as Dogpile (www.dogpile.com/) that are able to deploy multiple individual search engines in the service of a single search. These are very useful, particularly at the beginning of an Internet search on your topic. However, metasearch engines aren't quite as good as they sound because they skim off the top results from each individual search tool so you won't see the range of results you would get if you focus on one of the search engines with its own large database.

What's the key to maximizing the efficiency of your Internet research?

1. Maximize your coverage by using multiple search engines, not just your favorite one.
2. If possible, exploit subject directories put together by people, not software, concerned with quality content.
3. Be thoughtful about what and how many keywords you use to search. Generally, the more words—and especially phrases—you use, the more likely you are to generate relevant hits.

EXERCISE 2.2

Research on the Internet

STEP 1: Using some of the keyword combinations you developed for your topic, launch a search on one or more of the metasearch engines shown in the accompanying list. These tools are a good place to begin because of their breadth—you can quickly see the more popular sites on your topics and the various contexts in which information about it might be found.

METASEARCH ENGINES
Clusty (clusty.com)

Dogpile (www.dogpile.com)

Mamma (www.mamma.com)

Search.com (www.search.com)

Vivisimo (www.vivismo.com)

SurfWax (www.surfwax.com)

Remember to play around with keywords, and don't forget the search language you learned earlier in this chapter. The "Help" button on whatever metasearch tool you use will give you the specifics on what connectors, Boolean or others, that search engine accepts.

Develop a "working bibliography" of Web pages (see Figure 2.12) that seem promising and print copies of them for note taking. For each page, include the following information, if available. A Web-based citation machine can help you with this.

Author (if any). _____

Title of page. _____

Publication name and date of print version (if any). _____

Name of online publication or database. _____

Online publication (volume or issue, date, page or paragraph

numbers). _____

Date you accessed the page. _____

Full Internet address. _____

A brief summary of what you found particularly promising or

interesting about the site. _____

Internet Research
Topic: The Intelligence of Crows
Focusing Question: Do crows exhibit unusual intelligence when compared with similar birds?

Working Bibliography

1. Hutchins, Lisa. "The Intelligence of Crows." Pica Productions. March 99. 2 July 2002 <http://www.users.qwest.net/~lhutchins/intelli_crows.htm>. Article reviews crow's problem-solving abilities and specific social behaviors like "mobbing."
2. "ASCAR's Frequently Asked Questions About Crows and Ravens." American Society of Crows and Ravens. ASCAR Online. 3 July 2002 <http://www.ascaronline.org/crowfaq.html>. FAQ page that includes some useful but limited information about crow behavior and common myths about the bird.
3. "Crow Family." Crow City. 3 July 2002 <http://website.lineone.net/~crowseed/crowcity/info/family.html>. British-based site discusses crow species in England with especially useful information on crows in Celtic mythology. Seems like a personal site.
4. Davies, Garweth Huw. "Bird Brains." PBS Online. 3 July 2002 <http://www.pbs.org/lifeofbirds/brain/index.html>. Page tells story of crows in Japan that use cars at intersections to open nuts. Also examines intelligence of other bird species. Linked to David Attenborough PBS program "The Life of Birds."

FIGURE 2.12   A sample working bibliography of Web sites related to topic on the intelligence of crows.

To make assembling this information easier, open a blank page in Word or some other word-processing program in another window while you search the Web. When you find a page you want to keep, highlight the address in your browser's address window, right-click to copy, go to your open page in Word, and right-click to paste. Because it's so important to get Internet addresses right, this copy-and-paste function can be very helpful.

STEP 2: Select *at least* two other single-search engines (see list) for a keyword search on your topic. Try two that you didn't use in Exercise 1.3 in the last chapter. Bookmark useful sites, and add what you find useful for your project to the working bibliography you started in Step 1. Though it's a bit of a pain, this working bibliography will be enormously useful later as you assemble the final draft of your essay.

In the searches you conduct for both steps of the exercise, you'll likely find links to pages that didn't appear in response to your original query. Follow these, too. The Web is aptly named since it presents knowledge through hyperlinks as multidisciplinary and interconnected.

POPULAR SINGLE SEARCH ENGINES

Google (www.google.com)

Yahoo! Search (search.yahoo.com)

Ask.com (www.ask.com)

Live search (www.live.com)

AltaVista (www.altavista.com)

Hotbot (www.hotbot.com)

Search.com (www.search.com)

AlltheWeb.com (www.alltheweb.com)

Looksmart (www.looksmart.com)

STEP 3: Specialized search engines that are subject-focused have proliferated on the Web in recent years, and these can be a boon to researchers because they often generate quite different results than general search portals, like Yahoo!. Google Scholar, the site you used briefly in the last chapter, is one of the best of these. Return there and do a more thorough investigation using some of the refined search terms you've developed in the last week. You can also find additional specialized search at the following sites.

SPECIALIZED SEARCH ENGINES SITES

Search Engine Guide (www.searchengineguide.com)

Pandia Powersearch (www.pandia.com/powersearch)

Virtual Search Engines (www.virtualfreesites.com)

Webquest (webquest.sdsu.edu/searching/specialized.html)

As before, bookmark all the documents or pages you discovered that seem useful, and add them to your working bibliography.

By now you're well on your way to developing focused knowledge of your topic. If you've successfully completed Exercises 2.1 and 2.2 you will have the following:

1. A working bibliography, annotated with your initial comments, of books, periodicals, and Web pages relevant to your topic. This will be invaluable later as you develop the bibliography for your essay.

2. Copies of promising articles or Web documents for note taking.

Living Sources: Interviews and Surveys

Arranging Interviews

A few years ago, I researched a local turn-of-the-century writer named Sarah Orne Jewett for a magazine article. I dutifully read much of her work, studied critical articles and books on her writing, and visited her childhood home, which is open to the public in South Berwick, Maine. My research was going fairly well, but when I sat down to begin writing the draft, the material seemed flat and lifeless. A few days later, the curator of the Jewett house mentioned that there was an eighty-eight-year-old local woman, Elizabeth Goodwin, who had known the writer when she was alive. "As far as I know, she's the last living person who knew Sarah Orne Jewett," the curator told me. "And she lives just down the street."

The next week, I spent three hours with Elizabeth Goodwin, who told me of coming for breakfast with the famous author and eating strawberry jam and muffins. Elizabeth told me that many years after Jewett's death, the house seemed haunted by her friendly presence. One time, when Elizabeth lived in the Jewett house as a curator, some unseen hands pulled her back as she teetered at the top of the steep stairs in the back of the house. She likes to believe it was the author's ghost.

This interview transformed the piece by bringing the subject to life—first, for me as the writer, and then later for my readers. Ultimately, what makes almost any topic compelling is discovering why it matters to *people*—how it affects their lives. Doing interviews with people close to the subject, both experts and nonexperts, is often the best way to find that out.

If you'd like to do some interviews, now is the time to begin arranging them.

Finding Experts

You may be hesitant to consider finding authorities on your topic to talk to because, after all, you're just a lowly student who knows next to nothing. How could you possibly impose on that sociology professor who published the book on anti-Semitism you found in the library? If that's how you feel, keep this in mind: *Most people, no matter who they are, love the attention of an interviewer, no matter who she is, particularly if what's being discussed fascinates them both.* Time and again, I've found my own shyness creep up on me when I pick up the telephone to arrange an interview. But almost invariably, when I get there and start talking with my interview subject, the experience is great for us both.

How do you find experts to interview?

■ *Check your sources.* As you begin to collect books, articles, and Internet documents, note their authors and affiliations. I get calls from time to time from writers who come across my book on lobsters in the course of their research and discover that I am at Boise State University. Sometimes the caller will arrange a phone interview or, if he lives within driving distance, a personal interview.

■ *Check the phone book.* The familiar Yellow Pages can be a gold mine. Carin, who was writing a paper on solar energy, merely looked under that heading and found a local dealer who sold solar systems to homeowners. Mark, who was investigating the effects of sexual abuse on children, found a counselor who specialized in treating abuse victims.

■ *Ask your friends and your instructors.* Your roommate's boyfriend's father may be a criminal attorney who has lots to say about the insanity defense for your paper on that topic. Your best friend may be taking a photography course with a professor who would be a great interview for your paper on the work of Edward Weston. One of your instructors may know other faculty working in your subject area who would do an interview.

■ *Check the faculty directory.* Many universities publish an annual directory of faculty and their research interests. On my campus, it's called the *Directory of Research and Scholarly Activities.* From it, I know, for example, that two professors at my university have expertise in eating disorders, a popular topic with student researchers.

■ *Check the* Encyclopedia of Associations. This is a wonderful reference book that lists organizations with interests ranging from promoting tofu to preventing acid rain. Each listing includes the name of the group, its address and phone number, a list of its publications, and a short description of its purpose. Sometimes, these organizations can direct you to experts in your area who are available for live interviews or to spokespeople who are happy to provide phone interviews.

■ *Check the Internet.* You can find the e-mail addresses and phone numbers of many scholars and researchers on the Internet, including those affiliated with your own university and ones nearby. Often, these experts are listed in online directories for their colleges or universities. Sometimes, you can find knowledgeable people by subscribing to a listserv or Internet discussion group on your topic. Occasionally, an expert will have her own Web page, and her e-mail address will provide a hypertext link. (For more details, see "Finding People on the Internet," later in this chapter on page 105.)

Finding Nonexperts Affected by Your Topic

The distinction between *expert* and *nonexpert* is tricky. For example, someone who lived through twelve months of combat in Vietnam certainly has direct knowledge of the subject, though probably he hasn't published an article about the war in *Foreign Affairs.* Similarly, a friend who experienced an abusive relationship with her boyfriend or overcame a drug addiction is, at least in a sense, an authority on abuse or addiction. Both individuals would likely be invaluable interviews for papers on those topics. The voices and the stories of people who are affected by the topic you're writing about can do more than anything else to make the information come to life, even if they don't have Ph.D.'s.

You may already know people you can interview about your topic. Last semester, Amanda researched how mother-daughter relationships change when a daughter goes to college. She had no problem finding other women anxious to talk about how they get along with their mothers. A few years ago, Dan researched steroid use by student athletes. He discreetly asked his friends if they knew anyone who had taken the drugs. It turned out that an acquaintance of Dan's had used the drugs regularly and was happy to talk about his experience.

If you don't know people to interview, try posting notices on campus kiosks or bulletin boards. For example, "I'm doing a research project and interested in talking to people who grew up in single-parent households. Please call 555–9000." Also poll other students in your class for ideas about people you might interview for your paper. Help each other out.

Making Contact

By the end of this week, you should have some people to contact for interviews. First, consider whether to ask for a personal, telephone, or e-mail interview or perhaps, as a last resort, to simply correspond by mail. The personal interview is almost always preferable; you not only can listen, but you can watch, observing your subject's gestures and the setting, both of which can be revealing. When I'm interviewing someone in her office or home, for example, one of the first things I may jot down are the titles of books on the bookshelf. Sometimes, details about gestures and settings can be worked into your paper. Most of all, the personal interview is preferable because it's more natural, more like a conversation.

Be prepared. You may have no choice in the type of interview. If your subject is off campus or out of state, your only options may be the telephone, e-mail, or regular mail.

When contacting a subject for an interview, first state your name and then briefly explain your research project. If you were referred to the subject by someone she may know, mention that. A comment like "I think you could be extremely helpful to me," or "I'm familiar with your work, and I'm anxious to talk to you about it," works well. That's called *flattery,* and as long as it isn't excessive or insincere, we're all vulnerable to it.

It is gracious to ask your prospective subject what time and place for an interview may be convenient for her. Nonetheless, be prepared to suggest some specific times and places to meet or talk. When thinking about when to propose the interview with an expert on your topic, consider arranging it *after* you've done some research. You will not only be more informed, but you will have a clearer sense of what you want to know and what questions to ask.

Conducting Interviews

You've already thought about whether interviews might contribute to your paper. Build a list of possible interview subjects and contact several of them. By the end of this week, you should begin interviewing.

I know. You wouldn't mind putting it off. But once you start, it will get easier and easier. I should know. I used to dread interviewing strangers, but after making the first phone call, I got some momentum going, and I began to enjoy it. It's decidedly easier to interview friends, family, and acquaintances, but that's the wrong reason to limit yourself to people you know.

Whom to Interview?   Interview people who can provide you with what you want to know. And that may change as your research develops. In your reading, you might have encountered the names of experts you'd like to contact, or you may have decided that what you really need is some anecdotal material from someone with experience in your topic. It's still not too late to contact interview subjects who didn't occur to you earlier. But do so immediately.

What Questions to Ask?   The first step in preparing for an interview is to ask yourself, What's the purpose of this interview? In your research notebook, make a list of *specific questions* for each person you're going to interview. Often, these questions are raised by your reading or other interviews. What theories or ideas encountered in your reading would you like to ask your subject about? What specific facts have you been unable to uncover that your interview subject may provide? What don't you understand that he could explain? Would you like to test one of your own impressions or ideas on your subject? What about the subject's work or experience would you like to learn? Interviews are wonderful tools for clearing up your own confusion and getting specific information that is unavailable anywhere else.

Now make a list of more *open-ended questions* you might ask each or all of the people you're going to talk to. Frankly, these questions are a lot more fun to ask because you're more likely to be surprised by the answers. For example:

- In all your experience with _____, what has most surprised you?
- What has been the most difficult aspect of your work?
- If you had the chance to change something about how you approached _____, what would it be?
- Can you remember a significant moment in your work on _____? Is there an experience with _____ that stands out in your mind?
- What do you think is the most common misconception about _____? Why?
- What are significant current trends in _____?
- Who or what has most influenced you? Who are your heroes?
- If you had to summarize the most important thing you've learned about _____, what would it be?
- What is the most important thing other people should know or understand?

As you develop both specific and open-ended questions, keep in mind what you know about each person—his work in the field and personal experience with your topic. You may end up asking a lot of the same questions of everybody you interview, but try to familiarize yourself with any special qualifications a subject may have or experiences he may have had. That knowledge might come from your reading, from what other people tell you about your subject, or from your initial telephone call to set up the interview.

Also keep in mind the *kinds* of information an interview can provide better than other sources: anecdotes, strong quotes, and sometimes descriptive material. If you ask the right questions, a live subject can paint a picture of his experience with your topic, and you can capture that picture in your paper.

During the Interview.   Once you've built a list of questions, be pre-pared to ignore it. Interviews are conversations, not surveys. They are about human interaction between two people who are both inter-ested in the same thing.

I remember interviewing a lobsterman, Edward Heaphy, on his boat. I had a long list of questions in my notebook, which I dutifully asked, one after the other. My questions were mechanical, and so were his answers. I finally stopped, put my notebook down, and talked informally with Edward for a few minutes. Offhandedly, I asked, "Would you want your sons or daughter to get in the busi-ness?" It was a totally unplanned question. Edward was silent for a moment, staring at his hands. I knew he was about to say something important because, for the first time, I was attentive to him, not my notepad. "Too much work for what they get out of it," he said quietly. It was a surprising remark after hearing for the last hour how much Edward loved lobstering. What's more, I felt I had broken through. The rest of the interview went much better.

Much of how to conduct an interview is common sense. At the outset, clarify the nature of your project—what your paper is on and where you're at with it. Briefly explain again why you thought this individual would be the perfect person to talk to about it. I find it often helps to begin with a specific question that I'm pretty sure my subject can help with. But there's no formula. Simply be a good con-versationalist: Listen attentively, ask questions that your subject seems to find provocative, and enjoy with your subject sharing an interest in the same thing. Also don't be afraid to ask what you fear are obvious questions. Demonstrate to the subject that you *really* want to understand.

Always end an interview by making sure you have accurate background information on your subject: name (spelled correctly), position, affiliation, age (if applicable), phone number. Ask if you can call him with follow-up questions, should you have any. And always ask your subject if he can recommend any additional reading or other people you should talk to. Of course, mention that you're appreciative of the time he has spent with you.

Notetaking.   There are basically three ways to take notes during an interview: Use a digital recorder, a notepad, or both. I adhere to the third method, but it's a very individual choice. I like digital recorders because I don't panic during an interview that I'm losing information or quoting inaccurately, but I don't want to spend hours transcribing the files. So I also take notes on the information I think I want to use, and if I miss anything, I consult the recording later. It's a backup. Sometimes, I find that there is no recording—the machine decided not to participate in the interview—and at least I have my notes. Again, a backup.

Get some practice developing your own note-taking technique by interviewing your roommate or taking notes on the television news. Devise ways to shorten often-used words (e.g., *t* for *the, imp* for *important,* and *w/o* for *without*).

The E-Mail Interview

The Internet opens up new possibilities for interviews; increasingly, experts (as well as nonexperts interested in certain subjects) are accessible through e-mail and newsgroups. While electronic communication doesn't quite approach the conversational quality of the conventional face-to-face interview, the spontaneous nature of e-mail exchanges can come pretty close. It's possible to send a message, get a response, respond to the response, and get a further response—all in a single day. And for shy interviewers and interviewees, an e-mail conversation is an attractive alternative.

Finding People on the Internet. Finding people on the Internet doesn't have to involve a needle and hay if you have some information on whom you're looking for. If you know an expert's name, his organizational affiliation, and his geographical location, several search tools may help you track down his e-mail address, if he has one. But perhaps the easiest way to use the Net to find someone to interview is through a Web document on your topic. For example, when researching this new edition of this book, I encountered an online version of the Alliance for Computers and Writing's proposals for MLA-style electronic citations, authored by Janice Walker. Walker's e-mail address was a hyperlink in that document, so had I wanted to ask her some questions, all I would have had to do was click on her name. Authors of Web pages frequently provide their addresses as links, inviting comments about their texts and the like. Thus, it seems safe to assume that they are probably willing to entertain questions from researchers, too.

Plucking an e-mail address from a Web page is the easiest way to find an interview subject. But what if you just have someone's name and organizational affiliation? Google them! This has become second nature for most of us when we're trying to track down that girlfriend or boyfriend from the eigth grade. It can be equally useful to hunt down experts on your research topic.

You can also find academics by visiting the Web sites of the universities or colleges where they teach and use the online faculty/staff directories to find their addresses. Obviously, this won't work if you don't know the name of the institutions with which a scholar is affiliated, but this is often listed in an academic's articles, books, or Web page. To find the home pages of hundreds of American universities and colleges, visit the following site: The Yahoo Education Directory (http://dir.yahoo.com/Education/Higher_Education/Colleges_and_Universities/). This is a very easy to use search page that allows you to find the home pages of universities in the United States. It includes links to a number of sites that also index colleges and universities as well as their various programs.

Making Contact by E-Mail.   Once you find the e-mail address of someone who seems a likely interview subject, proceed courteously and cautiously. One of the Internet's haunting issues is its potential to violate privacy. Be especially careful if you've gone to great lengths in hunting down the e-mail address of someone involved with your research topic; she may not be keen on receiving unsolicited e-mail messages from strangers. It would be courteous to approach any potential interview subject with a short message that asks permission for an online interview. To do so, briefly describe your project and why you thought this individual might be a good source for you. As always, you will be much more likely to get an enthusiastic response from someone if you can demonstrate your knowledge of her work on or experience with your topic.

Let's assume your initial contact has been successful and your subject has agreed to answer your questions. Your follow-up message should ask a *limited* number of questions—say, four or five—that are thoughtful and, if possible, specific. Keep in mind that while the e-mail interview is conducted in writing rather than through talking, many of the methods for handling conventional interviews still apply.

The Discussion Board Interview.   Discussion or message boards don't involve live conversations, like instant messaging, but they can be good places to find people—and sometimes experts—who are passionately interested in your research topic or question. How do you find one that might be relevant to your project? Try visiting one of the following directories that list these sites by subject.

- Google Directory (www.google.com/Top/Computers/Interent/On_the_Web/Message_Boards)
- BoardReader (boardreader.com)

- BoardTracker (www.boardtracker.com)
- MSN Groups (groups.msn.com)
- Yahoo! Groups (groups.yahoo.com)

Deciding What to Ask.   Another way to get some help with knowing what to ask—and what not to—is to spend some time following the discussion of list participants before you jump in yourself. You might find, for example, that it would be far better to interview one participant with interesting views rather than to post questions to the whole list.

But if you do want to query the discussion board, avoid posting a question that may have already received substantial attention from participants. You can find out what's been covered by consulting the list's FAQs (frequently asked questions). The issue you're interested in may be there, along with a range of responses from list participants, which will spare you the need to ask the question at all.

Planning Informal Surveys

Christine was interested in dream interpretation, especially exploring the significance of symbols or images that recur in many people's dreams. She could have simply examined her own dreams, but she thought it might be more interesting to survey a group of fellow students, asking how often they dream and what they remember. An informal survey, in which she would ask each person several standard questions, seemed worth trying.

You might consider it, too, if the responses of a group of people to some aspect of your topic would reveal a pattern of behavior, attitudes, or experiences worth analyzing. Informal surveys are decidedly unscientific. You probably won't get a large enough sample size, nor do you likely have the skills to design a poll that would produce statistically reliable results. But you probably won't actually base your paper on the survey results, anyway. Rather, you'll present specific, concrete information that *suggests* some patterns in your survey group, or, at the very least, some of your own findings will help support your assertions.

Defining Goals and Audience

Begin planning your informal survey by defining what you want to know and whom you want to know it from. Christine suspected that many students have dreams related to stress. She wondered if there were any similarities among students' dreams. She was also curious about how many people remember their dreams and how often, and if this might be related to gender. Finally, Christine wanted to find out whether people have recurring dreams and, if so, what those were about. There were other things she wanted to know, too. But she knew she had to keep the survey short, probably no more than seven questions.

If you're considering a survey, make a list in your research notebook of things you might want to find out and specify the group of people you plan to talk to. College students? Female college students? Attorneys? Guidance counselors? Be as specific as you can about your target group.

Types of Questions

Next, consider what approach you will take. Will you ask *open-ended questions,* which give respondents plenty of room to invent their own answers? For example, Christine might ask, *Describe any dreams that seemed related to stress?* The payoff for open-ended questions is that sometimes you get surprising answers. The danger, which seems real with Christine's question, is that you'll get no answer at all. A more *directed question* might be, *Have you ever dreamed that you showed up for class and didn't know that there was a major exam that day?* Christine will get an answer to this question—yes or no—but it doesn't promise much information. A third possibility is the *multiple-choice question.* It ensures an answer and is likely to produce useful information. For example:

Have you ever had any dreams similar to these?

a. You showed up for a class and didn't know there was a major exam.
b. You registered for a class but forgot to attend.
c. You're late for a class or an exam but can't seem to move fast enough to get there on time.
d. You were to give a presentation but forgot all about it.
e. None of the above.*

Ultimately, Christine decided to combine the open-ended question about stress and the multiple-choice approach, hoping that if one didn't produce interesting information, the other would (see Figure 2.13). She also wisely decided to avoid asking more than seven questions, allowing her subjects to respond to her survey in minutes.

---

*Reprinted with permission of Christine Bergquist.

The following survey contains questions about dreaming and dream content. The findings gathered from this survey will be incorporated into a research paper on the function of dreaming and what, if anything, we can learn from it. I'd appreciate your honest answers to the questions. Thank you for your time!

General Subject Information

Gender: ☐ Male ☐ Female
Age: _____
Major: _____

Survey Questions
(circle all letters that apply)

1. How often do you remember your dreams?
   A. Almost every night
   B. About once a week
   C. Every few weeks
   D. Practically never
2. Have you ever dreamt that you were:
   A. Falling?
   B. Flying?
3. Have you ever dreamt of:
   A. Your death?
   B. The death of someone close to you?
4. Have you ever had a recurring dream?
   A. Yes
   B. No
   If yes,   How often? _____
               What period of your life? _____
               Do you still have it? _____
5. Have you ever had any dreams similar to these?
   A. You showed up for a class and didn't know there was a major exam.
   B. You're late for a class or an exam but can't seem to move fast enough to get there.
   C. You were to give a presentation but forgot all about it.
6. Do you feel your dreams:
   A. Hold some deep, hidden meanings about yourself or your life?
   B. Are meaningless?
7. Please briefly describe the dream you best remember or one that sticks out in your mind. (Use the back of this survey.)

FIGURE 2.13   **Sample Informal Survey**
Source: Reprinted with permission of Christine Bergquist.

Survey Design

A survey shouldn't be too long (probably no more than six or seven questions), it shouldn't be biased (asking questions that will skew the answers), it should be easy to score and tabulate results (especially if you hope to survey a relatively large number of people), it should ask clear questions, and it should give clear instructions for how to answer.

As a rule, informal surveys should begin as polls often do: by getting vital information about the respondent. Christine's survey began with questions about the gender, age, and major of each respondent (see Figure 2.13). Depending on the purpose of your survey, you might also want to know things such as whether respondents are registered to vote, whether they have political affiliations, what year of school they're in, or any number of other factors. Ask for information that provides different ways of breaking down your target group.

Avoid Loaded Questions.   Question design is tricky business. An obviously biased question—*Do you think it's morally wrong to kill unborn babies through abortion?*—is easy to alter by removing the charged and presumptuous language. (It is unlikely that all respondents believe that abortion is killing.) One revision might be, *Do you support or oppose providing women the option to abort a pregnancy during the first twenty weeks?* This is a direct and specific question, neutrally stated, that calls for a yes or no answer. The question would be better if it were even more specific.

Controversial topics, like abortion, are most vulnerable to biased survey questions. If your topic is controversial, take great care to eliminate bias by avoiding charged language, especially if you have strong feelings yourself.

Avoid Vague Questions.   Another trap is asking vague questions: *Do you support or oppose the university's alcohol policy?* In this case, don't assume that respondents know what the policy is unless you explain it. Since the campus alcohol policy has many elements, this question might be redesigned to ask about one of them: *The university recently established a policy that states that underage students caught drinking in campus dormitories are subject to eviction. Do you support or oppose this policy?* Other equally specific questions might ask about other parts of the policy.

Drawbacks of Open-Ended Questions.   Open-ended questions often produce fascinating answers, but they can be difficult to tabulate.

Christine's survey asked, *Please briefly describe the one dream you best remember or one that sticks out in your mind.* She got a wide range of answers—or sometimes no answer at all—but it was hard to quantify the results. Almost everyone had different dreams, which made it difficult to discern much of a pattern. She was still able to use some of the material as anecdotes in her paper, so it turned out to be a question worth asking.

Designing Your Multiple-Choice Questions. The multiple-choice question is an alternative to the open-ended question, leaving room for a number of *limited* responses, which are easier to quantify. Christine's survey had a number of multiple-choice questions.

The challenge in designing multiple-choice questions is to provide choices that will likely produce results. From her reading and talking to friends, Christine came up with what she thought were three stress-related dreams college students often experience (see question 5, Figure 2.13). The results were interesting (45 percent circled "B") but unreliable, since respondents did not have a "None of the above" option. How many respondents felt forced to choose one of the dreams listed because there was no other choice? Design choices you think your audience will respond to, but give them room to say your choices weren't theirs.

Continuum Questions. Question 6 (see Figure 2.13) has a similar choice problem in that it asks a direct either/or question: *Do you feel your dreams: (A) Hold some deep, hidden meanings about yourself or your life? or (B) Are meaningless?* Phrased this way, the question forces the respondent into one of two extreme positions. People are more likely to place themselves somewhere in between.

A variation on the multiple-choice question is the *continuum,* where respondents indicate how they feel by marking the appropriate place along a scale. Christine's question 6 could be presented as a continuum:

> How do you evaluate the significance of your dreams? Place an "X" on the continuum in the place that most closely reflects your view.
>
> _____
>
> | | | | | |
>
> *My dreams always*   *My dreams are*
> *hold some meaning*   *meaningless*

Though it is a bit more difficult to tabulate results of a continuum, this method often produces reliable answers if the instructions are clear.

Planning for Distribution

Surveys can be administered in person, by phone, or online. Although there are some real advantages to administering the survey yourself (or lining up friends to help you do it), reflect on how much time you want to devote to gathering the information. How important will the survey be to your paper? Are the results crucial to your argument? If not, consider doing what Christine did: Print several hundred survey forms that are easy for respondents to fill out themselves, and distribute them with some help from your instructor or friends.

Conducting Surveys

Last week, you considered whether your topic lends itself to an informal survey. If it does, you generated three types of questions you might ask: *open-ended, multiple choice,* and *directed.* After all the reading you did this week, you likely have some fresh ideas of questions you might ask. Finalize the questions, and begin distributing the survey to the target group you defined earlier.

Distribution.   Surveys administered by telephone have some advantages. People are more likely to be direct and honest over the phone, since they are relatively anonymous. Surveys are also more likely to be completed correctly, since the answers are recorded by the survey giver. However, making multiple phone calls can be tedious and expensive, if your target group goes beyond the toll-free calling area. But you may have no choice, especially if the target group for your survey isn't exclusively on campus.

One alternative to conducting a telephone survey is to distribute the survey yourself. The university community, where large numbers of people are available in a confined area, lends itself to administering surveys this way, if there's a university audience you're interested in polling. A survey can be distributed in dormitories, dining halls, classes, or anywhere else the people you want to talk to gather. You can stand outside the student union and stop people as they come and go, or you can hand out your survey to groups of people and collect them when the participants have finished. Your instructor may be able to help distribute your survey to classes. I asked a number of my colleagues to distribute Christine's survey (see Figure 2.13) in their Freshman English classes, a required course representing a relatively random sample of freshmen. Since the survey only took five minutes to fill out, other instructors were glad to help, and in one day Christine was able to sample more than ninety students.

The campus and its activities often self-select the group you want to survey. Anna, writing a paper on date rape, surveyed exclusively women on campus, many of whom she found in women's dormitories. For his paper on the future of the fraternity system, David surveyed local "Greeks" at their annual awards banquet.

How large a sample should you shoot for? Since yours won't be a scientific survey, don't bother worrying about statistical reliability; just try to survey as many people as you can. Certainly, a large (say, more than one hundred) and representative sample will lend more credence to your claims about any patterns observed in the results.

The Internet Survey

You can create an online survey easily using a program like surveymonkey.com. These programs are remarkably easy to use, walking you through the process of designing questions, posting the survey, and even analyzing the results. For example, Survey-Monkey's free "basic" service will allow you to create a ten-question survey and collect up to a hundred responses. You can then post the survey on your blog, send it out to an email mailing list, or put a link on your web site. The challenge, as usual, is reaching the people you'd like to survey and getting them to respond.

Listservs, discussion boards, and even real-time communication tools such as chat rooms, all organize people with similar interests—and in some cases similar demographics. This makes cyberspace a potentially appealing place to conduct survey work. Consider, for example, posting three or four questions on your topic to a relevant discussion group or to a group that may reach an audience you'd like to survey. For example, Marty was working on an essay that explored the extent to which college students felt a generational identity. A search on Google Groups produced a Usenet group (alt.society.generation-x) that proved an ideal forum to respond to her questions.

CHAPTER 3

The Third Week

Writing in the Middle

I was never crazy about taking notes for a research paper. Notetaking seemed so tedious. Instead, I developed a love affair with the photocopier and walked around sounding like a slot machine, my pockets full of change, ready to bolt to the nearest copier whenever I encountered a promising article. I collected these articles to read later. I also checked out scores of books that seemed useful, rather than taking the time to skim them in the library and jot down notes on what seemed important. I was quite a sight at the end of the day, walking back to my dormitory or apartment, reeling under the weight of a mound of books and articles, all precariously balanced, defying natural laws.

When the time came to begin writing my paper, the work seemed agonizingly slow. I would consult my meager notes, thumb through two or three books from the stack, reread a dog-eared copy of an article, stop and think, write a line or two, stop and go back to a book, and then maybe write another line or two. I was always a slow writer, but I now realize that one major reason I got bogged down writing my research paper drafts was my inattention to note-taking. I paid the price for doing so little writing before I had to do the writing.

I now believe that the writing that takes place in the *middle* of the research process—the notetaking stage—may be as important, if not more so, than the writing that takes place at the end—composing the draft. Writing in the middle helps you take possession of your sources and establish your presence in the draft. It sharpens your thinking about your topic. And it is the best cure for unintentional plagiarism.

I realize I have a sales job to do on this. Writing in the middle, particularly if you've been weaned on notecards, feels like busywork. "It gets in the way of doing the research," one student told me. "I just want

115

to collect as much stuff as I can, as quickly as I can. Notetaking slows me down." Though it may seem inefficient, writing as you read may actually make your research *more* efficient. Skeptical? Read on.

Becoming an Activist Notetaker

Notetaking can and probably should begin the process of writing your paper. Notetaking is not simply a mechanical process of vacuuming up as much information as you can and depositing it on notecards or in a notebook with little thought. Your notes from sources are your first chance to *make sense* of the information you encounter, to make it your own. You do need more time to take thoughtful notes, but doing so pays off in writing a draft more quickly and in producing a paper that reflects your point of view much more strongly.

I'll show you what I mean. Here's a passage from the essay "How the Web Destroys the Quality of Students' Research Papers" by David Rothenberg.

> But too much of what passes for information these days [on the Web] is simply *advertising* for information. Screen after screen shows you where you can find out more, how you can connect to this place or that. The acts of linking and networking and randomly jumping from here to there become as exciting or rewarding as actually finding anything of intellectual value.

As part of a conference presentation, I decided to write an essay that explores some of the issues raised in the article. I wondered, "Is David Rothenberg right when he argues that so far Web research has had a mostly negative impact on student writing?" The passage above struck me, and I wrote it down—word for word—on the left page of my journal. On the opposing page I began an open-ended fastwrite, exploring my reaction to Rothenberg's claim.

Here's what I found myself saying about four minutes into the fastwriting:

> It strikes me that the real virtue of the Web might be its central weakness: Because so much of the Web is, as Rothenberg claims, insubstantial and unreliable, we have a wonderful opportunity to get students to consider that distinction between information and knowledge, between legitimate and specious claims to authority
>
> . . . Where Rothenberg sees pitfalls, I see opportunities, I guess.

And here's what I ended up writing in my own essay, "A Net Full of Nothing?":

> I don't think most of my students think that the Internet makes research easier. It makes research more *convenient,* and that's why students' first instinct these days is to pull up a chair in front of a monitor rather than to journey into the stacks. For the foreseeable future, the campus library will remain the best place to cast a net for term papers, but I'm coming around to seeing that the Web may be an even better place for students to practice how to evaluate their catch. *Can the Internet's weakness as a source of knowledge tutor students in the opportunities for knowlege-making?* I'm not sure yet.

It's quite possible, of course, that I could have used some other way to come up with the idea that the Web's weaknesses as an information source might be one of its virtues. But time and again I've seen in my own writing—and in my students'—that this kind of open-ended, often messy writing *as I'm reading* a book or article or even a Web page produces suprises: new ways of seeing things, and sometimes even new ways of saying things. It is also a great way to talk to, with, and sometimes against the published author. Talking freely to yourself in writing about what you're reading, how you understand it, and how it relates to what you already think (or may have never thought of) is one of the best ways to make outside sources your own. Such writing to yourself also allows you to indulge in "the gift of perhaps," trying out ideas and posing questions you wouldn't dare to do in a draft because it would complicate things.

Writing in the middle is basically something you do everyday: Have a conversation. In this case you're doing it with a stranger who shares your interest in something and you're talking with texts. The exercise that follows is an opportunity to practice this new kind of dialog.

Something like 85 percent of all American college students use the social networking site Facebook. Writer Christine Rosen speculates that sites like Facebook and MySpace have fundamentally changed the "taxonomy of friendship." Where we once developed good friendships with people by privately sharing the intimate details of our lives face-to-face, these social networking sites place a premium on divulging these details in public. In fact, the weirder you come across, the more you can distinguish yourself as unique and quirky, the more successful you can be at "acquiring" friends. Rosen argues that the kinds of things that earn you status on Facebook or MySpace are not the kinds of things that generally encourage meaningful relationships. Her essay, excerpted in Exercise 3.1, is titled "Virtual Friendship and the New Narcissism." You can find the full essay later in this chapter, on page 134.

EXERCISE 3.1

Getting a Word in Edgewise

Have a conversation with Christine Rosen about what you think about her argument. To get in the spirit of this, imagine that you are actually going to sit across from her at lunch as she explains some of her key claims. Rosen obviously knows more about the influence of social networking sites on our relationships with each other than you do; after all, you haven't thought about it as much as she has. But she is interested in what you think.

First, think to yourself about these issues by fastwriting for four minutes in your notebook in response to one or more of the following questions. Follow the writing wherever it goes.

1. If you're a Facebook or MySpace user, what kind of "portrait" do you think you've tried to paint of yourself on your site?
2. If you've never used a social networking site online, what do you think of the idea that Facebook or MySpace are "great places to connect with people and make friends?"
3. Tell a story of one of your experiences on one of these sites.

Now that you've prepared a little for your conversation with Rosen, imagine that you've met her at a restaurant and she says suddenly, "There are some things I've been thinking about and I'd really like to know your thoughts about them, particularly as a college student."

"Shoot," you say.

And then Rosen says this:

Today's online social networks are congeries of mostly weak ties— no one who lists thousands of "friends" on MySpace thinks of those people in the same way as he does his flesh-and-blood acquaintances, for example. It is surely no coincidence, then, that the activities social networking sites promote are precisely the ones weak ties foster, like rumor-mongering, gossip, finding people, and tracking the ever-shifting movements of popular culture and fad. If this is our small world, it is one that gives its greatest attention to small things.*

STEP 1: Begin a five-minute fastwrite in which you respond to Rosen's comment. Try to hold up your end of the conversation. Whenever the writing stalls, return to the passage above and find something else to respond to—ask questions, react, present your own ideas, try to restate what you think Rosen seems to be saying.

Lunch continues. Rosen seems genuinely interested in your response to her ideas. She sets her glass of water down after a sip, looks you in the eye, and says, "Okay, what do you think of this?":

> . . . [I]n the offline world, communities typically are responsible for enforcing norms of privacy and general etiquette. In the online world, which is unfettered by the boundaries of real-world communities, new etiquette challenges abound. For example, what do you do with a "friend" who posts inappropriate comments on your Wall? What recourse do you have if someone posts an embarrassing picture of you on his MySpace page? What happens when a friend breaks up with someone—do you defriend the ex? If someone "friends" you and you don't accept the overture, how serious a rejection is it? Some of these scenarios can be resolved with split-second snap judgments; others can provoke days of agonizing.

STEP 2: Begin another five-minute fastwrite in your notebook in which you respond to this latest proposition by your luncheon partner. Again, try to preserve the relatively informal, conversational quality of the situation.

Lunch is nearly over, and Rosen seems finished talking. You're wondering about who will pick up the check. Suddenly, Rosen says, "Sorry. There's just one more thing I'd like to say. Will you hear me out?"

Your pen is at the ready.

She says:

> The implications of the narcissistic and exhibitionistic tendencies of social networkers also cry out for further consideration. There are opportunity costs when we spend so much time

---

*Christine Rosen, "Virtual Friendship and the New Narcissism," *The New Atlantis: A Journal of Technology and Society* (Summer 2007): 15–31.

carefully grooming ourselves online. Given how much time we already devote to entertaining ourselves with technology, it is at least worth asking if the time we spend on social networking sites is well spent. In investing so much energy into improving how we *present* ourselves online, are we missing chances to genuinely *improve* ourselves?

STEP 3: You graciously respond to Rosen once more in a five-minute fastwrite.

Your instructor may have you read the full text of Rosen's article (Exercise 3.5) and ask you to compose an essay that grows out of this written conversation. What I most want you to notice at this point, however, is whether this dialog with a published author has anything in common with conventional notetaking. If not, what are the differences? Later in this chapter, I suggest an approach to notetaking that combines conventional quotation, summary, and paraphrase with the kind of open-ended writing you accomplished here. It's a process that encourages the kind of *dialectical* thinking that is at the heart of inquiry, the movement back and forth between your observations and your ideas about them, between generating and judging, and collecting evidence and developing theories about what it might mean.

A Variation in Responding: Believing and Doubting

In each fastwrite response to Rosen, consider spending the first two minutes playing "the believing game" and the next two minutes "the doubting game." In other words, begin by thinking through writing about why Rosen might see things the way she does. What can you *understand* about her point of view? What might you agree with? Then shift your stance, and critically examine her claims. What is she ignoring? What fault do you find with her reasoning? How does your own experience offer contrary evidence?

Most *good* conversations make demands on both speakers. The most important of these is simply to listen carefully to what the other person is saying, even (and perhaps especially) if you don't agree. In couples therapy there's a method to help this along called "say back"—each partner has to listen first and then repeat what he or she heard the other say. Response or reaction comes later. Researchers entering into a conversation with their sources need to engage in the same practice: Listen or read carefully, first making an effort to understand a subject or author's arguments or ideas, and then exploring your response to them, as you did in the preceding exercise.

The academic equivalent of "say back" is paraphrasing or summarizing. Both are undervalued skills, I think, that require practice. Try your hand at it in the following exercise.

EXERCISE 3.2

"Say Back" to a Source

The following passage is from an article by linguist Deborah Tannen on the complexity of communication within families.

> Through talk, we create and shape our relationships. Through talk, we are comforted; through talk we are hurt. We look to family members for come-as-you-are acceptance, but instead of an intimate ally, we sometimes find an intimate critic. A small remark can spark a big conflict because with the family, no utterance stands alone. Every remark draws meaning from innumerable conversations that came before.*

In your notebook, rewrite the passage in your own words in roughly the same length—a *paraphrase*. You'll find it's easier to do if you first focus on understanding what Tannen is trying to say and then write without looking much at the passage, if possible. If this is an in-class exercise, exchange your rewrite with a partner. Then read the following section on plagiarism.

Recognizing Plagiarism

Simply put, *plagiarism* is using others' ideas *or* words as if they were your own. The most egregious case is handing in someone else's work with your name on it. Some schools also consider using one paper to meet the requirements of two classes to be a grave offense. But most plagiarism is unintentional. I remember being guilty of plagiarism when writing a philosophy paper my freshman year in college. I committed the offense largely because I didn't know what plagiarism was and I hadn't been adequately schooled in good scholarship (which is no excuse).

*Deborah Tannen, "I Heard What You Didn't Say," *The Washington Post,* May 13, 2001: B1.

I Read What You Said and Borrowed It, Okay?

Here's another passage from the same article by Deborah Tannen. In this excerpt she is talking about a situation with which we're all familiar. We're talking with a loved one and he or she makes a comment that seems innocuous—"I'll put the dishes in the dishwasher because I can pack more in"—but the comment is heard as a larger criticism: "You're not good at housework." There are what seem to be simple messages with equally simple motives, and then there are "metamessages" that we sometimes hear instead of the simple ones. What follows is Tannen's original passage, and what seems like a pretty good paraphrase.

> **Original passage:** *Distinguishing the message from the metamessage (terms I have adopted from anthropologist Gregory Bateson) is necessary to ensure that family members work things out rather than working each other over. It's frustrating to have the same arguments again and again. But some arguments can be constructive—if family members use them to articulate and understand the metamessages they are intending and hearing.*

> **Paraphrase:** Sometimes family members can have the same argument over and over and not realize that they're arguing about two different things. Linguist Deborah Tannen writes that it's important to distinguish between the message and the metamessages; a message may have a simple intention but it is heard as something quite different, something the speaker didn't intend at all. By articulating what was said and what was heard, arguments can be constructive rather than frustrating.

There are a couple of problems with this paraphrase but they might, at first, seem pretty subtle. Notice that the first line uses the phrase "have the same argument over and over" which, though worded slightly different, copies the pattern of Tannen's original "have the same arguments again and again." That won't do.

Worse, the paraphrase fails to include quotation marks around the borrowed phrase "the message and the metamessage." It also lifts "constructive" from the original without quotation marks and uses the word "articulating" in the paraphrase, without quotation marks, which also is uncomfortably close to Tannen's "articulate." But the bigger problem is not one I would expect you to notice yet. Even though the paraphrase uses an attribution tag—"Linguist Deborah Tannen writes . . . "—the paraphrase doesn't include a parenthetical

What Is Plagiarism?

Each college or university has a statement in the student handbook that offers a local definition. But that statement probably includes most or all of the following forms of plagiarism.

1. Handing in someone else's work—a downloaded paper from the Internet or one borrowed from a friend—and claiming that it's your own.
2. Using information or ideas that are not common knowledge from any source and failing to acknowledge that source.
3. Handing in the same paper for two different classes.
4. Using the exact language or expressions of a source and not indicating through quotation marks and citation that the language is borrowed.
5. Rewriting a passage from a source by minor substitutions of different words but retaining the same syntax and structure of the original.

citation, something like (Tannen 2) indicating the page number from which the passage was borrowed. We'll talk later about citation, but here's the key thing to remember: *Whenever you quote, paraphrase, or summarize a source, it must always be cited, even if you mention the author's name.*

> **Corrected paraphrase:** Old family arguments may not really be about what family members have always thought they were about. Linguist Deborah Tannen writes that it's important to distinguish between **"the message and the metamessage"**; a message may have a simple intention but is heard as something quite different, something the speaker didn't intend at all. Even old family arguments can be **"constructive,"** says Tannen, if family members are careful to talk openly about this difference (**Tannen 2**).

Here are some simple tactics for avoiding plagiarism:

- It's fine to borrow distinctive terms or phrases from a source, but also signal that you've done so with quotation marks.
- Make a habit of using attribution tags, signaling to your reader who is the source of the idea, quotation, or fact. These tags include things such as, *Tannen argues, Tannen writes, According*

to Tannen, etc. For a lengthy list of these tags, see the box, "Active Verbs for Discussing Ideas," in Chapter 5.

■ *Always* cite borrowed material (more about how to do that later).

As a follow up to Exercise 3.2, return to the paraphrase you composed of the Tannen passage on talk within families. Do you need to edit or alter the paraphrase you wrote to avoid possible plagiarism problems? If you're in class, your instructor may ask you to work in pairs on this. What are the common plagiarism mistakes—almost always unintentional—that students in the class made when they paraphrased the passage in Exercise 3.2?

Why Plagiarism Matters

It may seem that all the fuss over plagiarism is just another example of English teachers' obsession with rules. In fact, the saddest days I've ever had as a writing teacher have always been when I've talked with a student about a paper she downloaded from the Internet or borrowed from her roommate. Most instructors hate dealing with plagiarism. It is, of course, a moral issue, but the motive to be careful about distinguishing what is yours and what you've borrowed isn't just a matter of "being good." It's really a gesture of gratitude. Research is always built on the work that came before it, and as you read and write about your topic, I hope that you come to appreciate the thoughtful writing and thinking of people before you who may have given you a new way of seeing or thinking.

Knowledge is a living thing (see Figure 3.1), growing like a great tree in multiple directions, adding and losing branches which keep reaching higher toward new understandings and truths.

The Common Knowledge Exception

While you always have to tell readers what information you have borrowed and where it came from, things that are "common knowledge" are excluded from this. Everyone knows, for example, that John Kennedy died in Dallas in November 1963. These and other widely known facts need not be cited. Neither do observations that anyone could make or common sayings, such as "home is where the heart is."

Why Cite?

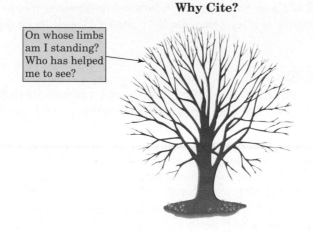

On whose limbs am I standing? Who has helped me to see?

FIGURE 3.1   Like a tree, knowledge in a discipline is a living thing, from time to time losing and adding branches, growing in new directions.

As researchers we are tree climbers, ascending the branches in an effort to see better. It's only natural that as we make this climb, we feel grateful for the strength of certain limbs under our feet. Citing and acknowledging sources is a way of expressing this gratitude.

Sources Are from Mars, Notetakers Are from Venus

I have to admit that I never read John Gray's bestseller about the complexity of communication between men and women, *Men Are from Mars, Women Are from Venus,* but I like the metaphor that sometimes it seems as if men and women are from different planets; I think the metaphor applies to notetaking, too. Consider how awkward it is to read someone else's words, make a concerted effort to understand what they mean, and then find your own words to restate the ideas. What's worse is that sometimes the authors are experts who use language you may not easily grasp or use reasoning in ways you can't easily follow. And then there are those authors who write so beautifully, you wonder how you could possibly say it better. Finally, there might be the fear that somehow you will goof and plagiarize the source's ideas or words.

For all of these reasons, the relationship between a source and a research writer is often complex. Both might as well be on different planets.

Paraphrasing

In Exercise 3.2, you practiced "say back," a technique that helps many married couples who are headed for divorce. As I mentioned, *paraphrase* is the academic equivalent of this therapeutic method for getting people to listen to each other. Try to say in your own words— and in about the same length as the author said it—what you understand that author to mean. This is hard, at first, because instead of just mindlessly quoting—a favorite alternative for many students— you have to *think*. Paraphrasing demands that you make your own sense of something. The time is well worth it. Why? Because not only are you lowering the risk of unintentional plagiarism and being fair to the source's ideas, *you are essentially writing a fragment of your draft*. Exercise 3.3 will help you develop these skills.

EXERCISE 3.3

Paraphrase Practice

At the heart of paraphrasing is this very simple idea: *Good writers find their own way of saying things*. That's your challenge here. Read each line or passage below until you think you thoroughly understand it, and then don't look at it again. Paraphrase the passage on a separate piece of paper finding your own way of saying what you understand the original passage to mean. Finally, review your paraphrase to make sure that any borrowed words or phrases from the original are within quotation marks in your paraphrase.

The lines and passages get progressively harder to paraphrase.

1. For most of the last 500 years, imitation was the sincerest form of architectural flattery.*

2. According to the National Institutes of Health,
   - Percentage of U.S.-born *Mexican* Americans who have suffered from some psychological disorder: 48
   - Percentage of Mexican immigrants who have: 29
   - Percentage of Mexico City residents who have: 23

---

*Witold Rybczynski, "When Architects Plagiarize It's Not Always Bad," *Slate,* Sept. 14, 2005; www.slate.com/id/2126270/?nav=tap3, Sept. 15, 2005.

3. Houseflies not only defecate constantly, but do so in liquid form, which means they are in constant danger of dehydration.*

4. An increasing number of Americans have come to view Islam as a religion that encourages violence while a declining number say Islam has a lot in common with their own religion. The public remains divided over whether churches should stay out of politics, even as large numbers say they are comfortable with expressions of faith by political leaders.†

Exercise 3.3 returns me to my original argument: Thoughtful notetaking pays off in the long run because you're essentially writing your essay in the middle of the process. Imagine what an advantage you'll have over those who wait until the night before the paper is due. Rather than pages of journal notes ripe for the picking, the night-before-it's-due clan is looking at bare branches. In a few pages, I'll suggest several notetaking methods that I think will give you the most to harvest; one of these, the double-entry journal, is a method that combines both the kind of listening that paraphrase demands and the open-ended exploratory thinking that you enjoyed in Exercise 3.1, the conversation with Rosen. But first, let's review another listening technique useful for academic writers: summary.

Summarizing

In order to sell a movie to Hollywood, a screenwriter should be able to summarize what it's about in a sentence. "*Juno* is a film about a smart, single, pregnant teenager who finds unexpected humor in her situation but finally finds that her wit is not enough to help her navigate the emotional tsunami her pregnancy triggers in the lives of those around her." That statement hardly does justice to the film—which is about so much more than that—but I think it basically captures the story and its central theme.

Obviously, that's what a *summary* is: a reduction of longer material into some brief statement that captures a basic idea, argument, or theme from the original. Like paraphrasing, summarizing often requires careful thought, since you're the one doing the distilling, especially if you're trying to capture the essence of a whole movie, article, or chapter that's fairly complex. But many times,

*Richard Conniff, "Why Did God Make Flies?" *Wonders* (New York: Owl, 1997).
†Pew Forum on Religion and Public Life, "Religion and Politics: Contention and Consensus," www.pewforum.org/docs/index.php?DocID=26, July 25, 2005.

summarizing involves simply boiling down a passage—not the entire work—to its basic idea.

EXERCISE 3 . 4

Summary Practice

Does Madonna make art? Does Jay-Z? Certainly Mozart did, right? Simon Frith, a scholar who writes about theories of popular music, thinks that we need an "aesthetic theory" to talk about pop music of all kinds but sees resistance to the idea. In the following passage, an excerpt from his book *Popular Music: Critical Concepts in Media and Cultural Studies*, Frith writes about this problem.

The excerpt is typical of the kinds of writing you'll encounter in scholarly books—it seems to use some unfamiliar jargon and follows a line of reasoning that may not be immediately obvious to you. That's why it will be a great opportunity for you to practice summary.

Carefully read the passage, and write a brief (two to four sentences) summary of his main point. Make sure to say it in your own words, and if you borrow any words from Frith, don't forget those quotation marks.

> Underlying all the other distinctions critics draw between "serious" and "popular" music is an assumption about the source of musical value. Serious music matters because it transcends social forces; popular music is aesthetically worthless because it is determined by them (because it is "useful" or "utilitarian"). This argument, common enough among academic musicologists, puts sociologists in an odd position. If we venture to suggest that the value of, say, Beethoven's music can be explained by the social conditions determining its production and subsequent consumption we are dismissed as philistines—aesthetic theories of classical music remain decidedly non-sociological. Popular music, by contrast, is taken to be good only for sociological theory. Our very success in explaining the rise of rock' n' roll or the appearance of disco proves their lack of aesthetic interest. To relate music and society becomes, then, a different task according to the music we are treating. In analyzing serious music, we have to uncover the social forces concealed in the talk of "transcendent" values; in analyzing pop, we have to take seriously the values scoffed at in the talk of social functions.*

*Simon Frith, *Popular Music: Critical Concepts in Media and Cultural Studies* (London: Routledge, 2004) 32.

A summary, where you distill only part of a larger source, is selective. You choose to emphasize some key part of a source because it fits your paper's purpose. But the same warning applies to selective summarizing as was given earlier about paraphrasing: Don't misrepresent the general thrust of the author's ideas. Ask yourself, Does my selective use of this source seem to give it a spin the author didn't intend? Most of the time, I think you will discover the answer is no.

Quoting

The quotation mark may be the student researcher's best friend, at least as demonstrated by how often papers are peppered by long quotes!

As a general rule, the college research paper should contain no more than 10 or 20 percent quoted material, but it's an easy rule to ignore. For one thing, quoting sources at the notetaking and drafting stages is quicker than restating material in your own words. When you quote, you don't have to think much about what you're reading; you just jot it down the way you see it and, if you have to, think about it later. That's the real problem with verbatim copying of source material: There isn't much thinking involved. As a result, the writer doesn't take possession of the information, shape it, and allow herself to be shaped by it.

That's not to say that you should completely avoid quoting sources directly as a method of notetaking. If you're writing on a literary topic, for example, you may quote fairly extensively from the novel or poem you're examining. Or if your paper relies heavily on interviews, you'll want to bring in the voices of your subjects, verbatim.

When to Quote. As a rule, jot down a quote when someone says or writes something that is distinctive in a certain way and when restating it in your own words wouldn't possibly do the thought justice. I'll never forget a scene from the documentary *Shoah,* an eleven-hour film about the Holocaust, which presented an interview with the Polish engineer of one of the trains that took thousands of Jews to their deaths. Now an old man and still operating the same train, he was asked how he felt now about his role in World War II. He said quietly, "If you could lick my heart, it would poison you."

It would be difficult to restate the Polish engineer's comment in your own words. But more important, it would be stupid even to try. Some of the pain and regret and horror of that time in history is embedded in that one man's words. You may not come across such a distinctive quote as you read your sources this week, but be alert to *how* authors (and those quoted by authors) say things. Is the prose unusual, surprising, or memorable? Does the writer make a point in an interesting way? If so, jot it down.

Heidi, in a paper on the children's television program *Sesame Street,* began by quoting a eulogy for Muppets creator Jim Henson. The quote is both memorable and touching. Heidi made an appropriate choice, establishing a tone that is consistent with her purpose: to respond to certain critics of the program. The fact that a quote sounds good isn't reason enough to use it. Like anything else, quotes should be used deliberately, with purpose.

There are several other reasons to quote a source as you're notetaking. Sometimes, it's desirable to quote an expert on your topic who is widely recognized in the field. Used to support or develop your own assertions, the voice of an authority can lend credit to your argument and demonstrate your effort to bring recognized voices into the discussion.

Another reason to quote a source is that his explanation of a process or idea is especially clear. Such quotes often feature metaphors. Robert Bly's *Iron John,* a book that looks at American men and their difficult journey into manhood, is filled with clear and compelling explanations of that process. As a son of an alcoholic father, I found Bly's discussion often hit home. Here, using a metaphor, he explains in a simple but compelling way how children in troubled homes become emotionally unprotected, something that often haunts them the rest of their lives:

> When a boy grows up in a "dysfunctional" family (perhaps there is no other kind of family), his interior warriors will be killed off early. Warriors, mythologically, lift their swords to defend the king. The King in a child stands for and stands up for the child's mood. But when we are children our mood gets easily overrun and swept over in the messed-up family by the more powerful, more dominant, more terrifying mood of the parent. We can say that when the warriors inside cannot protect our mood from being disintegrated, or defend our body from invasion, the warriors collapse, go into a trance, or die.*

I'm sure there's a more technical explanation for the ways parents in dysfunctional families can dominate the emotional lives of their children. But the warrior metaphor is so simple; that is, partly, its power. As you read or take notes during an interview, be alert to sources or subjects who say something that gets right to the heart of an important idea. Listen for it.

If your paper is on a literary topic—involving novels, stories, poems, and other works—then purposeful and selective quoting

*Robert Bly, *Iron John: A Book About Men* (Reading, MA: Addison-Wesley, 1990), 147.

is especially important and appropriate. The texts and the actual language the writers use in them are often central to the argument you're making. If you're writing about the misfit heroes in J. D. Salinger's novels, asserting that they embody the author's own character, then you'll have to dip freely into his books, quoting passages that illustrate that idea. (See Appendix C for an essay on literary topics that use quotes effectively.)

Quoting Fairly.   If you do choose to quote from a source, be careful to do three things: (1) Quote accurately, (2) make sure it's clear in your notes that what you're jotting down is quoted material, and (3) beware of distorting a quote by using it out of context. The first two guidelines protect you from plagiarism, and the last ensures that you're fair to your sources.

To guarantee the accuracy of a quote, you may want to photocopy the page or article with the borrowed material. A tape recorder can help in an interview, and so can asking your subject to repeat something that seems especially important. To alert yourself to which part of your notes is a quote of the source's words, try using oversized quotation marks around the passage so that it can't be missed.

Guarding against out-of-context quotations can be a little more difficult. After all, an isolated quote has already been removed from the context of the many other things a subject has said. That shouldn't be a problem if you have represented her ideas accurately. However, sometimes a quote can misrepresent a source by what is omitted. Simply be fair to the author by noting any important qualifications she may make to something said or written, and render her ideas as completely as possible in your paper.

EXERCISE 3.5

Dialogic Notetaking: Listening In, Speaking Up

There's the skills part of note taking—knowing how to cite, summarize, paraphrase, and quote correctly—and then there's the more interesting, harder part—making *use* of what you're reading to discover what you think. So far, we've talked about this latter process using the metaphor of conversation. In Exercise 3.1, you tried out this idea, responding in writing to Christine Rosen's ideas about the influence of social networking sites like Facebook on how we think about friendship. I asked you to imagine that this was literally a conversation between you and Rosen, except that the voices you heard were in writing rather than speech.

The Unending Conversation

Imagine that you enter a parlor. You come late. When you arrive, others have long preceded you, and they are engaged in a heated discussion, a discussion too heated for them to pause and tell you exactly what it is about. In fact, the discussion had already begun long before any of them got there, so that no one present is qualified to retrace for you all the steps that had gone before. You listen for a while, until you decide that you have caught the tenor of the argument; then you put in your oar. Someone answers; you answer him; another comes to your defense; another aligns himself against you, to either the embarrassment or gratification of your opponent, depending upon the quality of your ally's assistance. However, the discussion is interminable. The hour grows late, you must depart. And you do depart, with the discussion still vigorously in progress.

Kenneth Burke

This conversation metaphor doesn't originate with me. Lots of people use it to describe how all knowledge is made. One theorist, Kenneth Burke, famously explained that we might imagine that all scholarship on nearly any subject is much like a parlor conversation between people in the know (see box above). These are the experts who, over time, have contributed to the discussions about what might be true and who constantly ask questions to keep the conversation going.

As newcomers to this conversation, we don't really have much to contribute. It's important that we listen in so that we begin to understand what has already been said and who has said it. But at some point, even novices like us, are expected to speak up. We're not there to simply record what we hear. We're writers. We're supposed to discover something to say.

A lot of people have weighed in on the impact of technology on how we live, think, and feel. That conversation won't be contained by any parlor. Think convention hall, or maybe football stadium. But imagine that in one corner of that hall a smaller group is talking about the impact of social networking on our relationships with each other. Coincidentally, the moment you arrive Christine Rosen, who you met earlier, has the floor, and she's talking in more detail about the things she mentioned in the earlier exercise. You can hear what she's saying by reading a portion of her longer essay, "Virtual Friendship and the New Narcissism," starting on page 134.

STEP 1:

1. Begin by listening in. Read Christine Rosen's essay once straight through. Underline and mark passages that you think are:
   a. important to your understanding of the article,
   b. puzzling in some way,
   c. surprising, or
   d. connected with your own initial ideas and experiences.

2. Reread the opening paragraph, ending few paragraphs, and all of your marked passages, and then, without looking at the article, compose a two- or three-sentence summary of what you understand to be the most important thing the article is saying. Write this down on the left page of your notebook.

3. Find two passages in the article that you think are good examples of what you state in your summary. Copy these on the left page of your notebook, too.

STEP 2: Now speak up. Use the right side of your notebook to explore your thinking about what Rosen is saying. Look on the opposing left pages to remind yourself of some of her ideas and assertions. This is an open-ended fastwrite, but here are some prompts to get you writing and thinking:

- Tell the story of your thinking:
    - When I first started thinking about this topic, I thought _____, and then I thought _____, and then, and then . . . but now I think _____.

- Consider ways you've begun to think differently:
    - I used to think _____, but now I'm starting to think _____.

- Try both believing and doubting:
    - *The most convincing points Rosen makes in her essay are _____. or Though I don't necessarily agree with Rosen, I can understand why she would think that _____.*
    - And then: *The thing that Rosen ignores or fails to understand is _____. or The least convincing claim she makes is _____ because _____.*

- Use questions:
    - The most important question Rosen raises is _____.
    - The question that she fails to ask is _____.

Discuss in class how this notetaking exercise worked. What went well? What was difficult? How did your initial thoughts influence your reading of the article? Did your thinking change? Which of these techniques will you continue to use in your notetaking?

*Virtual Friendship and the New Narcissism**
by Christine Rosen

Christine Rosen *is a senior editor of The New Atlantis and a fellow at the Ethics and Public Policy Center.*

For centuries, the rich and the powerful documented their existence and their status through painted portraits. A marker of wealth and a bid for immortality, portraits offer intriguing hints about the daily life of their subjects—professions, ambitions, attitudes, and, most importantly, social standing. Such portraits, as German art historian Hans Belting has argued, can be understood as "painted anthropology," with much to teach us, both intentionally and unintentionally, about the culture in which they were created.

Self-portraits can be especially instructive. By showing the artist both as he sees his true self and as he wishes to be seen, self-portraits can at once expose and obscure, clarify and distort. They offer opportunities for both self-expression and self-seeking. They can display egotism and modesty, self-aggrandizement and self-mockery.

Today, our self-portraits are democratic and digital; they are crafted from pixels rather than paints. On social networking websites like MySpace and Facebook, our modern self-portraits feature background music, carefully manipulated photographs, stream-of-consciousness musings, and lists of our hobbies and friends. They are interactive, inviting viewers not merely to look at, but also to respond to, the life portrayed online. We create them to find friendship, love, and that ambiguous modern thing called connection. Like painters constantly retouching their work, we alter, update, and tweak our online self-portraits; but as digital objects they are far more ephemeral than oil on canvas. Vital statistics, glimpses of bare flesh, lists of favorite bands and favorite poems all clamor for our attention—and it is the timeless human desire for attention that emerges as the dominant theme of these vast virtual galleries.

Although social networking sites are in their infancy, we are seeing their impact culturally: in language (where *to friend* is now a verb), in politics (where it is *de rigueur* for presidential aspirants to catalogue their virtues on MySpace), and on college campuses (where *not* using Facebook can be a social handicap). But we are only beginning to come to grips with the consequences of our use of these sites: for friendship, and for our notions of privacy, authenticity, community, and identity. As with any new technological advance, we must consider what type of behavior online social networking encourages. Does this technology, with its constant demands to collect (friends and status), and perform (by marketing ourselves), in some ways undermine our ability to attain what it promises—a surer sense of who we are and where we belong? The Delphic oracle's guidance was *know thyself*. Today, in the world of online social networks, the oracle's advice might be *show thyself*. . . .

Won't You Be My Digital Neighbor?

According to a survey recently conducted by the Pew Internet and American Life Project, more than half of all Americans between the ages of twelve and seventeen use some online social networking site. Indeed, media coverage of social networking sites usually describes them as vast teenage playgrounds—or wastelands, depending on one's perspective. Central to this narrative is a nearly unbridgeable generational divide, with tech-savvy youngsters redefining friendship while their doddering elders look on with bafflement and increasing anxiety. This seems anecdotally correct; I can't count how many times I have mentioned social networking websites to someone over the age of forty and received the reply, "Oh yes, I've heard about that MyFace! All the kids are doing that these days. Very interesting!"

Numerous articles have chronicled adults' attempts to navigate the world of social networking, such as the recent *New York Times* essay in which columnist Michelle Slatalla described the incredible embarrassment she caused her teenage daughter when she joined Facebook: "everyone in the whole world thinks its super creepy when adults have facebooks," her daughter instant-messaged her. "unfriend paige right now. im serious. . . . i will be soo mad if you dont unfriend paige right now. actually." In fact, social networking sites are not only for the young. More than half of the visitors to MySpace claim to be over the age of *35*. And now that the first generation of college Facebook users have graduated, and the site is open to all, more than half of Facebook users are no longer students. What's more, the proliferation of niche social networking sites, including those aimed at adults, suggests that it is not only teenagers who will nurture relationships in virtual space for the foreseeable future.

What characterizes these online communities in which an increasing number of us are spending our time? Social networking sites have a peculiar psychogeography. As researchers at the Pew project have noted, the proto-social networking sites of a decade ago used metaphors of *place* to organize their members: people were linked through virtual cities, communities, and homepages. In 1997, GeoCities boasted thirty virtual "neighborhoods" in which "homesteaders" or "GeoCitizens" could gather—"Heartland" for family and parenting tips, "SouthBeach" for socializing, "Vienna" for classical music aficionados, "Broadway" for theater buffs, and so on. By contrast, today's social networking sites organize themselves around metaphors of the *person,* with individual profiles that list hobbies and interests. As a result, one's entrée into this world generally isn't through a virtual neighborhood or community but through the revelation of personal information. And unlike a neighborhood, where one usually has a general knowledge of others who live in the area, social networking sites are gatherings of deracinated individuals, none of whose personal boastings and musings are necessarily trustworthy. Here, the old arbiters of community—geographic location, family, role, or occupation—have little effect on relationships.

Also, in the offline world, communities typically are responsible for enforcing norms of privacy and general etiquette. In the online world, which is unfettered by the boundaries of real-world communities, new etiquette challenges abound. For example, what do you do with a "friend" who posts inappropriate comments on your Wall? What recourse do you have if someone posts an embarrassing picture of you on his MySpace page? What happens when a friend breaks up with someone—do you defriend the ex? If someone "friends" you and you don't accept the overture, how serious a rejection is it? Some of these scenarios can be resolved with split-second snap judgments; others can provoke days of agonizing.

Enthusiasts of social networking argue that these sites are not merely entertaining; they also edify by teaching users about the rules of social space. As Danah Boyd, a graduate student studying social networks at the University of California, Berkeley, told the authors of *MySpace Unraveled,* social networking promotes "informal learning. . . . It's where you learn social norms, rules, how to interact with others, narrative, personal and group history, and media literacy." This is more a hopeful assertion than a proven fact, however. The question that isn't asked is how the technology itself— the way it encourages us to present ourselves and interact—limits or imposes on that process of informal learning. All communities expect their members to internalize certain norms. Even individuals in the transient communities that form in public spaces obey these rules, for the most part; for example, patrons of libraries are expected to keep noise to a minimum. New technologies are challenging such norms—cell phones ring during church sermons; blaring televisions in doctors' waiting rooms make it difficult to talk quietly—and new norms must develop to replace the old. What cues are young, avid social networkers learning about social space? What unspoken rules and communal norms have the millions of participants in these online social networks internalized, and how have these new norms influenced their behavior in the offline world?

Social rules and norms are not merely the strait-laced conceits of a bygone era; they serve a protective function. I know a young woman—attractive, intelligent, and well-spoken—who, like many other people in their twenties, joined Facebook as a college student when it launched. When she and her boyfriend got engaged, they both updated their relationship status to "Engaged" on their profiles and friends posted congratulatory messages on her Wall.

But then they broke off the engagement. And a funny thing happened. Although she had already told a few friends and family members that the relationship was over, her ex decided to make it official in a very twenty-first century way: he changed his status on his profile from "Engaged" to "Single." Facebook immediately sent out a feed to every one of their mutual "friends" announcing the news, "Mr. X and Ms. Y are no longer in a relationship," complete with an icon of a broken heart. When I asked the young woman how she felt about this, she said that although she assumed her friends and acquaintances would eventually hear the news, there was something disconcerting about the fact that everyone found out about it instantaneously; and since the message came from Facebook, rather than in a face-to-face exchange initiated by her, it was devoid of context—save for a helpful notation of the time and that tacky little heart.

Indecent Exposure

Enthusiasts praise social networking for presenting chances for identity-play; they see opportunities for all of us to be little Van Goghs and Warhols, rendering quixotic and ever-changing versions of ourselves for others to enjoy. Instead of a palette of oils, we can employ services such as PimpMySpace.org, which offers "layouts, graphics, background, and more!" to gussy up an online presentation of self, albeit in a decidedly raunchy fashion: Among the most popular graphics used by PimpMySpace clients on a given day in June 2007 were short video clips of two women kissing and another of a man and an obese woman having sex; a picture of a gleaming pink handgun; and an image of the cartoon character SpongeBob SquarePants, looking alarmed and uttering a profanity.

This kind of coarseness and vulgarity is commonplace on social networking sites for a reason: it's an easy way to set oneself apart. Pharaohs and kings once celebrated themselves by erecting towering statues or, like the emperor Augustus, placing their own visages on coins. But now, as the insightful technology observer Jaron Lanier has written, "Since there are only a few archetypes, ideals, or icons to strive for in comparison to the vastness of instances of everything online, quirks and idiosyncrasies stand out better than grandeur in this new domain. I imagine Augustus' MySpace page would have pictured him picking his nose." And he wouldn't be alone. Indeed, this is one of the characteristics of MySpace most striking to anyone who spends a few hours trolling its millions of pages: it is an overwhelmingly dull sea of monotonous uniqueness, of conventional individuality, of distinctive sameness.

The world of online social networking is practically homogenous in one other sense, however diverse it might at first appear: its users are committed to self-exposure. The creation and conspicuous consumption of intimate details and images of one's own and others' lives is the main activity in the online social networking world. There is no room for reticence; there is only revelation. Quickly peruse a profile and you know more about a potential acquaintance in a moment than you might have learned about a flesh-and-blood friend in a month. As one college student recently described to the *New York Times Magazine:* "You might run into someone at a party, and then you Facebook them: what are their interests? Are they crazy-religious, is their favorite quote from the Bible? Everyone takes great pains over presenting themselves. It's like an embodiment of your personality."

It seems that in our headlong rush to join social networking sites, many of us give up one of the Internet's supposed charms: the promise of anonymity. As Michael Kinsley noted in *Slate,* in order to "stake their claims as unique individuals," users enumerate personal information: "Here is a list of my friends. Here are all the CDs in my collection. Here is a picture of my dog." Kinsley is not impressed; he judges these sites "vast celebrations of solipsism." . . .

The New Taxonomy of Friendship

There is a Spanish proverb that warns, "Life without a friend is death without a witness." In the world of online social networking, the warning might be simpler: "Life without hundreds of online 'friends' is virtual death." On these sites, friendship is the stated *raison d'être.* "A place for friends," is the slogan of MySpace. Facebook is a "social utility that connects people with friends." Orkut describes itself as "an online community that connects people through a network of trusted friends." Friendster's name speaks for itself.

But "friendship" in these virtual spaces is thoroughly different from real-world friendship. In its traditional sense, friendship is a relationship which, broadly speaking, involves the sharing of mutual interests, reciprocity, trust, and the revelation of intimate details over time and within specific social (and cultural) contexts. Because friendship depends on mutual revelations that are concealed from the rest of the world, it can only flourish within the boundaries of privacy; the idea of public friendship is an oxymoron.

The hypertext link called "friendship" on social networking sites is very different: public, fluid, and promiscuous, yet oddly bureaucratized. Friendship on these sites focuses a great deal on collecting, managing, and ranking the people you know. Everything about MySpace, for example, is designed to encourage users to gather as many friends as possible, as though friendship were philately. If you are so unfortunate as to have but one MySpace friend, for example, your page reads: "You have 1 friends," along with a stretch of sad empty space where dozens of thumbnail photos of your acquaintances should appear.

This promotes a form of frantic friend procurement. As one young Facebook user with 800 friends told John Cassidy in *The New Yorker,* "I always find the competitive spirit in me wanting to up the number." An associate dean at Purdue University recently boasted to the *Christian Science Monitor* that since establishing a Facebook profile, he had collected more than 700 friends. The phrase universally found on MySpace is, "Thanks for the add!"—an acknowledgment by one user that another has added you to his list of friends. There are even services like FriendFlood.com that act as social networking pimps: for a fee, they will post messages on your page from an attractive person posing as your "friend." As the founder of one such service told the *New York Times* in February 2007, he wanted to "turn cyberlosers into social-networking magnets."

The structure of social networking sites also encourages the bureaucratization of friendship. Each site has its own terminology, but among the words that users employ most often is "managing." The Pew survey mentioned earlier found that "teens say social networking sites help them manage their friendships." There is something Orwellian about the management-speak on social networking sites: "Change My Top Friends," "View All of My Friends" and, for those times when our inner Stalins sense the need for a virtual purge, "Edit

Friends." With a few mouse clicks one can elevate or downgrade (or entirely eliminate) a relationship.

To be sure, we all rank our friends, albeit in unspoken and intuitive ways. One friend might be a good companion for outings to movies or concerts; another might be someone with whom you socialize in professional settings; another might be the kind of person for whom you would drop everything if he needed help. But social networking sites allow us to rank our friends publicly. And not only can we publicize our own preferences in people, but we can also peruse the favorites among our other acquaintances. We can learn all about the friends of our friends—often without having ever met them in person.

Status-Seekers

Of course, it would be foolish to suggest that people are incapable of making distinctions between social networking "friends" and friends they see in the flesh. The use of the word "friend" on social networking sites is a dilution and a debasement, and surely no one with hundreds of MySpace or Facebook "friends" is so confused as to believe those are all real friendships. The impulse to collect as many "friends" as possible on a MySpace page is not an expression of the human need for companionship, but of a different need no less profound and pressing: the need for status. Unlike the painted portraits that members of the middle class in a bygone era would commission to signal their elite status once they rose in society, social networking websites allow us to *create* status—not merely to commemorate the achievement of it. There is a reason that most of the MySpace profiles of famous people are fakes, often created by fans: Celebrities don't need legions of MySpace friends to prove their importance. It's the rest of the population, seeking a form of parochial celebrity, that does.

But status-seeking has an ever-present partner: anxiety. Unlike a portrait, which, once finished and framed, hung tamely on the wall signaling one's status, maintaining status on MySpace or Facebook requires constant vigilance. As one 24-year-old wrote in a *New York Times* essay, "I am obsessed with testimonials and solicit them incessantly. They are the ultimate social currency, public declarations of the intimacy status of a relationship. . . . Every profile is a carefully planned media campaign."

The sites themselves were designed to encourage this. Describing the work of B.J. Fogg of Stanford University, who studies "persuasion strategies" used by social networking sites to increase participation,

The New Scientist noted, "The secret is to tie the acquisition of friends, compliments and status—spoils that humans will work hard for—to activities that enhance the site." As Fogg told the magazine, "You offer someone a context for gaining status, and they are going to work for that status." Network theorist Albert-László Barabási notes that online connection follows the rule of "preferential attachment"—that is, "when choosing between two pages, one with twice as many links as the other, about twice as many people link to the more connected page." As a result, "while our individual choices are highly unpredictable, as a group we follow strict patterns." Our lemming-like pursuit of online status via the collection of hundreds of "friends" clearly follows this rule.

What, in the end, does this pursuit of virtual status mean for community and friendship? Writing in the 1980s in *Habits of the Heart*, sociologist Robert Bellah and his colleagues documented the movement away from close-knit, traditional communities, to "lifestyle enclaves" which were defined largely by "leisure and consumption." Perhaps today we have moved beyond lifestyle enclaves and into "personality enclaves" or "identity enclaves"—discrete virtual places in which we can be different (and sometimes contradictory) people, with different groups of like-minded, though ever-shifting, friends.

Beyond Networking

This past spring, Len Harmon, the director of the Fischer Policy and Cultural Institute at Nichols College in Dudley, Massachusetts, offered a new course about social networking. Nichols is a small school whose students come largely from Connecticut and Massachusetts; many of them are the first members of their families to attend college. "I noticed a lot of issues involved with social networking sites," Harmon told me when I asked him why he created the class. How have these sites been useful to Nichols students? "It has relieved some of the stress of transitions for them," he said. "When abrupt departures occur—their family moves or they have to leave friends behind—they can cope by keeping in touch more easily."

So perhaps we should praise social networking websites for streamlining friendship the way e-mail streamlined correspondence. In the nineteenth century, Emerson observed that "friendship requires more time than poor busy men can usually command." Now, technology has given us the freedom to tap into our network of friends when it is convenient for us. "It's a way of maintaining a friendship without having to make any effort whatsoever," as a recent graduate of Harvard explained to *The New Yorker*. And that ease admittedly makes it possible to stay in contact with a wider circle of offline acquaintances than might have been possible in the era before Facebook. Friends you haven't heard from in years, old buddies from elementary school, people you might have (should have?) fallen out of touch with—it is now easier than ever to reconnect to those people.

But what kind of connections are these? In his excellent book *Friendship: An Exposé*, Joseph Epstein praises the telephone and e-mail as technologies that have greatly facilitated friendship. He writes, "Proust once said he didn't much care for the analogy of a book to a friend. He thought a book was better than a friend, because you could shut it—and be shut of it—when you wished, which one can't always do with a friend." With e-mail and caller ID, Epstein enthuses, you can. But social networking sites (which Epstein says "speak to the vast loneliness in the world") have a different effect: they discourage "being shut of" people. On the contrary, they encourage users to check in frequently, "poke" friends, and post comments on others' pages. They favor interaction of greater quantity but less quality.

This constant connectivity concerns Len Harmon. "There is a sense of, 'if I'm not online or constantly texting or posting, then I'm missing something,'" he said of his students. "This is where I find the generational impact the greatest—not the use of the technology, but the *overuse* of the technology." It is unclear how the regular use of these sites will affect behavior over the long run—especially the behavior of children and young adults who are growing up with these tools. Almost no research has explored how virtual socializing affects children's development. What does a child weaned on Club Penguin learn about social interaction? How is an adolescent who spends her evenings managing her MySpace page different from a teenager who spends her night gossiping on the telephone to friends? Given that "people want to live their lives online," as the founder of one social networking site recently told *Fast Company* magazine, and they are beginning to do so at ever-younger ages, these questions are worth exploring.

The few studies that have emerged do not inspire confidence. Researcher Rob Nyland at Brigham Young University recently surveyed 184 users of social networking sites and found that heavy users "feel less socially involved with the community around them." He also found that "as individuals use social networking more for entertainment, their level of social involvement decreases." Another recent study conducted by communications professor Qingwen Dong and colleagues at the University of the Pacific found that "those who engaged in romantic communication over MySpace tend to have low levels of both emotional intelligence and self-esteem."

The implications of the narcissistic and exhibitionistic tendencies of social networkers also cry out for further consideration. There are opportunity costs when we spend so much time carefully grooming ourselves online. Given how much time we already devote to entertaining ourselves with technology, it is at least worth asking if the time we spend on social networking sites is well spent. In investing so much energy into improving how we *present* ourselves online, are we missing chances to genuinely *improve* ourselves?

We should also take note of the trend toward giving up face-to-face for virtual contact—and, in some cases, a preference for the latter. Today, many of our cultural, social, and political interactions take place through eminently convenient technological surrogates— Why go to the bank if you can use the ATM? Why browse in a bookstore when you can simply persue the personalized selections Amazon.com has made for you? In the same vein, social networking sites are often convenient surrogates for offline friendship and community. In this context it is worth considering an observation that Stanley Milgram made in 1974, regarding his experiments with obedience: "The social psychology of this century reveals a major lesson," he wrote. "Often it is not so much the kind of person a man is as the kind of situation in which he finds himself that determines how he will act." To an increasing degree, we find and form our friendships and communities in the virtual world as well as the real world. These virtual networks greatly expand our opportunities to meet others, but they might also result in our valuing less the capacity for genuine connection. As the young woman writing in the *Times* admitted, "I consistently trade actual human contact for the more reliable high of smiles on MySpace, winks on Match.com, and pokes on Facebook." That she finds these online relationships more *reliable* is telling: it shows a desire to avoid the vulnerability and uncertainty that true friendship entails. Real intimacy requires risk—the risk of disapproval, of heartache, of being thought a fool. Social networking websites may make relationships more reliable, but whether those relationships can be humanly satisfying remains to be seen.

Notetaking Techniques

In the first edition of *The Curious Researcher,* I confessed to a dislike of notecards. Apparently, I'm not the only one. Mention notecards, and students often tell horror stories. It's a little like talking about who has the most horrendous scar, a discussion that can prompt participants to expose knees and bare abdomens in public places. One student even mailed me her notecards—fifty bibliography cards and fifty-three notecards, all bound by a metal ring and color coded. She assured me that she didn't want them back—ever. Another student told me she was required to write twenty notecards a day: "If you spelled something wrong or if you put your name on the left side of the notecard rather than the right, your notecards were torn up and you had to do them over."

It is true, of course, that some students find recording information on notecards an enormously useful way of organizing information. And some teachers have realized that it's pretty silly to turn notetaking into a form that must be done "correctly" or not at all. For these reasons, I included suggestions about how to use notecards effectively in the first edition of this text. But in good conscience, I can't do it anymore. I no longer believe that 3" × 5" or 4" × 6" cards are large enough to accommodate the frequently messy and occasionally extended writing that often characterizes genuinely useful notes. Little cards get in the way of having a good conversation with your sources.

If conventional notecards encourage a monologue, then what method will encourage dialogue? Basically any notetaking strategy that encourages the two things that you've practiced so far in this chapter: listening and responding, collecting and evaluating. It's that movement back and forth between information and what you think of that information, between your observations of things and your ideas about them, between what you once understood and what you *now* understand, that will involve you in the process of *knowledge-making,* rather than simple information retrieval and reporting. Now this probably sounds pretty grandiose. Your research essay will probably not earn space in an academic journal. But as you begin to understand the difference between knowledge and information, you will earn yourself a place in an academic community that values people with their own ideas. Isn't that inviting?

I'm convinced that something as seemingly mundane as notetaking can be a key part of becoming a knower rather than a parrot. One method, in particular, seems especially effective at encouraging dialogue between the researcher and his sources: the double-entry journal.

The Double-Entry Journal

The double-entry approach (see Figure 3.2) is basically this: Use opposing pages of your research notebook (or opposing columns in a word document). On each left side, compile your notes from a source—paraphrases, summaries, quotes—and on each right side,

Four Motives for Using a Source

My daughter Julia wants a pug. This isn't good news because I don't think much of little dogs with sinus problems. I also heard a rumor that if a pug sneezes hard enough its eyes might pop and dangle by the optical nerve until the eyeball is greased and popped back into the eye socket. This posed a research question: *Are pugs typical of overbred dogs that tend to suffer from a range of physiological and psychological problems?*

Since this is a question that goes way beyond my personal experience, I naturally turn to outside sources to learn more. When most of us do research for an academic paper, we typically search for sources that exemplify or support a point we want to make. But inquiry-based projects often begin with questions, not a preconceived argument, so the search for sources becomes much more than an exercise in finding sources that support what you already want to say. For example:

1. **Sources Can Extend Your Thinking.** This is an essential motive for doing research, particularly early in the process. You want to learn more about your subject so that you can refine your research question and understand more fully what it is you're asking. For example, in an article in *Economist* magazine, I learn that kennel clubs, which began in England in the second half of the nineteenth century, have played a key role in "genetic painting" of dog breeds, a euphemism for genetic

(continued)

manipulation (1).* The article goes on to argue that it is the demands of these associations for a kind of "racial purity" that have contributed to overbreeding (2). Perhaps I should revise my research question: *What role has the Pug Dog Club of America (PDCA) played in promoting or confronting the problem of inbreeding in the dog?*

2. **Sources Can Provide Necessary Background.** In order to fully understand your topic there may be things you—and ultimately your readers—should know. For example, the *Encyclopedia of Animals*† tells me that pugs are one of the oldest breeds and live an average of eight years. The dog's genetic history is a long one, which may be a significant fact. The average life span of a pug also means that Julia will be a sophomore in college when the dog dies, which means her pug becomes my pug.

3. **Sources Can Support or Exemplify a Point You Want to Make.** This is the default approach to using a source. We have a point, claim, or assertion we want to support with the information we've found. For instance, here's a quotation that seems to confirm the claim that kennel clubs have indeed contributed to medical problems in dogs:

The Kennel Club, the top canine body in Britain, working with breed-specific dog clubs has laid out the "right" looks—a narrow set of desirable characteristics that breeders try to match. "Judges judge against a standard, and it's rewarding and challenging for breeders to try to meet those standards," says Geoff Sampson, a geneticist who works for the Kennel Club. But that kind of judging has too often been unrewarding for the dog. In the quest to create the perfect pooch, close relatives will often be mated, sometimes even brother and sister or mother and son. The danger of this practice is that it increases the

---

*"It's a Dog's Life," *Economist*, December 12, 2002: 1–5; *Academic Search Premier,* EBSCOhost, Boise State University, www.epnet.com., August 8, 2005.
†"Pug," *Encyclopedia of Animals,* EBSCO Animals, Boise State University, www.epnet.com, August 8, 2005.

likelihood that puppies will inherit genetic diseases—some 400 have now been identified in dogs.*

4. **Sources Can Present Opportunities for Analysis and Interpretation.** Sometimes you encounter information that raises new questions, and when it does, you have a chance to offer your own analysis or interpretation of how that information or assertion might be understood. For example, one article asserted that the whole movement to promote purebred dogs for show, which originated with the British Kennel Clubs in the nineteenth century, might be part of a larger, social push toward racial purity in people. That dog breeding may have "racist" origins is an explosive and fascinating assertion. While I concede this might have been true, is it a relevant claim today? Isn't it faulty reasoning to infer that the motives of some people 150 years ago remain the motives of people today?

By the way, I could not find evidence that pugs blow out their eyeballs when they sneeze. Sadly, I can't use that as a reason for discouraging Julia about pug ownership unless I find some convincing evidence to support it. But I'll keep looking.

comment on them. Imagine that line down the middle of the page—or that spiral binder that divides opposing pages—as the lunch table at which you sat with Christine Rosen in the opening exercise of this chapter. On the left sits the published author. You sit on the right. Take care to listen to what the author said through paraphrase, summary, and quotation on the left, and then on the right respond with your own commentary, questions, interpretations, clarifications, or even feelings about what you heard. Your commentary can be pretty open ended: What strikes you? What was confusing? What was surprising? How does the information stand up to your own experiences and observations? Does it support or contradict your thesis (if you have one at this point)?

How might you use the information in your paper? What purpose might it serve? What do you think of the source? What further

*Helen Gibson, "A Flawed Beauty," *Time Europe,* August 8, 2001: 2–3. MasterFile Premier, EBSCOhost, Boise State University, www.epnet.com, August 8, 2005.

Notes from Source

- On the left page collect direct quotations, paraphrases, and summaries of key ideas that you cull from your source.

- Collect material that's relevant to your project, but also write down passages, facts, and claims from the source that you find surprising or puzzling or that generate some kind of emotional response in you.

- Make sure you write down this material carefully and accurately.

- Don't forget to include the page number from the source to the left of the borrowed material or idea.

Fastwrite Response

- On the right page, think through writing about some of the information you collected in the other column. This will likely be a messy fastwrite but a focused one.

- Try shifting between two stances: believing and doubting. Spend a few minutes writing about the possible merits of an author's ideas, assertions, or study. Then spend a few minutes writing about questions, doubts, or counterclaims you would raise.

- Whenever your writing dies, skip a space, look to the left, and find something else to respond to.

- Some questions to ponder as you're writing might include:
  1. What strikes me about this?
  2. What are my first thoughts when I consider this? And then what? And then? And then?
  3. What exactly does this make me think of or remember?
  4. How would I qualify or challenge this author's claim? In what ways do I agree with it?
  5. What else have I read that connects with this?
  6. How do I feel about this?

FIGURE 3.2   Double-Entry Journal Method

questions does the information raise that might be worth investigating? How does the information connect to other sources you've read?

There are a variety of ways to approach the double-entry journal. If you're taking notes on a photocopied article or a book you own, try reading the material first and underlining passages that seem important. Then, when you're done, transfer some of that underlined material—quotes, summaries, or paraphrases—into the left column of your journal. Otherwise, take notes in the left column *as* you read.

While you take notes, or after you've finished, do some exploratory writing in the right column. This territory belongs to you. Here, through language, your mind and heart assert themselves over the source material. Use your notes in the left column as a trigger for writing in the right. Whenever your writing stalls, look to the left. The process is a little like watching tennis—look left, then right, then left, then right. Direct your attention to what the source says and then to what *you* have to say about the source. Keep up a dialogue.

Figures 3.3, 3.4, and 3.5 illustrate how the double-entry journal works in practice. Note these features:

- Bibliographic information is recorded at the top of the page. Do that first, and make sure it's complete.
- Page numbers are included in the far-left margin, right next to the information that was taken from that page. Make sure you keep up with this as you write.
- While the material from the source in the left column may be quite formal or technical—as it is in Figure 3.4—the response in the right column should be informal, conversational. Try to write in your own voice. Find your own way to say things. And don't hesitate to use the first person: *I*.
- As you read the writers' responses to their sources in Figures 3.3 and 3.4, notice how often the writers use their own writing to try to question a source's claim or understand better what that claim might be (e.g., "What the authors seem to be missing here . . ." and "I don't get this quote at all . . .").
- Seize a phrase from your source, and play out its implications; think about how it pushes your own thinking or relates to your thesis. For example, the student writing about the rise of home video (Figure 3.3) plays with the phrase "mode of consumption"—a particular way of using film that the author believes home video encourages—and she really takes off on it. It leads her to a meditation on what it's like to see movies in theaters and what might be lost in the transition to home viewing.
- Use questions to keep you writing and thinking. In both Figure 3.3 and 3.4, the writers frequently pause to ask themselves questions—not only about what the authors of the original sources might be saying but what the writers are saying to themselves as they write.

Ehrenstein, David. "Film in the Age of Video." <u>Film Quarterly</u> 49.3 (1996): 38–42. Print.

38 ". . . today the once distinct spheres of theatrical and home exhibition have been radically conflated."

Let's see. So the "spheres" of showing films in theaters and in home video have been "conflated." What I think he means is that movies are now produced with both means of showing them in mind, which would seem to have implications for *how* they're made these days. E. talks later in the article about this, I think, when he mentions how only the dimension of sound has been preserved from the old days of big screens in dark theaters. The "big image" is lost. I'm not sure what this means, exactly.

39 <u>That's Entertainment 3</u>, which started as video, is "less a spectacular to be enjoyed in a darkened theater than a work of historical and cultural research that invites detailed analysis—a mode of consumption that home video, by its very nature, encourages."

I like this phrase that home video represents a particular "mode of consumption" for film. You may see more than one film at a sitting, in a lighted room, and you can rewind and reexamine favorite scenes and images. There is something about sitting in the dark, too, watching a big screen with a few hundred other people. It's like you experience nothing but image because there's nothing else to see. And somehow the act of watching with strangers, instead of in your living room by yourself or with friends, creates a kind of community. But E. talks here about how even the theater experience is no longer "distinctive." But he doesn't really say why. What exactly was lost with the disappearance of the "movie palace?" Size, for one thing. Maybe that's one way that home video and movies in theater have been "conflated." Because, as E. says, films are now made for both video and theaters, and the "illusion

40 "There are any number of (video) sets devoted to films, old and new, that enable the average everyday consumer to examine cinema now as never before."

"The illusion of depth" is destroyed on home video.

41 "To remember the movie palaces, with enormous images floating in a velvety darkness, framed by curtains that never seemed to close on an ever-shifting

---

FIGURE 3.3   Sample Double-Entry Journal. This writer, taking notes on an article from a scholarly journal, collects and responds to summaries, quotes, and paraphrases from the source.

program (features, cartoons, shorts, news, coming attractions) is not to indulge in nostalgia but rather to note how radically cinematic object relations have changed. There's nothing in any way distinctive about the modern theatrical movie-going experience, save the sound.

42 "We have entered an era of lowered cinematic expectations."

Jacque Rivette: "The cinema is necessarily fascination and rape, that is how it acts on people; it is something pretty unclear, something one sees shrouded in darkness."

of depth" as well as size of the image is destroyed by home video, then there's really no need for the really big screen of the "movie palace." Instead, we now have theaters divided and subdivided into eight theaters. Screens have shrunk, rooms have shrunk, and the theater experience begins to approximate home video. That leads to this "era of lowered cinematic expectations."

I don't get this quote at all. How can Rivette compare the experience of watching a film as both "fascination and rape?" Does he mean that film does violence in the dark to viewers in the same way a rapist would?

Check Rivette cite.

FIGURE 3.3   (Continued)

What I like about the double-entry journal system (see Figure 3.5) is that it turns me into a really active reader as I'm taking notes for my essay. That blank column on the right, like the whirring of my computer right now, impatiently urges me to figure out what I think through writing. All along, I've said the key to writing a strong research paper is *making the information your own.* Developing your own thinking about the information you collect, as you go along, is one way to do that. Thoughtful notes are so easy to neglect in your mad rush to simply take down a lot of information. The double-entry journal won't let you neglect your own thinking, or at least, it will remind you when you do.

The double-entry system does have a drawback. Unlike index card systems, double-entry journals don't organize your information particularly well. A lot of page flipping is involved to find pieces of information as you draft your paper. But I find I often remember which sources have what information, partly because I thought about what might be important as I read and took notes on each source.

Prior, Molly. "Bright On: Americans' Insatiable Appetite for Whiter-Than-White Teeth Is Giving Retailers Something to Smile About." <u>Beauty Biz</u> 1 Sept. 2005: 36–43. Print.

Teeth are no longer just for eating with—their appearance is becoming more important as a factor in a person's image, and they need to be perfectly white. (36)

Cosmetics companies are now entering territory once reserved for dentists as more and more people care mostly about the aesthetics of their teeth and smile. (36)

"Sephora is so enthusiastic about the [tooth whitening] category, it named "smile" its fifth retail pillar, joining the four others (makeup, fragrance, skin care and hair care) earlier this year." (37)

"The trend has shed its clinical beginnings and assumed a new identity, smile care. Its new name has been quickly adopted by a growing troupe of retailers, who hope to lure consumers with a simple promise: A brighter smile will make you look younger and feel more confident." (37)

Instead of going to the dentist and taking care of their teeth so they function well, people are investing a cosmetic interest in their teeth. People selling tooth whitening products hope people associate whiter, more perfect teeth with higher self-esteem and social acceptance. (40)

"What says health, youth and vitality like a great smile?" (40)

I have noticed the increasing amount of importance that people put on the whiteness of their teeth, but this also seems to have increased with the amount of advertising for whitening products on TV and in magazines. I wonder if the whole thing is profit driven: hygiene companies wanted to make more money, so instead of just selling toothbrushes and toothpaste, they created a whitening product and then worked to produce a demand for it. I almost feel really manipulated, like everyone's teeth were fine the way they naturally existed, and then all the sudden a big company decided it needed to create a new product and sell it by making us feel bad about our smiles, and thus bad about ourselves.

The whole thing is sad, because once something becomes the societal "norm," we start to become obligated to doing it. If everyone's teeth are beige, it's no problem when yours are too. But when everyone has sparkling white teeth, then it looks funny if you let yours stay brown. It either says "I don't have the money to whiten my teeth," or "I don't care about my appearance."

Sometimes it feels people might also judge you as being dirty, because white teeth seem healthier and cleaner than brown teeth, or lazy, for not spending the time to whiten your teeth. All those things are negative, and create a negative cloud around our teeth where we once felt good, or at least ambivalent. I don't like the way I'm being told my smile isn't good enough the way it is. I feel like when I smile it should just be about showing happiness and conveying that to others, not a judgment about me as a person.

FIGURE 3.4 **Amanda's Double-Entry Journal.** Here, Amanda concentrates on collecting and responding to quoted material from the source.

Oppenhiemer, Todd. "The Computer Delusion." <u>TheAtlantic.com</u>. *Atlantic Monthly Group*, July 1997. Web. 15 Apr. 2009.

4 Alan Lesgood, director of Learning and Development Center at U of Pitt: The computer is an "amplifier," involves both sound "study practices and thoughtless ones." Which of the two will predominate?

5 Are computers "the filmstrips of the 90s"? Clifford Stoll, author of <u>Silicon Snake Oil</u>: "We loved them (filmstrips) because we didn't have to think for an hour, teachers loved them because they didn't have to teach and parents loved them because it showed their schools are high tech. But no learning happened."

8 Children with disabilities show most evidence of improvement with computer use.

10 A number of experts argue that visual learning produces much less than sensory learning.

". . . the senses have little status after kindergarten."

The article upended some of my thinking about the virtues of computer technology. What was most helpful for my project, though, were the comments about the need for learners to engage in sensory activity, and the idea that computers do not seem to encourage creativity. I'm not sure that the analysis holds for the activity of research, which unlike some of the examples—mostly high school and elementary—seem directed toward a whole range of teacher-guided instruction. The task of collecting research off the Web seems more directed and purposeful. But maybe not.

One quote that really stands out: "School is not about information, it's about <u>using</u> information." And here this seems relevant. The Web offers the student the illusion she's getting somewhere if she simply collects information, something that is easy to do surfing the Web. Like the photocopying machine, the Web will help the student research accumulated material but at what point will she think about it? How much does the student, for example, have to reflect before she decides to click the printer icon? At least with the photocopy machine, it costs money to print a copy, an incentive to think about whether the material is <u>worth</u> copying; this incentive is missing on the Web.

FIGURE 3.5   Here's one of my double-entry scribbles. I was researching how students use the Web for research and found a related article in the *Atlantic Monthly* titled "The Computer Delusion." In the right-hand column, I found myself taking off on a quotation: "Schooling is not about information, it's about using information."

Other Notetaking Techniques

The Research Log: A Jay Leno Approach

The research log is an alternative to the double-entry journal that promotes a similar "conversation" between writer and source, but with a few differences. One is that, like Jay Leno, the researcher starts with a monologue and always gets the last word. Another difference is that the research log may be more adaptable than the double-entry journal for researchers who prefer to write on computers. The standard format of the research log can serve as a template, which can be retrieved whenever you're ready to take notes on another source. Those notes can then be easily dropped into the draft as needed, using the "Cut and Paste" feature of your word-processing program. Obviously, the research log format works just as well in a paper notebook.

The basic approach is this:

1. Take down the full bibliographic information on the source (see Figure 3.6). Then read the article, book chapter, Web page, or whatever first, marking up your personal copy in the usual fashion by underlining, making marginal notes, and so on.
2. Your first entry will be a fastwrite that is an *open-ended response* to the reading under the heading "What Strikes Me Most." You could take the following stances or pose the following questions to guide this writing:
   - Begin by playing the "believing game," exploring how the author's ideas, arguments, or findings are sensible. Then shift to the "doubting game," looking for gaps, questions, and doubts you have about what the source says.
   - What strikes you as the most important thing the author is trying to say?
   - What surprises you most?
   - What do you remember best?
   - What seems most convincing? Least convincing?
   - How has it changed your thinking on the topic?
   - How does it compare to other things you've read?
   - What other research possibilities does it suggest?
3. Next, mine the source for nuggets. Take notes under the heading "Source Notes." These are quotations, summaries, paraphrases, or key facts you collect from the reading. They are probably some of the things you marked as you read the source initially.
4. Finally, follow up with one more fastwrite under the heading "The Source Reconsidered." This is a second, *more focused* look at the source in which you fastwrite about what stands out in the notes you took. Which facts, findings, claims, or arguments that you jotted down shape your thinking now? If the writing stalls, skip a line, take another look at your source notes, and seize on something else to write about.

Project: The Newest Commodity: The Smile

Citation: Tanner, Marty. "American Choppers." *New York Times*. New York Times, 20 Feb. 2005. Web. 4 Apr. 2009.

Date: 4/5/2009

What Strikes Me Most:
A prosthodontist is a dentist that specializes in making teeth look a certain way. While many people are born with smiles they are proud of, a prosthodontist can take any smile and modify it in any way. Unfortunately, more and more people are falling into a trap that there is only one "perfect" smile, and they are asking for their own mouths to be modified to create the perfect smile. This disgusts me because I think there should be as many smiles as there are people. It's becoming like a nose job or a face lift—some modification people make to their appearance to make it less like the countenance they were born with, and more like that "perfect" face. It makes me sad that another thing that is so distinctive to each person has actually become something we want to normalize. As a woman I feel like I'm told to be a size two, have straight, shiny hair, and have a little, cute nose, and have perfectly arched eyebrows, and have thick, pink lips. Now too I have to have the correct length and width teeth that are a sparkly B1 white. It makes me wonder why our culture goes from accepting one part of ourselves as standard and imperfect but acceptable, and makes it into something we need to modify.

I also think the prosthodontist to the stars, Dr. Levine, is really disingenuous in this article. While his job depends on people being unhappy with the way their teeth look, he tries to play the "good guy" card and say that people's smiles are looking too perfect, and that people need to have a great set of choppers, but not overly great. He

FIGURE 3.6 Amanda's Research Log

seems to want to make the polite statement that
nobody has a perfect smile, but then through his
profession his job is to make people believe they
can get a perfect smile—and they don't already have
one. I think that's kind of slimy.

Source Notes:
"Within certain strict boundaries, Levine likes to
see some imperfection because it renders the hand
of the dentist invisible. This is his art." Many
famous people, like actors and actresses, think of
their smile as a sort of symbol of their status
that they can flash to attract attention. Many of
these smiles are exactly the same, with the golden
mean the proportion of the length of their top six
front teeth, and with each individual tooth having
a width that is 80% of the length. There is even a
"perfect" amount of tooth that should show when a
person's mouth is closed: around 3.7 mm. Patients
can wear a fake set of teeth around their home
before they have their smiles modified to see if
what they imagine as being perfect actually looks
bad. They can test drive their new set of teeth
for friends and family so they don't end up with
a mistake that looks like a pair of too-perfect
dentures.

"Smiles are looking too much alike."
" . . . the man who credits himself with shaping
Christie Brinkley's 'iconic American smile.'" Reality
makeover programs like The Swan often use a
prosthodontist as part of the makeover.

The Source Reconsidered:
When the article mentions Julia Roberts or the
"iconic American smile" I know exactly what it
means. In my mind, I truly have an image of that
smile, and I realize now that's because every single starlet and commercial model seems to have
that smile. Yet, when I look at my friends and all
the people around me, there are so many different
smiles. I have one friend with really short, stubby

FIGURE 3.6   (Continued)

teeth that are pretty brown around the edges, and I
admit that I notice it. But when she smiles, I tend
to look more at the rest of her face and the fact
that she's really happy than I do at her imperfect
teeth. It's like it's turning some natural human
emotion into some mass produced carbon copy. That's
why the whole smile care thing really bothers me.
Changing somebody's nose changes only their nose.
Changing someone's smile seems to control and modify the way they communicate a feeling, and that
is really bothersome. They are modifying something
far more personal than just their appearance,
they are changing the way they emote. That's
freaky.

FIGURE 3.6   (Continued)

Narrative Notetaking

Narrative notetaking (see Figure 3.7) is an episodic approach to
reading for research. It documents the writer's narrative of thought
about a source, developing several "layers" of response with each
reading and rereading; in that sense, it's a bit like the research log.
Narrative notetaking essentially turns the double-entry journal on

Focusing Question: How has cosmetic dentistry changed the way we
think of the smile, and what are the repercussions?

Source: Walker, Rob. "Consumed; Unstained Masses." New York Times.
New York Times, 2 May 2004. Web. 10 Apr. 2009.

First Layer: Story the Source
The prosthodontist Jonathan Levine works to change the way people's
teeth look. He created a product called GoSmile that works to whiten
people's teeth. At first he didn't think there was much use for it, but
then normal people started to want whiter teeth, and his business
has boomed.

FIGURE 3.7   Amanda's Narrative Notets

For a while many celebrities have cosmetically enhanced their teeth, but now normal people are as well. Saks and Sephora, two upscale retailers, started selling the product. Colgate and Crest, traditionally known for their toothpaste, also created products for over the counter whitening. These products seem to be booming in the early 2000s.

Many people are now feeling that white teeth are as much of a necessity as a washed face or brushed hair. It seems to be a sign of the times. Retailers are also making out hand over fist as more and more people buy whitening products.

One of the clever ways whitening products work is they tell consumers that they don't have to change their lifestyles to get whiter teeth. They can still drink dark beverages and eat colored foods, but just use a whitener to keep their teeth looking pristine. Americans seem to like products that make sure they can indulge in all the things they'd like, but avoid the negative repercussions of doing so.

People are now going to the dentist to make sure their teeth look good, rather than just for oral health. This can actually be seen as a benefit, because it means that people are at least going to the dentist.

It's not completely irrational that many people are hopping on the bandwagon of a more celebrity-like smile. People who are generally considered attractive make more money than average looking people, and it's another way to stand out positively in the crowd.

Second Layer: Rapid Summary

The American public is getting more and more vain, as evidenced by the fact that tooth whitening is growing in popularity. While only celebrities used to modify the appearance of their teeth, now average people are

---

FIGURE 3.7   (Continued)

doing it. Because of the value of appearance in our society, once we realize we can modify the way we look to our advantage, we seem to flock to it quickly. That's what's happening with the whole trend of smile care—we're using whiteners to change the way our teeth look so maybe we will be judged more profitably. And when a large percentage of society decides to buy something, there will always be corporations and retailers standing alongside to reap a profit.

Third Layer: Narrative of Thought

Before I started reading this article I thought that it was the capitalistic profit motive that had introduced whitening products and created a consumer demand for them. Now I understand that all of us as consumers have an equal responsibility with the companies that make and market such products, because we're the ones that buy them and change our standards of beauty. That makes me think that this is a complicated issue. While it's frustrating to feel like I can never be attractive enough, because the standard of attractiveness to which I'm held keeps getting harder and harder to meet, I'm the one that is interested in meeting it in the first place. While it would be easy to denigrate that as vanity, however, I can also see that being judged by others as attractive does have actual benefits, be it a higher salary or better treatment from strangers. In that case I'm put in a tough spot—I can work against the culture that tells me I don't look the right way, and feel negatively judged, or I can conform to it, and feel disappointed that I folded to social pressure. This isn't just an issue about people whitening their teeth for fun, it's about how society changes its standards and how quickly we assimilate to them— and why.

FIGURE 3.7   (Continued)

its side, creating layers of thought and information rather than columns, each layer building on the other; yet it also preserves the contrary thinking that makes the double-entry journal so valuable. The number of layers the writer makes depends on the value of the source to his or her project.

First Layer: Story the Source.   Read the source carefully from beginning to end, marking up your personal copy with underlining, marginal notes, highlighter, or whatever you use to signal important passages. Then in your notebook (or on your computer) quickly tell the story of the text and how it developed from beginning to end. This should be a rough chronological account or the source's chain of reasoning or development.

- How did the piece begin?
- And then where did it go from there?
- And then?
- How did it end?

When finished, draw a line under your entry.

Second Layer: Rapid Summary.   This step involves a rereading, but a selective one. Review the text, including your underlining and other marks to find ideas, concepts, or claims that seem to be *repeated* or that seem to be important assertions, claims, or findings. Circle or mark with Post-its® the lines or passages that seem most important to your understanding of the source's argument or findings, or that seem most relevant to your project. Now, *in your own words,* compose a few sentences that summarize your understanding of what the source is saying about your topic. Remember that a summary doesn't simply state the topic of the passage, but what the reading *says* about the topic.

Draw another line under this entry.

Third Layer: Narrative of Thought.   Now push the text aside for a moment and reflect on how it has contributed to your thinking about the topic. Begin a fastwrite that tells the story of your thinking since reading and writing about this source. Start with this "seed" sentence or ones like it:

Before I started reading this article / book / Web document / etc.,

I thought _____, but now I understand that _____. That

makes me think _____.

These three layers certainly don't have to be the end of the writing you do about a source, and you may find that one or more of the layers command most of your attention, perhaps generating much longer entries than those in the model, Figure 3.7. Customize this approach to make it most productive for you. For example, you might find that the third layer, "Narrative of Thought," might be more useful as an initial step, or you might find that the second layer of notes is a collection of quotes, summaries, or paraphrases from the source, rather than the rapid summary. Experiment and make narrative notetaking work for you. The most important thing with all of these notetaking techniques—the double-entry journal, the research log, or narrative notetaking—is that you're using writing to think *when you're in the middle,* engaging with the voices, views, and findings of the people you're reading.

Online Research Notebooks

Google Notebook offers some easy ways to organize yourself during the notetaking stage, especially if a lot of your research is taking place online. (See Figure 3.8.) To use it, create a Google account, and then follow the "more" link on the Google homepage to "even more." Scroll down to the "notebook" function.

Once you're in the notebook, start piecing together the research you have so far. A helpful thing to do is to cut and paste text from the Internet site you're using, and put that into the general body of the notebook. Make sure you keep track of all the citation information you'll need for the site here as well. Then, use the "comments" feature that shows up at the bottom of the text bubble to use some of the notetaking techniques you've learned in this chapter. Take your time—this isn't so much about copying information from the Internet but spending time mentally digesting it. Because you can take writing directly from the notebook and put it in your draft later on, making keen observations at this stage will lighten your writing workload later on.

Once you have both the information—which can include both text and images, whatever you find helpful—use the "add labels" function to help organize the information. That way when you go back through the data, it will be easy to piece together similar pieces of information into the same place. You can also divide your notes up into sections by following the "add section" link to break your notes up into different categories. It might be helpful to make each source a different section, so you can flip through and see what each independent author is saying.

If you want to find a specific phrase in your notebook, the search function at the top of the notebook lets you hunt down exactly the words you're looking for. If you can't remember who said what, the search is an easy way to minimize the fogginess that sometimes comes with an abundance of research.

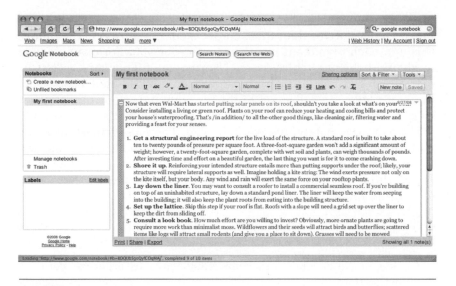

FIGURE 3.8   Sites like Google Notebook, seen here, or Zotero provide researchers with new methods of collecting and commenting on sources online. The key is to go beyond the cut-and-paste reflex and use the notetaking features as you would with a double-entry journal.

Whatever you choose to do, the notebook allows you to keep track of all the different perspectives you're getting, as well as all your own thoughts and ideas about the information. A little time put into keeping things straight will make your life easier when you start writing the body of your paper.

When You're Coming Up Short: More Advanced Searching Techniques

At the end of the third week of the research assignment last semester, Laura showed up at my office, looking pale.

"I spent all night at the library, and I couldn't find much on my topic," she said. "What I *could* find, the library didn't have—it was missing, or checked out, or wasn't even part of the collection. I may have to change my topic."

"I hate libraries!" she said, the color returning to her face.

Laura's complaint is one that I hear often at this point in the research process, especially from students who have dutifully tried to find a narrow focus for their papers, only to realize—they think—that there isn't enough information to make the topic work. They have tried the online catalog, periodical databases, and the Internet. The students found a few articles but not enough for a ten-page paper. Like Laura, they may decide to broaden their focus or bail out on their topic altogether, even though they're still interested in it.

I always give these frustrated students the same advice: Don't despair yet. And don't give up on your narrow focus or your topic until you've dug more deeply for information. There are still some more specialized indexes to try and some nonlibrary sources to consider. You are, in a sense, like the archaeologist who carefully removes the dirt from each layer of a dig site, looking to see what it might reveal. If little turns up, the next layer is systematically explored and then the next, until the archaeologist is convinced she's digging in the wrong place. Student researchers too often give up the dig before they've removed enough dirt, believing too quickly there's nothing there.

Advanced Library Searching Techniques

Here are some things you might not have considered to unearth more useful information on your research question. They are listed in the order you might try them.

1. *Vary search terms.* If you ignored the *Library of Congress Subject Headings* in Exercise 2.1, those huge red books in the library reference room, now is the time to crack them open. These will provide language for searches that is most likely to produce the best results in books and article databases. At the very least, try using some other search terms suggested by your research so far. You might, for instance, try searching using the names of people who have published on your topic.

2. *Search other databases.* Okay, so you've tried a general subject database like Academic OneFile, and even a specialized database like PsychINFO. But have you tried another general database like Academic Search Premier, or another specialized database like InfoTrac Psychology? Broaden your coverage.

3. *Check bibliographies.* Academic books and articles always include a list of references at the end. These can be gold mines. Look at all the sources like these that you've collected so far and scan the titles in the bibliographies that seem promising. Find these by searching the library databases.

4. *Use a bibliographic index.* These are databases that will provide you with a list of references on many topics. For example, the Bibliographic Index Plus not only will allow you to search for articles on your topic but may also return links to full-text versions.

5. *Consider using interlibrary loan services.* Your campus library will get you that article or book they don't have by borrowing the materials from another library. This is an incredibly useful service, often available online, but it's useless to procrastinators since delivery can take a week or two.

6. *Troll government documents.* The U.S. Government is the largest publisher in the world. If your research question is related to some issue of public policy, then there's a decent chance you'll find some government documents on the subject. Try the site FirstGov (see Figure 3.9), a useful index to the gazillions of government publications and reports.

Advanced Internet Search Techniques

It's more likely that you've tapped out relevant sources on the Internet than those in the library since many of us seem to always begin there. But make sure that you've tried some of the following search strategies on the Web.

1. *Vary search terms.* By now, you've gathered enough information on your topic to have some new ideas about terms or phrases that might yield good results. Say you're researching the origins of American blues music, and you discover that among its many traditions is something called the Piedmont style. Try searching using that phrase in quotation marks. Also consider doing Web searches on the names of experts who have contributed significantly to the conversation on your topic.

2. *Use advanced search features.* Few of us use the advanced search page on Google and other search engines. By habit, we just type in a few terms in the simple search window. But advanced searching will allow you to exploit methods that will give you better results—things like phrase searching in conjunction with Boolean operators like AND and OR.

3. *Use multiple search engines.* Don't call for retreat until you've gone beyond Google. Try Yahoo!, Ask.com, and similar search

FIGURE 3.9 FirstGov is a useful starting point for a search of government documents on your topic.

engines. Also try specialized search engines that are relevant to your subject (see Chapter 2).

4. *Search the invisible Web.* The vast majority of information on the Web is not accessible to everyday search engines. Much of this information exists in databases that web crawlers don't know how to categorize or is blocked from listing in search hits. That's unfortunate for academic researchers because educational institutions post many of these databases and documents. As usual, some savvy people have come up with methods of searching this frontier. Try some of the following:

- **Direct Search** http://www.freepint.com/gary/direct.htm
- **Infomine** http://infomine.ucr.edu/
- **Invisible Web Directory** http://www.invisible-web.net/

Thinking Outside the Box: Alternative Sources

Sometimes you need to be creative. Try finding sources on your research question in places you don't think to look.

1. *Search blogs.* It is easy to dismiss blogs as merely self-indulgent musings of people with nothing better to do, except that some blogs are written by people who really know what they're talking about. In addition, bloggers can be vigilant observers of new developments, breaking news stories, and cutting-edge opinion. There are a number of specialized search engines to scour the blogosphere. Perhaps the best is Google's.

2. *Search images.* Another source of material you may not have thought of is images available on the Internet. A photograph of a collapsed school building following the 2008 earthquake in central China will do much to dramatize your essay on the vulnerability of buildings to such a disaster. Or a historical essay on lynching in the South might be more powerful with a picture of a murder from the Library of Congress archives.

3. *Listen to archived radio or podcasts.* Suppose your research question focuses on Martin Luther King Jr. Why not listen to an interview of Taylor Branch, the man who wrote a three-volume biography of the civil rights leader? You can find it on NPR.org (see Figure 3.10). National Public Radio is a particularly good

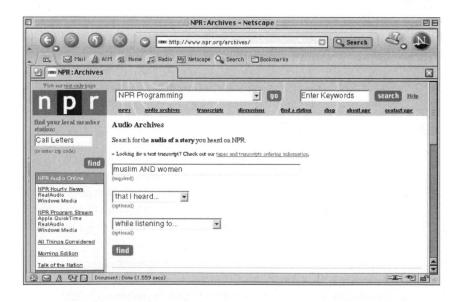

FIGURE 3.10   **Searching the Archives at National Public Radio**

source for material for academic projects. There are also a variety of search engines that will help you find podcasts on nearly any subject.

4. *Check out YouTube.* It isn't just about laughing babies anymore. YouTube is a rich archive of video that can provide material on many topics. For the project on Martin Luther King Jr., for example, you might watch a video of his last speech. There are, of course, other sites that archive video, too. Truveo (http://www.truveo.com/) will help you search them all.

5. *Search iTunes U.* Across the U.S., colleges and universities are going online through Apple's iTunes U, putting up video and audio speeches, lectures, and other academic content. You can find iTunes U on iTunes, of course, and you can do a keyword search on multiple sites using "power search." The terms "global warming" produced 90 hits, including lectures, opinion, and reports from some of America's top universities. See Figure 3.11 for more advanced searching techniques.

Library	**Internet**	**Alternative Sources**
• Vary search terms	• Vary search terms	• Search blogs
• Search other databases	• Use advanced search features	• Search images
• Check bibliographies	• Use multiple search engines	• Listen to archived radio and podcasts
• Use a bibliographic index	• Search the invisible Web	• Watch videocasts
• Use interlibrary loan		• Search iTunes U
• Troll government documents		

FIGURE 3.11   **More Advanced Searching Techniques**

CHAPTER 4

The Fourth Week

Getting to the Draft

It is *not* 2 A.M. Your paper is *not* due in twelve hours but in one or two weeks. For some students, beginning to write a research paper this early—weeks before it's due—will be a totally new experience. An early start may also, for the first time, make the experience a positive one. I know that starting early will help ensure writing a better paper.

Still, there are those students who say they thrive on a looming deadline, who love working in its shadow, flirting with failure. "I work best that way," they say, and they wait until the last minute and race to the deadline in a burst of writing, often sustained by cigarettes and strong doses of caffeine. It works for some students. Panic is a pretty strong motivator. But I think most who defend this habit confuse their relief at successfully pulling off the assignment once again with a belief that the paper itself is successful.

Papers done under such pressure often aren't successful, and that is particularly true of the last-minute research paper, where procrastination is especially deadly. Research writing is recursive. You often have to circle back to where you've already been, discovering holes in your research or looking at your subject from new angles. It's hard to fit in a trip back to the library the night before the paper is due, when you've just started the draft and need to check some information. This book is designed to defeat procrastination, and if, in the past few weeks, you've done the exercises, taken thoughtful notes, and attempted a thorough search for information, you probably have the urge to begin writing.

On the other hand, you may feel as if you don't know enough yet about your topic to have anything to say. Or you may be swamped with information, and your head may be spinning. What do you do with it all?

When Christy came to my office, she was three weeks into her research on a paper that asked, Why do diets fail? She really wanted to know, since she was having such a hard time with her own diet. Though she'd really done a good job collecting information, she was exasperated.

"I found a whole bunch of articles on how heredity affects obesity," she said, "and all this stuff on how people's upbringing determines how they eat. I also found some articles that said our bodies *want* to be certain weights."

It sounded pretty interesting to me.

"I've got all this information, but I'm worried that I'll lose my focus," she said. *"And so much of it seems contradictory.* I don't know what to think."

When the Experts Disagree

Christy was pretty sure she was in trouble because her sources sometimes didn't agree on the same things. I thought she was right where she should be: standing on the curb at a busy intersection, watching the experts on her topic collide and then go off in different directions. Knowledge in any field—nutrition, literature, or entomology—is not static. It is contested—pushed, pulled, probed, and even sometimes turned over completely to see what is underneath. Scholars and experts devote their lifetimes to disagreeing with each other, not because they enjoy being disagreeable but because when knowledge is contested, it is advanced.

When I researched lobsters, I discovered a fascinating scientific mystery: More than 90 percent of the lobsters that grow to the minimum legal size every year end up on someone's dinner table. At that size, most lobsters haven't even had a chance to breed. How is it possible, asked the scientists, that there are any lobsters left at that rate of exploitation? I discovered several explanations. Some people argued that the millions of lobster traps—each of which is designed to allow undersize lobsters to escape—serve as a kind of giant soup kitchen, providing extra food to lobsters. That, some experts said, accounts for lobsters' resilience. Other experts believed that laws protecting females carrying eggs have worked remarkably well. Still others believed that lobsters migrate into areas depleted by overfishing. Recently, another idea won favor with scientists. They suggested that large lobsters at the edge of the continental shelf are the "parental stock" for coastal lobsters, sending their larval offspring inshore on tides and currents.

Evaluating Conflicting Claims

As a writer—and in this case, a nonexpert—I had to sort through these conflicting opinions and decide which I thought were most convincing. I had to claim my point of view and later make it convincing to my own readers.

That was Christy's challenge, and it's your challenge, too. When you're thorough in your research, you're bound to find sources that square off against each other or come at your subject from different directions. What do you make of these competing claims and differing perspectives?

EXERCISE 4 . 1

Do Concealed Guns Reduce Crime?

Soon after the Virginia Tech and Northern Illinois University shooting rampages, a group called Students for Concealed Carry on Campus (SCCC) started organizing on American campuses. The group is determined to overturn gun bans at most schools and allow students who are otherwise legally qualified to carry concealed weapons on campus.

SCCC is part of a larger national debate about whether allowing people to carry concealed weapons will reduce crime. Currently, a number of states have either "shall issue" or more restrictive "may issue" laws regulating whether citizens can carry concealed weapons. The "shall issue" states are required to give their residents a permit to carry if they meet other legal qualifications to own a gun. The "may issue" states have more latitude to reject applicants. Considerably fewer states now have the "may issue" laws.

At the heart of the issue is the very sensible theory that if gun-toting criminals know that their potential victims might be carrying too, the criminals are much less likely to behave violently. But is this theory true? Certainly the NRA thinks so. On its Web site, the interest group notes that there is "not a single academic study that claims Right to Carry laws have increased state crime rates. The debate among academics has been over how large the benefits have been."

Actually, there is a lively academic debate about the impact of concealed gun laws on crime. What follows are the conclusions of two academic studies that come to two quite different conclusions about the issue. Read each claim carefully and then think about how you might decide which to believe.

Claim #1

In a landmark study that has profoundly influenced the debate over the potential benefits of right-to-carry laws, two researchers, John Lott and David Mustard, studied crime rates in U.S. counties, some of which have "shall issue" (SI) laws. This is what they found:

> Using cross-sectional time-series data for U.S.
> counties from 1977 to 1992, we find that allowing
> citizens to carry concealed weapons deters violent
> crimes, without increasing accidental deaths. If
> those states without right-to-carry concealed gun
> provisions had adopted them in 1992, county- and
> state-level data indicate that approximately 1,500
> murders would have been avoided yearly. Similarly,
> we predict that rapes would have declined by over
> 4,000, robbery by over 11,000, and aggravated
> assaults by over 60,000. We also find criminals
> substituting into property crimes involving stealth,
> where the probability of contact between the
> criminal and the victim is minimal. Further, higher
> arrest and conviction rates consistently reduce

crime. The estimated annual gain from all
remaining states adopting these laws was at least
$5.74 billion in 1992. The annual social benefit
from an additional concealed handgun permit is as
high as $5,000.*

Claim #2

After Lott and Mustard published their study, researchers
engaged in a lively debate about its findings that "shall issue"
laws reduced crime. Among those that found different results was
a 2005 study excerpted below. Kovandzic, Marvel, and Vieratas
looked at U.S. cities with 100,000 or more residents to determine
the effect of "shall issue" laws on crime. This is what they found:

Our results provide little support for the findings
of Lott and Mustard (1997)and Lott (1998b, 2000),
that SI laws reduce violent crime. . . . Even if
criminals have timely information regarding the
passage of SI laws and the number of people
lawfully carrying guns in public, such information
is unlikely to have a significant impact on their
behavior and violent crime rates. According to
ethnographic research on active offenders, most
crime is opportunistic and does not involve
elaborate planning and potential costs are given
relative little consideration (Jacobs, 2000;
Jacobs, Topalli & Wright, 2003; Shover, 1996;
Wright & Decker, 1994, 1997). Even when offenders
do calculate the costs, they also factor in
their ability to manage or eliminate these

---

*John R. Lott and David B. Mustard, "Crime, Deterrence, and Right to Carry
Concealed Handguns," *Journal of Legal Studies* 26 (January 1997): 1–68.

potential costs (Hochstetler & Copes, 2003; Miller
& Jacobs, 1998). Research suggests that criminals
are extremely confident about their abilities to
control a situation and deal with whatever may
arise, including encountering an armed victim
(Jacobs, 2000; Wright & Decker, 1997).*

Who to Believe?

You have two competing claims from two respected sources.

1. How would you decide which of these claims is true? What else
   might you need to know to answer that question?
2. Now imagine two different situations. In one, you're writing a
   research essay that *explores* the question of whether SI laws
   reduce crime. In another, you're writing a paper that *argues*
   that these laws are effective at reducing crime. Would either
   situation affect how you might use these competing claims in
   your paper?
3. If you were going to come up with some general principles for
   evaluating the claims in sources what might they be?

Careful researchers are systematic in their evaluation of competing claims. After reading these two excerpts, can you imagine a
series of questions you might ask to help you determine whom to
believe when faced with this situation in the future? In groups, brainstorm such a list of questions on a piece of newsprint. Do these fall
into any categories?

Finally, on a fresh piece of newsprint, refine your list. Which
questions and in what order might you ask yourself when trying to
decide between conflicting claims? Discuss these lists in class.

EXERCISE 4 . 2

Reclaiming Your Topic

More than two weeks ago, you began researching a topic that
you may have known little about. But you were curious enough to

---

*Tomislav V. Kovandzic, Thomas B. Marvel, and Lynne M. Vieratas, "The Impact of
'Shall-Issue' Concealed Handgun Laws on Violent Crime Rates," *Homicide Studies*
9 (November 2005): 292–323.

dive in and immerse yourself in the research, listening to the voices of people who know more than you. You may feel, as Christy did, that your paper is beginning to slip away from you; there is just too much information, or the contradictions can't possibly be sorted out. It might seem presumptuous to think that your ideas matter. You may feel as if you're in over your head. After all, you're not an expert.

If you're not at all confused at this stage in the research process, that's great. Now is the time, through writing, to tighten your grasp on the material. But if you're feeling overwhelmed, writing now can help you get a grip. Try this exercise, which will take about forty minutes.

STEP 1: Spend ten or fifteen minutes reviewing all of the notes you've taken so far and skimming key articles or passages from books. Glance at your most important sources. Let your head swim with information.

STEP 2: Now clear your desk of everything but your research notebook. Remove all your notes and all your sources. You won't use them while doing the rest of this exercise. Trust that you'll remember what's important.

STEP 3: Now fastwrite about your topic for eight minutes. Tell the story of how your own thinking about your topic has evolved. When you began the project, what did you think? Then what happened, and what happened after that? What were your preconceptions about your topic? How have they changed? This is an open-ended fastwrite. Don't let the writing stall out. If you run out of things to say, talk to yourself through writing about your research, thinking about other trails you might follow. Time yourself.

STEP 4: Skip a few lines in your notebook. Write "Moments, Stories, People, and Scenes." Now fastwrite for another ten minutes, this time focusing on more specific case studies, situations, people, experiences, observations, and so on that stand out in your mind from the research done so far or perhaps from your own experience with the topic. Keep your pen moving for a full ten minutes. Time yourself.

STEP 5: Skip a few more lines. For ten minutes, quickly write a dialogue between you and someone else about your topic. You choose whom to converse with—a friend, your instructor. Don't plan the dialogue. Just begin with the question most commonly asked about your topic, and take the conversation from there, writing both parts of the dialogue.

STEP 6: Finally, skip a few more lines and write these two words in your notebook: "So What?" Now spend a few minutes trying to summarize the most important thing *you* think people should understand about your topic based on what you've learned so far. Distill these comments down to a sentence or two. This may be hard, but it's important. Remember, you can change your mind later.

An Application Example

What did doing Exercise 4.2 accomplish, besides giving you a cramp in your writing hand? If the exercise worked, you probably already know. By freeing yourself from the chorus of expert voices in your sources and thinking to yourself about what the ideas you've collected mean, you've taken possession of the information again. You may have reaffirmed your purpose in writing the paper.

In the preceding chapters, we've followed Amanda as she tackled her research questions about teeth whitening. (You can see her final research essay in Appendix A.) Here's how Exercise 4.2 helped her get a handle on where she wanted to go in the draft.* Notice how her project began with a relatively small question about whether the now widely available teeth whiteners worked to making a larger point about the fluidity of beauty standards, and how hard it is for people to keep up with them.

Amanda is thinking like a researcher. One question leads to another, and each allows her to see her topic in a fresh way. As she becomes more knowledgeable, Amanda begins to see what it is she might say. A thesis is emerging.

STEP 3

I first thought about this topic because I noticed how many whitening products were being advertised on TV and I looked for one in the store. I couldn't believe that it was $30 for an over-the-counter whitening system. Then I wondered if they actually worked. I know that looking at people in Hollywood, they do have really bright white teeth, and it seems like now more than ever makeover shows are focusing on the color of teeth. I started to wonder why we're whitening our teeth at all. Is it healthier? In a word, no. But when everyone else starts doing something, our standard of beauty begins to change, and then it's important for the rest of us to conform. This creates a challenge because standards of beauty keep

*The following excerpts are reprinted with permission of Amanda Stewart.

increasing more and more, and we keep increasing our expectations for ourselves. We add things to our beauty routines rather
than subtract them. It also seems to make disadvantaged and
lower class people more obvious—almost like a caste system. They
can't afford laser hair removal, acne treatments, and cosmetic
dentistry, so the rich people start to look more and more different
from less wealthy people. We're creating dividing lines through
appearance that segregate us even more.

Wow, does this all have to do with tooth whitening? A little
bit, I guess. It has to do with appearance and the way we modify
our appearance. I'm concerned I've strayed a little bit too far
from my original topic, but that might be okay. Rather than
looking at the health implications and the effectiveness of tooth
whitening and all the "hows" I want to look more at the "whys."

I also am interested in the birth of mass cosmetic
dentistry. As people have started to take better care of their
teeth and hygiene has improved, dentists were making less
money on all sorts of health procedures. They had to find a way
to recoup that money, so they created a new niche of services—
smile care. They found an endless source of revenue when they
tapped into Americans' desire for improved appearance, and
they can't ever underestimate our willingness to spend money
to look better. It's funny how profit motive can piggyback on our
vanity and create a sort of loop wherein we spend money to look
better, and then companies know we're willing to spend money
to look better, so they create a higher standard of beauty and a
product that will help us meet that standard.

By focusing on specifics in Step 4, the second fastwrite, you
should discover some ways to anchor your ideas about the topic to
particular people, situations, and case studies you discovered in your

reading or from your own experience. Making these connections will not only strengthen your own thinking; case studies and personal accounts often make compelling examples, important to your paper.

STEP 4

One intriguing character in tooth whitening is Dr. Levine, who talked about the perfect celebrity smile. He gave exact dimensions and proportions that create the same smile in all those Hollywood glamour gals that are known for their beautiful teeth. I can't believe that there's nearly a mathematical formula that tells us exactly what a perfect smile should look like. It's disturbing to me that we have standardized our smile as one thing.

One story that intrigued me was a female corporate worker that had her teeth worked on several times to change her image. She talked about big, powerful teeth and the way they made her look more assertive than small, dainty teeth. I never realized all the character judgments that are made based on teeth. Not only does the whiteness convey associations of youth, vitality, and health, but apparently a lot more than that. Also, we're not aware that we make these judgments the majority of the time. If a person walks around with a mouth full of brown snaggle-teeth, we assume they take poor care of themselves and are low-income.

I was shocked when I learned that tooth-brushing didn't become a common American phenomenon until after World War II, when soldiers picked up the habit of brushing their teeth while in the army, and then continued it when they got home and spread it to their families. The Europeans and Asians had popularized the habit much earlier, in the mid 19th century. I knew oral hygiene was a relatively new phenomenon, but I didn't realize it was that new. It makes me amazed by the number of advances we've made in five decades. We've gone from chewing on sticks to help freshen our breath, to brushing and flossing, to having veneers placed on and teeth realigned for better aesthetics. I couldn't believe the statistics on the number of Americans that felt dissatisfied with the appearance of their teeth, and couldn't shake the feeling that the numbers had probably doubled in the past ten years. I think something like 34 percent of people had tried a whitening product, while a much larger number had considered it. When I was young I never heard of anyone mentioning the whiteness of his or her teeth, and now it's nearly a universal concern.

Step 5, the dialogue writing activity, invites someone else to the discussion of your topic, challenging you to consider an audience. What might most people want to know about your topic? How might you explain the answers? These questions may later shape how you organize your paper.

Amanda's dialogue started with the question that began her research—Why do people whiten their teeth?—and then went from there, getting more and more specific. Can you visualize the inverted pyramid progression of her questions and answers?

It actually might be more productive to construct a more free-wheeling dialogue than Amanda's. Have a real conversation with an imagined reader. Push yourself with questions that really get you thinking about your topic and that might help you see it in a fresh way.

Here's Amanda's dialogue:

STEP 5

Why do people whiten their teeth?

People seem to have started whitening their teeth because other people whiten their teeth, and they want to "keep up with the Joneses" so to speak. Once it's a societal beauty standard to have white teeth, you almost have to do it to stay in line with everyone else.

Why did the beauty standard change in the first place?

Dentists and big corporations like Colgate and Crest seem to have created the desire in consumers to have whiter teeth.

They wanted to make more money, so they created more products to be sold to Americans—like whiteners. Now there are gums, gel trays, toothpastes, mouthwashes, and even laser treatments that can get teeth white.

What if you don't whiten your teeth?

A lot of judgments are made about us based on our teeth—like our overall health, hygiene, and age. By keeping more natural-colored teeth, you are unconsciously sending a message to other people about yourself that may not be what you'd prefer they think of you. It's funny how for eons people accepted eggshell-colored teeth as being natural, but now they're unacceptable.

Doesn't this just make people feel bad?

To some degree, yes. Once advertisers are promoting an image and certain people are living up to it, the rest of us feel required to live up to it too. But the people creating whitening products don't really care whether or not we feel secure about ourselves in a natural state. They want money. But I'm not bashing them, because we also create the demand by buying products, and if nobody purchased them, there wouldn't be anymore placed on the market.

Finally, asking "So What?" in Step 6 should help you redefine your thesis, or the controlling idea of your paper. In fact, your thesis may change. But for now, you need some brief statement—a sentence or two—that summarizes the most important thing you want your readers to understand.

STEP 6

So what?

Rather than being just a simple conveyance of positive feeling, smiles have become status symbols—and models to be improved through tooth-whiteners and cosmetic dentistry. Tooth-whitening products have changed the way people feel about their natural smiles, and are now used to create a prototype perfect smile.

If you're not happy with your answer to "So What?" spend some more time thinking about it. Don't proceed too much further with writing until you have some kind of tentative thesis statement to keep in mind. Put your thesis on an index card or piece of paper, and post it over your desk as a reminder. Pull it down and revise it, if necessary, as you continue with research and writing. But keep that thesis up there on the wall, at least while you're writing the first draft.

If Exercise 4.2 didn't work for you, you may need to collect more information. Consider circling back to some of the advanced search strategy suggestions made in the third week (see Chapter 3). But if you feel ready to begin writing a draft, read on.

Deciding Whether to Say *I*

I'm a writer who seems unable to stop talking about myself. As a reader of this textbook, that should be apparent to you by now. I share anecdotes about my photography failures, my high school girlfriend, and my predilection for lobsters. I've chosen to do this, though I know that getting personal in a piece of writing is somewhat risky business. If it's excessive, self-disclosure can seem egotistical or narcissistic. Constant self-reference—"I believe that . . . " or "I always wondered about . . . " or "I feel that . . . "—is usually unnecessary. (After all, if you simply make the assertion without the attribution, it's pretty obvious that you believe it or feel it.) The overuse of *I* can also seem to get in the way of the real subject, which may not be you. The personal profile is one genre of nonfiction writing that often suffers from explicit authorial intrusion. And teachers of research papers, as you know, often seem downright hostile to the intruding *I*.

By now, you know I don't agree with the view that all research writing should be objective (as if such a thing were possible). And in the research *essay* that you are about to draft this week, I certainly invite you to consider using the first person, presenting your own observations and experiences as evidence (if they're relevant) and yes, even talking about yourself.

There are many reasons this might be a good idea. First, by signaling our personal experiences and prejudices about a topic, we make explicit not only our particular purposes in exploring it but also why we might have a reason for (or even a vested interest in) seeing it a certain way. Readers like to know a writer's motivation for writing about something and appreciate knowing how her experiences might influence her ways of seeing. But maybe even more important, when a writer stops pretending that the *text* talks instead of the *author* (e.g., "This paper will argue that . . .") and actually enters into her text, she is much more likely to initiate a genuine conversation with her readers *and* with her sources. This dialogue might very well lead to some new ways of seeing her topic—that is, after all, the purpose of inquiry.

Getting Personal Without Being Personal

Conversation takes place between people, and in writing that embodies conversation, readers sense what Gordon Harvey* called *presence*—an awareness that a writer is making sense of things in his own particular ways, that he has a personal stake in what is being said. This is most easily achieved when the writer *gets* personal by using the first person, sharing personal experiences and perspectives. I hope that you sense my presence in *The Curious Researcher* through my willingness to do such things.

But I also want you to see, as Harvey observes, that presence in writing can be registered in ways other than simply talking about yourself. That is, you can write a research essay this week that *doesn't* use the first person or isn't autobiographical and still provides your readers with a strong sense of your presence as an individual writer and thinker. This presence may be much more subtle when it's not carried on the first-person singular's sturdy back. But it still makes writing come to life.

Before you begin drafting your essay this week, you'll have to decide how you'd prefer to get personal—explicitly or implicitly. For some of you, the choices may be limited. For instance, if your essay is on the causes of World War I, then integrating your own personal experience with the subject is obviously not an option. Most topics, however, offer the possibility of self-disclosure, and unless your instructor advises otherwise, almost all can accommodate *I*. But when you choose not to get personal in direct ways, you can still establish a strong presence in your essay.

Beginning at the Beginning

John McPhee, a staff writer for *The New Yorker* magazine and one of the masters of writing the research-based essay, gave a talk some years back about beginnings, which vex many writers.

*Gordon Harvey, "Presence in the Essay," *College English* 56 (1994): 642–54.

Making Your Presence Felt

Here are some ways to establish your presence in your research essay without necessarily using the first person.

- *Control quotation.* Carefully consider how you use the voices of others—where in your essay and for what purpose—as well as what you choose to emphasize in what those voices said.
- *Find your own way of saying things.* Even when talking about what someone else has said, say it in a way that only you can.
- *Find your own way of seeing things.* How do others usually see your topic, and how do you see it differently?
- *Seize opportunities to comment.* More than anything else, what you **do** with information—evaluating it, relating it, defining it, interpreting it, establishing its significance—gives the essay your signature.

The first part—the lead, the beginning—is the hardest part of all to write. I've often heard writers say that if you have written your lead you have written 90 percent of the story. You have tens of thousands of words to choose from, after all, and only one can start the story, then one after that, and so forth. And your material, at this point, is all fresh and unused, so you don't have the advantage of being in the middle of things. You could start in any of many places. What will you choose?* Leads must be sound. They should never promise what does not follow. Leads, like titles, are flashlights that shine down into the story.

Flashlights or Floodlights?

I love this: *"Leads . . . are flashlights that shine down into the story."* An introduction, at least the kind I was taught to write in high school, is more like a sodium vapor lamp that lights up the whole neighborhood. I remember writing introductions to research papers that sounded like this:

```
There are many critical problems that face

society today. One of these critical problems is
```

*John McPhee, University of New Hampshire, 1977.

environmental protection, and especially the
conservation of marine resources. This paper
will explore one of these resources--the
whale--and the myriad ways in which the whale-
watching industry now poses a new threat to this
species' survival. It will look at what is happening today and what some people concerned with
the problem hope will happen tomorrow. It will
argue that new regulations need to be put
into effect to reduce boat traffic around our
remaining whales, a national treasure that
needs protection.

This introduction isn't that bad. It does offer a statement of purpose, and it explains the thesis. But the window it opens on the paper is so broad—listing everything the paper will try to do—that readers see a bland, general landscape. What's to discover? The old writing formula for structuring some papers—"Say what you're going to say, say it, and then say what you said"—breeds this kind of introduction. It also gets the writer started on a paper that often turns out as bland as the beginning.

Consider this alternative opening for the same paper:

Scott Mercer, owner of the whale-watching vessel
Cetecea, tells the story of a man and his son who
decide that watching the whales from inside their
small motorboat isn't close enough. They want to
swim with them. As Mercer and his passengers
watch, the man sends his son overboard with
snorkel and fins, and the boy promptly swims
towards a "bubble cloud," a mass of air exhaled
by a feeding humpback whale below the surface.
What the swimmer doesn't know is that, directly
below that bubble cloud, the creature is on

```
its way up, mouth gaping. They are both in for a
surprise. "I got on the P.A. system and told my
passengers, just loud enough for the guy in the
boat to hear me, that either that swimmer was
going to end up as whale food or he was going to
get slapped with a $10,000 fine. He got out of
the water pretty fast."
```

I think this lead accomplishes nearly as much as the bland version but in a more compelling way. It suggests the purpose of the paper—to explore conflicts between whale lovers and whales—and even implies the thesis—that human activity around whales needs more regulation. This lead is more like McPhee's "flashlight," pointing to the direction of the paper without attempting to illuminate the entire subject in a paragraph. An interesting beginning will also help launch the writer into a more interesting paper, for both reader and writer.

It's probably obvious that your opening is your first chance to capture your reader's attention. But how you begin your research paper will also have a subtle yet significant impact on the rest of it. The lead starts the paper going in a particular direction; it also establishes the *tone,* or writing voice, and the writer's relationships to the subject and the reader. Most writers at least intuitively know this, which is why beginnings are so hard to write.

Writing Multiple Leads

One thing that will make it easier to get started is to write three leads to your paper, instead of agonizing over one that must be perfect. Each different opening you write should point the "flashlight" in a different direction, suggesting different trails the draft might follow. After composing several leads, you can choose the one that you—and ultimately, your readers—find most promising.

Writing multiple openings to your paper might sound hard, but consider all the ways to begin:

■ *Anecdote.* Think of a little story that nicely frames what your paper is about, as does the lead about the man and his son who almost became whale food.

■ *Scene.* Begin by giving your readers a look at some revealing aspect of your topic. A paper on the destruction of tropical rain forests might begin with a description of what the land looks like after loggers have left it.

■ *Profile.* Try a lead that introduces someone who is important to your topic. Amanda's essay on the relationship between the popularity of tooth whitening and our changing notions of beauty might begin, for example, by describing Dr. Levine, the man who determined with mathematical precision the dimensions of the "perfect smile."

■ *Background.* Maybe you could begin by providing important and possibly surprising background information on your topic. A paper on steroid use might start by citing the explosive growth in use by high school athletes in the last ten years. A paper on a novel or an author might begin with a review of what critics have had to say.

■ *Quotation.* Sometimes, you encounter a great quote that beautifully captures the question your paper will explore or the direction it will take. Heidi's paper on whether *Sesame Street* provides children with a good education began by quoting a tribute from *U.S. News and World Report* to Jim Henson after his sudden death.

■ *Dialogue.* Open with dialogue between people involved in your topic. Dan's paper on the connection between spouse abuse and alcoholism began with a conversation between himself and a woman who had been abused by her husband.

■ *Question.* Pointedly ask your readers the questions you asked that launched your research or the questions your readers might raise about your topic. Here's how Kim began her paper on adoption: "Could you imagine going through life not knowing your true identity?"

■ *Contrast.* Try a lead that compares two apparently unlike things that highlight the problem or dilemma the paper will explore. Dusty's paper "Myth of the Superwoman" began with a comparison between her friend Susan, who grew up believing in Snow White and Cinderella and married at twenty-one, and herself, who never believed in princes or white horses and was advised by her mother that it was risky to depend on a man.

■ *Announcement.* Sometimes the most appropriate beginning *is* one like the first lead on whales and whale-watchers mentioned earlier, which announces what the paper is about. Though such openings are sometimes not particularly compelling, they are direct. A paper with a complex topic or focus may be well served by simply stating in the beginning the main idea you'll explore and what plan you'll follow.

E X E R C I S E   4 . 3

Three Ways In

STEP 1: Compose three different beginnings, or leads, to your research paper. Each should be one or two paragraphs (or perhaps more, depending on what type of lead you've chosen and on the length of your paper). Think about the many different ways to begin, as mentioned earlier, and experiment (see Figure 4.1). Your instructor may ask you to write the three leads in your research notebook or type them on a separate piece of paper and bring them to class.

STEP 2: Get some help deciding which opening is strongest. Circulate your leads in class, or show them to friends. Ask each person to check the one lead he likes best, that most makes him want to read on.

STEP 3: Choose the lead you like (even if no one else does). To determine how well it prepares your readers for what follows, ask a friend or classmate to answer these questions: Based on reading only the opening of the paper: (a) What do you predict this paper is about? What might be its focus? (b) Can you guess what central question I'm trying to answer? (c) Can you predict what my thesis might be? (d) How would you characterize the tone of the paper?

Amanda's Three Leads

Here are three openings that Amanda crafted for her draft on our cultural obsession with the "perfect smile." Which do you think is strongest?

1. I haven't felt much like smiling recently. It isn't that I've been particularly melancholy, or deprived of necessary joy. I've actually been hesitant to smile because lately I've felt insecure about my teeth. I brush and floss every day and see my dentist twice a year, just like any responsible hygiene patient does—but that doesn't seem to be enough anymore. My teeth need to be white. Now when I feel the corners of my mouth pucker upwards and I start to grin at someone, I can't stop thinking about my teeth. What once was a

David Hancock
Brock Dethier
English 201
12 March 1998

Leaping Dog Awakens Locals' Curiosity

LOGAN, UT—A dog with seemingly supernatural abilities astounded observers on the Quad at Utah State University Friday when it leaped nearly twenty feet high while trying to catch a frisbee.

The owner of the dog, Sam McDougle, aroused the suspicions of local residents when he suggested Logan water as a possible cause. "Don't feed him no special vitamins or nuthin', just dog food and tap water," McDougle said.

"I'm a little scared," commented Ruth Parkins about questionable elements in the water, "and I don't know that I'd want my kids turning into freaks." Authorities downplayed rumors of steroids and hormone stimulants contaminating the water source. "I wasn't there, but I'd say Mr. McDougle is quite a charlatan," said Doug Thompson, mayor of Logan.

According to witnesses, McDougle repeatedly tossed a frisbee high into the air, and the dog launched after it "like a Patriot Missile taking out some Scuds," said Air Force Lieutenant John Richards. "When I first saw him do it, I thought, 'well, ain't that neat,'" said McDougle. "But now I'm gonna need a lot bigger fence."

FIGURE 4.1   Here's the opening to a paper that doesn't fit neatly into any category. David's essay begins with a photograph of a dog jumping an unreasonable height and a mock newspaper article on the feat. His next page unravels the mystery—the photograph was doctored using a software program—and then the essay goes on to explore the dangers of digitally altered images. David asks, "Can we even trust photographs anymore?"

Source: Reprinted by permission of David Hancock.

simple visual expression of happiness has become a symptom of my overall doubts about my appearance.

2. Julie Beatty wants people to look at her as a more confident, strong person, so she's doing the only logical thing. She's shelling out over $12,500 for an overhaul on her teeth. While it sounds completely ridiculous to change a person's oral structure to create a different persona, Julie is a member of a booming group of people who are looking to change their smiles to change their lives. Whether or not Julie's straightening, whitening, and tooth reshaping will change her success as an executive is still unknown, but the popularity of cosmetic dentistry and smile care is an undeniable new phenomenon.

3. I can feel individual molecules of air battering at my teeth. It's the middle of the night, but I can't sleep because of the constant pain in my mouth. Even the weight of my lips pressing down on my teeth is agonizing, like I've spent the day being hit in the mouth with a hammer and have exposed nerves protruding throughout. I haven't been beaten up, though. The cause of all my agony is a 10 percent peroxide gel I've been smearing into trays and putting on my teeth for the past week to whiten them. All this pain is due to my vanity and desire for a bit more pearliness in my pearly whites. As I watch the numbers of the clock roll from 2:00 to 4:00, I wonder why I'm putting up with such dental distress just for a more gleaming smile.

It's easy to choose an opening that's catchy. But the beginning of your paper must also help establish your purpose in writing it, frame your focus, and perhaps even suggest your main point, or thesis. The lead will also establish the voice, or tone, the paper will adopt (see the following section). That's a big order for one or two paragraphs, and you may find that more than a couple of paragraphs are needed to do it. Tentatively select the one opening (or a combination of several) from this exercise that does those things best. I think you'll find that none of the leads you composed will be wasted; there will be a place for the ones you don't use somewhere else in the paper. Keep them handy.

Deciding on a Voice

How you begin has another subtle influence on your draft: It establishes the tone, or writing voice, you will adopt in your paper. Though you may think *writing voice* is not something you've considered much before, you probably paid a lot of attention to it when writing the essay that accompanied your college applications. Does this *sound* right? you wondered, considering whether what you wrote would impress the admissions officer. Did you sound like college material? You also know how to *change* your writing voice. You do it all the time. The voice you choose in an email to your professor with a question about an assignment will be different from the voice you use if you ask a friend about it. We develop this kind of rhetorical awareness through experience.

Of all the writing assignments you've done over the years, the research paper is probably the one in which you paid the most attention to writing voice. Research papers are supposed to sound a certain way, right? They're supposed to be peppered with words such as *myriad* and *thus* and *facilitate*. They're supposed to sound like, well, nobody you know—detached, mechanical, and ponderous.

These are understandable assumptions. So many of the sources you've read in the past weeks have sounded that way. It's also difficult to avoid sounding detached when you're writing about a topic that holds little interest for you. But the writing voice you choose for this or any other paper you write *is* a choice. Don't assume that all research papers are supposed to sound a certain way and that you must mindlessly conform to that voice.

Considering Purpose, Audience, Subject, and Who You Are

How do you choose a writing voice for a research paper? A lot of the decisions, including an appropriate voice or tone for your essay, depend on this: *for whom are you writing and how knowledgeable are they already about your topic*? This has a huge impact on many things—how you structure your essay, the kind of information you use, and even the genre you choose (see Figure 4.2). Generally, the more knowledgeable your audience is about your research topic, the more likely it is that you will need to minimize your personal presence in the work, organize the information using conventions that expert readers expect, and consider what kinds of information these people will find most persuasive, sometimes called "rules of evidence."

In some classes, you may write for your instructors about subjects in which they are experts, and you may need to adjust your approach. But most composition courses invite students to write for their peers. These are general readers, an audience that is not likely to know nearly as much as you already do about your research topic. Therefore you're probably not writing a technical paper for an audience of experts. And though your primary purpose is not to entertain readers, you *are* trying to make your essay as interesting to others as it is to you.

But no text, even the most formal, is completely voiceless. And in an essay, even a research essay, readers' sense that they are

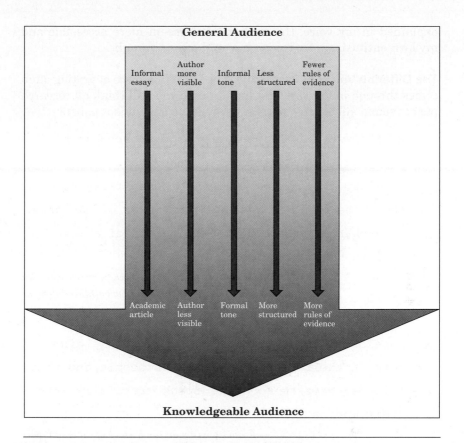

General Audience

| Informal essay | Author more visible | Informal tone | Less structured | Fewer rules of evidence |

| Academic article | Author less visible | Formal tone | More structured | More rules of evidence |

Knowledgeable Audience

FIGURE 4.2   The Reader Effect. As your audience varies from those less informed about your research topic to those who are knowledgeable about it, your approach changes.

listening to the sound of a human being with a particular way of seeing things makes the writing come alive.

Fundamentally, your writing voice is a reflection of *who you are.* Your natural writing voice is different from mine, just as your spoken voice is. You can change your spoken voice, something you're probably pretty experienced at already. But you may need to learn to know and appreciate your writing voice—the voice that sounds like you. It might even be appropriate for this paper.

I faced a difficult decision about voice in writing this text. My purpose was to instruct students in research skills as well as to motivate them to find some enthusiasm for the assignment. In order to motivate my readers, I wanted to present the research paper in a new way. That purpose would not be served, I thought, by writing in the detached, impersonal voice most people associate with textbooks (and research papers). I chose to sound like *me,* hoping that when explained in my voice, the subject would seem more accessible and my own enthusiasm for research would come through.

The Differing Voices of Research.   The voice in a piece of writing often comes through in the very first line. In case you still think all research papers sound alike, listen to these first lines from student papers:

Ernst Pawel has said that *The Metamorphosis* by Franz Kafka "transcends the standard categories of literary criticism; it is a poisoned fairy tale about the magic of hate and the power of hypocrisy . . . charting the transmogrification of a lost soul in a dead bug" (279).

> *—From a paper on how Kafka writes the story to deal with*
> *his own childhood demons*

As a waiter in a classy restaurant, I observe considerable variation in the way people dine, both in their treatment of other people and their skill at getting food and drink gracefully into their mouths.

> *— From an essay on the history of table manners*

Even the sound of the word is vulgar.

> *—From a paper on ticks*

Living during a period of war was something I had never experienced until the escalation of the recent Gulf crisis.

> *—From a paper on Igor Stravinsky's* The Soldier's Tale

I have often worried in the past months if there was either something wrong with or missing from my brain.

> *—From a paper on dream interpretation*

No more fat jokes.

> *—From a paper on a daughter coming to terms*
> *with her mother's cancer*

These *are* different beginnings. But notice something all these beginnings share: They are concrete. None begins with a bland, broad stroke—some sweeping generalization or obvious statement (e.g., "War is an unhappy reality in today's society" or "Richard Wright's *Native Son* is about the African-American experience in America"). Rather, each gives the reader a specific handle on the topic. In some cases, the reader is given not only a concrete point of view but also, through a distinctive voice, is introduced to an individual writer, as well.

The voices in the previous examples could be considered along a continuum, beginning with the more formal and moving to the much less formal, ranging from the impersonal to the personal, from a less visible writer to one who steps forward immediately. Any one of these voices might be appropriate for your paper, depending on your subject, purpose, and audience, and on who you are.

As suggested earlier in this book, ask your instructor if you have some latitude in choosing a voice for your paper. (See "Things to Ask Your Instructor" in the Introduction.) If so, review the lead you tentatively chose in Exercise 4.3. Does it establish a voice that's appropriate, given your topic, purpose, and audience? Do you like the way it sounds? Should you change it? Would another lead sound better? If so, write a new lead or choose another from the several leads you wrote earlier.

Writing for Reader Interest

You've tentatively chosen a lead for your paper. You've selected it based on how well you think it frames your tentative purpose, establishes an appropriate tone or voice, and captures your readers' attention. Before you begin writing your draft, consider these four other strategies for writing a lively, interesting paper that will help keep readers turning pages.

1. How does your topic intersect with your readers' experiences?

2. Is there a way to put faces on your topic, to dramatize how it affects or is affected by particular people?

3. Can you find an ending that further clarifies, dramatizes, or emphasizes what you've come to understand about the answers to your research question?

4. Are there opportunities to surprise your readers, with interesting facts, arresting arguments, or highlighting a way of seeing something that is unexpected?

Working the Common Ground

Here's how David Quammen, a nature writer, begins an essay on the sexual strategy of Canada geese:

> Listen: *uh-whongk, uh-whongk, uh-whongk, uh-whongk,* and then you are wide awake, and you smile up at the ceiling as the calls fade off to the north and already they are gone. Silence again, 3 A.M., the hiss of March winds. A thought crosses your mind before you roll over and, contentedly, resume sleeping. The thought is: "Thank God I live here, right here exactly, in their path. Thank God for those birds." The honk of wild Canada geese passing overhead in the night is a sound to freshen the human soul. The question is why.*

If you live in Puerto Rico or anywhere beyond the late-night call of geese flying overhead, this lead paragraph may not draw you into Quammen's article on the birds' sexual habits. But for the many of us who know the muttering of geese overhead, suddenly the writer's question—why this is a sound "to freshen the human soul"—becomes our question, too. *We want to know what he knows because he starts with what we both know already:* the haunting sound of geese in flight.

David Quammen understands the importance of working the common ground between his topic and his readers. In "The Miracle of Geese," he begins with an experience that many of us know, and once he establishes that common ground, he takes us into the less familiar territory he encountered while researching Canada geese. And we willingly go. Quammen gives us a foothold on his topic that comes from our own experience with it.

One of my interests in writing an essay about pigeons was the conviction that I'm not alone in feeling ambivalent about the birds. Though "The Bothersome Beauty of Pigeons" doesn't begin, as David Quammen's essay does, by establishing this common ground, on several occasions I exploit moments I think readers will find familiar, including the anecdote about the war I waged on pigeons roosting under the eaves of my house. In smaller ways, I work common ground by using it in explanations, particularly when I'm trying to bring research information to life. For

---

*David Quammen, *The Flight of the Iguana* (New York: Delacorte, 1988), 233.

example, here's how I described the drinking habits of pigeons in the essay:

```
[Pigeons] have other evolutionary advantages as
well, some of which save them from the well-placed
kicks of pigeon-haters or the tires of speeding
taxis. For one thing, they "suck" puddle water
rather than take it in their beaks and throw their
heads back to swallow it, something like the dif-
ference between drinking a juice box and slinging
back a shot of tequila. Sucking is quicker, appar-
ently, . . .
```

In an earlier draft, I had merely described the water sucking habits of pigeons, but I sensed that the information would be far more interesting and understandable if I exploited a comparison that readers would find familiar: drinking juice boxes and taking shots of tequila.

As you draft your research paper, look for ways to work the common ground between your topic and your readers: What typically is their relationship to what you're writing about? What might they know about the topic but not have noticed? How does it touch their world? What would they want to know from their own experiences with your topic?

Steve, writing a paper about the town fire department that services the university, began by describing a frequent event in his dormitory: a false alarm. He then went on to explore why many alarms are not really so false after all. He hooked his readers by drawing on their common experience with his topic.

Some topics, like geese and divorce and alcoholism, may have very real connections to the lives of your readers. Many people have heard geese overhead, seen families broken apart, or watched parents or friends destroy themselves with booze. As you revise your paper, look for opportunities to encourage readers to take a closer look at something about your topic they may have seen before.

Topics for Which Common Ground Is Hard to Find.   Some topics don't yield common ground so directly. They may be outside the direct experiences of your readers. For example, Margaret was a history major, and, thankfully, she had never had the bubonic plague. Neither have the rest of us. But she was interested in writing a research essay on the impact of the fourteenth century epidemic on the lives of European women. This is an age and a disaster that in some ways is beyond the imagining of modern readers, though a skillful writer will look to highlight some of the similarities between our lives and those of the people she's writing about. One of these connections might be the modern AIDS epidemic in Africa, a disaster of truly epic proportions though it seems largely ignored by many Americans. Margaret might begin her essay with a brief glimpse at the devastation of families in South Africa today as a way of establishing the relevance of her 500-year-old topic.

Literary topics may also present a challenge in establishing common ground with readers, unless the author or work is familiar. But there are ways. When I was writing a paper on notions of manhood in Wallace Stegner's novels *The Big Rock Candy Mountain* and *Recapitulation,* I brought the idea of manhood home to my readers by describing my relationship with my own father and then comparing it to the relationship of two key characters in the books. Comparison to other more popular works that readers may know is often a way to establish some common ground.

Though it's unlikely that any of your classmates served on the ground in the recent Afghan war, images of that conflict—the debris-laden streets of Kabul, and the emergence of women in their burkas following the fall of the Taliban—are familiar to most of us through TV. This familiarity with such a distant place and culture might be a great way to establish the common ground with readers if, say, you were writing about the resurgence of female participation in the affairs of that nation.

In writing your paper, imagine the ways in which your topic intersects with the life of a typical reader, and in that way, bring the information to life.

Putting People on the Page

Essayist E. B. White once advised that when you want to write about humankind, you should write about a human. The advice to look at the *small* to understand the *large* applies to most writing, not just the research paper.

Ideas come alive when we see how they operate in the world we live in. Beware, then, of long paragraphs with sentences that begin with phrases such as *in today's society,* where you wax on with generalization after generalization about your topic. Unless your ideas are anchored to specific cases, observations, experiences, statistics, and, especially, people, they will be reduced to abstractions and lose their power for your reader.

Using Case Studies.   Strangely, research papers are often people-less landscapes, which is one of the things that can make them so lifeless to read. Lisa wrote about theories of child development, citing studies and schools of thought about the topic yet never applying that information to a real child, her own daughter, two-year-old Rebecca. In his paper decrying the deforestation of the Amazon rain forest, Marty never gave his readers the chance to hear the voices of the Indians whose way of life is threatened.

Ultimately, what makes almost any topic matter to the writer or the reader is what difference it makes to people.

Candy's paper on child abuse and its effect on language development, for example, opened with the tragic story of Genie, who, for nearly thirteen years, was bound in her room by her father and beaten whenever she made a sound. When Genie was finally rescued, she could not speak at all. This sad story about a real girl makes the idea that child abuse affects how one speaks (the paper's thesis) anything but abstract. Candy gave her readers reason to care about what she learned about the problem by personalizing it.

Sometimes, the best personal experience to share is your own. Have you been touched by the topic? Kim's paper about the special problems of women alcoholics included anecdotes about several women gleaned from her reading, but the paper was most compelling when she talked about her own experiences with her mother's alcoholism.

Using Interviews.   Interviews are another way to bring people to the page. In "Why God Created Flies," Richard Conniff brought in the voice of a bug expert, Vincent Dethier, who not only had interesting things to say about flies but who also spoke with humor and enthusiasm. Heidi's paper on *Sesame Street* featured the voice of a school principal, a woman who echoed the point the paper made about the value of the program. Such research essays are filled not just with information about the topic but with people who are touched by it in some way.

As you write your paper, look for opportunities to bring people to the page. Hunt for case studies, anecdotes, and good quotes that will help your readers see how your topic affects how people think and live their lives.

Writing a Strong Ending

Readers remember beginnings and endings. We already explored what makes a strong beginning: It engages the reader's interest, it's more often specific than general, and it frames the purpose of the paper, defining for the reader where it is headed. A beginning for a research paper should also state or imply its thesis, or controlling idea.

We haven't said anything about endings yet, or "conclusions," as they are traditionally described. What's a strong ending? That depends. If you're writing a formal research paper (in some disciplines), the purpose of the conclusion is straightforward: It should summarize major findings. But if you're writing a less formal research essay, the nature of the conclusion is less prescribed. It could summarize major findings, but it could also suggest new directions worth exploring, highlight an especially important aspect of the topic, offer a rethinking of the thesis, or end the story of the search. The conclusion could be general, or it could be specific.

Endings to Avoid.   The ending of your research paper could be a lot of things, and in a way, it's easier to say what it should *not* be:

■ Avoid conclusions that simply restate what you've already said. This is the "kick the dead horse" conclusion some of us were taught to write in school on the assumption that our readers probably aren't smart enough to get our point, so we'd better repeat it. This approach annoys most readers who *are* smart enough to know the horse is dead.

■ Avoid endings that begin with *in conclusion* or *thus*. Words such as these also signal to your reader what she already knows: that you're ending. Language such as this often begins a very general summary, which gets you into a conclusion such as the one mentioned above: dead.

■ Avoid endings that don't feel like endings—that trail off onto other topics, are abrupt, or don't seem connected to what came before them. Prompting your readers to think is one thing; leaving them hanging is quite another.

In some ways, the conclusion of your research paper is the last stop on your journey; the reader has traveled far with you to get there. The most important quality of a good ending is that it should add something to the paper. If it doesn't, cut it and write a new one.

What can the ending add? It can add a further elaboration of your thesis that grows from the evidence you've presented, a discussion of solutions to a problem that has arisen from the information you've uncovered, or perhaps a final illustration or piece of evidence that drives home your point.

Student Christina Kerby's research essay on method acting explores the controversy over whether this approach is selfish, subverting the playwright's intentions about a character's identity and replacing it with the actor's focus on her own feelings and identity. Christina's ending, however, first transcends the debate by putting method acting in context: It is one of several tools an actor can use to tap her emotions for a role. But then Christina humorously raises the nagging question about selfishness once more: Can we accept that Juliet is not thinking about the fallen Romeo as she weeps by his side but about her dead cat Fluffy? Here's Christina's ending:

> Acting is no longer about poise, voice quality, and diction. It is also about feeling the part, about understanding the emotions that go into playing the part, and about possessing the skill necessary to bring those emotions to life within the character. . . . Whether an actor uses Stanislavski's method of physical actions to unlock the door to her subconscious or whether she attempts to stir up emotions from deep within herself using Strasberg's method, the actor's goal is to create a portrayal that is truthful. It is possible to pick out a bad actor from a mile away, one who does not understand the role because she does not understand the emotions necessary to create it. Or perhaps she simply lacks the means of tapping into them.
>
> If genuine emotion is what the masses want, method acting may be just what every star-struck actress needs. Real tears? No problem. The

```
audience will never know that Juliet was not
lamenting the loss of her true love Romeo but
invoking the memory of her favorite cat Fluffy,
who died tragically in her arms.*
```

An ending, in many ways, can be approached similarly to a lead. You can conclude with an anecdote, a quotation, a description, a summary, or a profile. Go back to the discussion earlier in this chapter of types of leads for ideas about types of conclusions. The same basic guidelines apply.

One of the easiest ways to solve the problem of finding a strong ending is to have the snake bite its tail. In other words, find some way in the end of your essay to return to where the piece began. For example, if your research essay began with an anecdote that dramatized a problem—say, the destruction of old growth forests in Washington—you might return to that opening anecdote, suggesting how the solutions you explored in your essay might have changed the outcome. If you pose a question in the first few paragraphs, return to the question in the last few. If you begin with a profile of someone relevant to your topic, return to him or her in the end, perhaps amplifying on some part of your picture of the person. Although this approach is formulaic, it often works well because it gives a piece of writing a sense of unity.

Using Surprise

The research process—like the writing process—can be filled with discovery for the writer if he approaches the topic with curiosity and openness. When I began researching the *Lobster Almanac,* I was constantly surprised by things I didn't know: Lobsters are bugs; it takes eight years for a lobster in Maine to grow to the familiar one-pound size; the largest lobster ever caught weighed about forty pounds and lived in a tank at a restaurant for a year, developing a fondness for the owner's wife. I could go on and on. And I did in the book, sharing unusual information with my readers on the assumption that if it surprised me, it would surprise them, too.

As you write your draft, reflect on the surprising things you discovered about your topic during your research and look for ways to weave that information into the rewrite. Later, after you have written your draft, share it with a reader and ask for his ideas about what is particularly interesting and should be further developed. For now, think about unusual specifics you may have left out.

*Reprinted with permission of Christina B. Kerby.

However, don't include information, no matter how surprising or interesting, that doesn't serve your purpose. Christine's survey on the dreams of college freshmen had some fascinating findings, including some accounts of recurring dreams that really surprised her. She reluctantly decided not to say much about them, however, because they didn't really further the purpose of her paper, which was to discover what function dreams serve. On the other hand, Bob was surprised to find that some politically conservative politicians and judges actually supported decriminalization of marijuana. He decided to include more information about who they were and what they said in his revision, believing it would surprise his readers and strengthen his argument.

Organizing the Draft

Like a lot of school kids, I learned to write something called the "five-paragraph theme": introduction with thesis, three topic sentences, and three supporting details under each topic sentence. This was the container into which I poured all of my writing back then. Though it didn't produce particularly interesting writing, the five-paragraph structure was a reliable way to organize things. It was very well-suited to outlines. I vaguely remember this one from sixth grade:

I. China is a really big country
   A. The population of China is really big
   B. The geographic size of China is really big
   C. The economic dreams of China are really big.

What's useful about thinking of structure this way is the notion of hierarchy. There are some ideas that are subordinated to others, and some information that is subordinated to each idea. A problem with it, however, is the assumption that hierarchy is *always* the best way to organize information. For instance, essays can often make relevant digressions, or they might play with one way of seeing the topic and then another.

Perhaps a more basic problem with forms like the five-paragraph theme is the idea that structure is this kind of inert container that stands apart from the things you put into it and that it is immune to your particular motives in writing about something.

Yet structure is important. And it's even more important when writers begin a draft with an abundance of information. John McPhee has written popular nonfiction essays on people who study animal road kills, a guy who still makes birch bark canoes, and McPhee's own exploration of Atlantic City using the game Monopoly as a guide. He is a careful and meticulous researcher, accumulating material in multiple binders from his interviews, observations, and reading. By the time he sits down to write, he's looking at pages and pages of notes. McPhee's solution to this problem is to use note cards to organize his information on bulletin boards, moving them around until he gets a satisfying arrangement. "The piece of writing has a structure inside it," he says, and before he begins drafting he seeks to find it.

If you don't have much information to begin with, structure isn't such a problem. You simply end up using everything you have.

I'd like to encourage you, as you start drafting this week, to think about organizing your essay in a way that is more flexible and more responsive to your purposes in the piece, the audience for whom you're writing, your topic, and the assignment. For example, here are two ways to imagine how your research essay might come together.

- *Delayed thesis structure*—characteristic of the exploratory essay
- *Question-claim structure*—characteristic of the argumentative paper

While each method of organizing your research essay is distinct, they all share certain characteristics. For example, nearly any academic research paper includes the following items:

1. A point, a claim, a thesis, one main thing you are trying to say about the research question.
2. A review of what has already been said by others about it.
3. Specific information—evidence—that is the data from which your interpretations, conclusions, assertions, and speculations arise.
4. A method of reasoning through the question, some pattern of thought—narrative, argument, essaying—that writer and reader finds a convincing way to try to get at the truth of things.

Delayed Thesis Structure

If you chose your topic because you wanted to learn what you think—to find out rather than to prove—then you are essaying your research question. That's what I was doing in the beginning of this book when I was trying to figure out what to make of my conflicting feelings about pigeons. What is it about these creatures that makes them so easy to love and hate at the same time and what does that say about our responses to the natural world?

Quite naturally, then, I didn't begin my draft with a thesis—an answer to these questions—but sought to use my essay to try to sort this out. The "delayed thesis" structure uses the information from your research to think through your research question (see Figure 4.3).

In one version of this, you essentially tell the story of your thinking, a kind of "narrative of thought." The plot is something like, "This seems to be the problem and this is the question is raises for me. And here's what this person and that person have said about it, and this is what they said that makes me think." The story ends with some kind of statement that addresses this question: "What do I understand now about the question I initially asked that I didn't understand when I first asked it?"

However, exploratory research essays can take any number of forms. The structure that follows highlights five parts a research essay *might* include and lists some specific options for developing each. It might help you think about how to organize your draft this week.

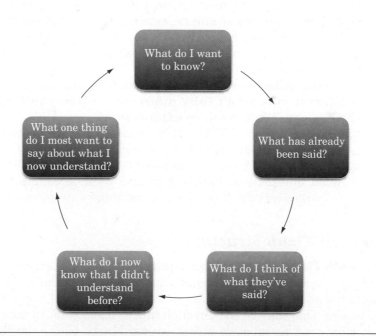

FIGURE 4.3   The Delayed Thesis Structure. This method of thinking through a research question might tell the story of your thinking and how what you've read and heard helps you to understand what you didn't understand before about your topic.

   I. **Introduce the research problem or question and then your motive for exploring it.**
      a. Tell a story that dramatizes the problem.
      b. Describe your own experiences with it.
      c. What did you read, observe, or experience that made you curious about it?
  II. **Establish the significance of the problem or question and why readers should care about it.**
      a. How many other people are affected?
      b. What difference will it make in people's lives?
      c. Why is this *particular* question significant?
 III. **Describe and analyze what has already been written or said by others about the problem or question, and how this advances your understanding.**
      a. Who has made a significant contribution to the conversation about this?
      b. What have they said and how does that relate to your research question?
      c. What important questions do these other voices raise for you?
  IV. **Explain what you find to be the most persuasive or significant answer to the research question (thesis)?**
      a. In the end, which voices were most convincing? Why?
      b. What might you add to the conversation?
      c. What do you want to say?
   V. **Describe what you've come to understand about the topic that you didn't fully appreciate when you began the project. What is left to explore?**
      a. What difference will the discoveries you made about your question make in your life? In your readers' lives?
      b. What do you remain curious about?
      c. What questions are unresolved and what directions might more inquiry take if you were to continue?

Question–Claim Structure

   While *The Curious Researcher* promotes essayed research as an excellent introduction to academic inquiry, most academic writing reports the products of the inquiry process in the form of argumentative papers. That may be the direction in which you want to take this draft after your research in recent weeks. Maybe you've developed strong feelings about your topic and you want to methodically build a case for a particular idea or assertion as a response to your research question.

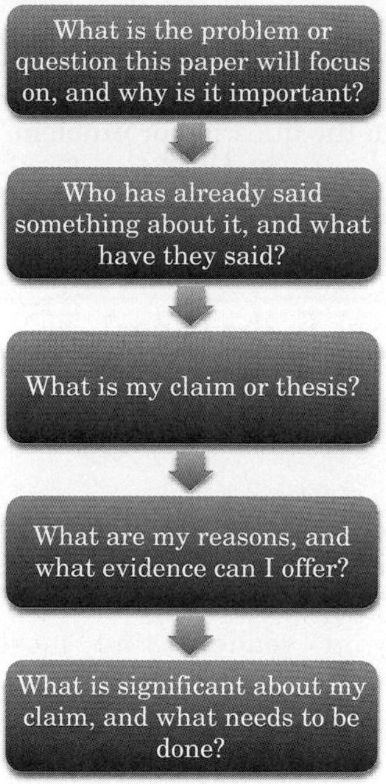

What is the problem or question this paper will focus on, and why is it important?

Who has already said something about it, and what have they said?

What is my claim or thesis?

What are my reasons, and what evidence can I offer?

What is significant about my claim, and what needs to be done?

FIGURE 4.4   **The Question–Claim Structure.** This structure, which is characteristic of the argumentative research paper, signals the writer's purpose and point early on and then sets out to prove it.

The question–claim structure is useful if your motive in the draft is to prove something. It has some similarities to the delayed thesis structure of the essay—for one thing it arises from a question—but this method for organizing your draft puts your answer to that question up front and then proceeds, using your research, to make the most convincing case (see Figure 4.4). It's a little like the automobile dealer who, after wandering the lot, decides to put the models he or she most wants to sell in the showroom window. You direct your readers' gaze away from the process of discovery to the product of that process: the point you want to make.

The question–claim structure may be the form of the research paper with which you're most familiar. Here's one way to think about organizing your draft using that approach.

I. Introduce the problem or research question that is the focus of the paper.
   a. Provide factual background.
   b. Dramatize with an anecdote.
   c. Establish the significance of the problem by citing experts or other observers.
   d. Explain your purpose: To change audience attitudes? To call for some kind of action? To merely inform?

II. **Review the literature. What have others already said about the question?**

   a. Cite published studies, interviews, commentaries, experiments, and so on that are relevant to the question or problem.

   b. Which ideas or voices seem most important? Are there identifiable camps in the debate, or certain patterns of argument?

   c. Address popular assumptions. What do most people believe to be true?

III. **What will be *your* argument or thesis in the paper?**

   a. What does your understanding of the ongoing conversation about your research question lead you to believe is true?

   b. What is your position?

   c. What will you try to prove?

IV. **What are your reasons for believing what you believe and, for each one, what specific evidence did you find that you thought was convincing?**

   a. What kinds of evidence will your readers find most persuasive?

   b. Are there various kinds of evidence that can be brought to bear?

   c. How do your reasons square with those who might disagree with you?

V. **What is the significance of your claim? What's at stake for your audience? What might be other avenues for research?**

   a. What should we do? What might happen if we don't act?

   b. How does the thesis or claim that you propose resolve some part of the problem? What part remains unresolved?

   c. What questions remain?

Essaying or Arguing: An Example

Susan was writing an exploratory research essay on the relationship between attendance at preschool and academic success in elementary school. She decided to introduce her topic by describing her own dilemma with her son, Sam. She wanted to send him to preschool, but as a working college student she wasn't sure she could afford it. Her personal anecdote highlighted the problem many parents face and the question behind her research: Will children who don't attend preschool be at a disadvantage in primary school or not? In the middle section of her essay, Susan reported on several studies that looked at a range of skills that were affected by preschool experience and discussed which of these she found most significant, particularly in the context of her personal interviews with several local teachers. In the second to last section of her draft, Susan concluded that preschool does indeed make a difference, but particularly in the areas of reading and reasoning.

Imagine that Susan wants to revise her exploratory research essay into an argumentative research paper, a more conventional form for academic research. Would it be organized differently? While she still might begin with a personal anecdote as a way to dramatize the problem, Susan instead might choose a more factual approach. How many children in the United States attend preschool? How many don't? What are the trends? Are more parents struggling to find affordable preschools? Are fewer preschools available in disadvantaged areas? Is there a shortage of teachers? A significant difference would be where in the paper Susan puts her thesis. In the argumentative paper, the thesis usually appears toward the beginning (see Figure 4.4) and is stated explicitly: "I will argue in this essay that the preschool experience, which is being denied to a growing number of children in the United States, will put them at a serious disadvantage in reading and reasoning skills when they enter elementary school." Her essay would then go on to methodically establish the truth of this claim using her research. Susan might end her essay by suggesting how elementary teachers could address the learning deficits these children bring into their classrooms.

Writing with Sources

The need for *documentation*—that is, citing sources—distinguishes the research paper from most other kinds of writing. And let's face it: Worrying about sources can cramp your style. Many students have an understandable paranoia about plagiarism and tend, as mentioned earlier, to let the voices of their sources overwhelm their own. Students are also often distracted by technical details: Am I getting the right page number? Where exactly should this citation go? Do I need to cite this or not?

As you gain control of the material by choosing your own writing voice and clarifying your purpose in the paper, you should feel less constrained by the technical demands of documentation. The following suggestions may also help you weave reference sources into your own writing without the seams showing.

Blending Kinds of Writing and Sources

One of the wonderful things about the research essay is that it can draw on all four sources of information—reading, interviews, observation, and experience—as well as the four notetaking strategies discussed earlier—quotation, paraphrase, summary, and the writer's own analysis and commentary. Skillfully blended, these elements can make music.

Look at this paragraph from Heidi's paper on *Sesame Street*:

> There is more to this show than meets the eye, cer-
> tainly. It is definitely more than just a crowd of
> furry animals all living together in the middle of
> New York City. Originally intended as an effort to
> educate poor, less privileged youth, Sesame Street
> is set in the very middle of an urban development on
> purpose (Hellman 52). As Jon Stone, one of the
> show's founders and co-producers sees it, the pro-
> gram couldn't be "just another escapist show set in
> a tree house or a badger den" (52). Instead, the
> recognizable environment gave something to the kids
> they could relate to. " . . . It had a lot more real
> quality to it than, say, Mister Rogers. . . . Kids say
> the reason they don't like Mister Rogers is that
> it's unbelievable," says Nancy Diamonti.*

The writing is lively here, not simply because the topic is interesting to those of us who know the program. Heidi has nicely blended her own commentary with summary, paraphrase, and quotation, all in a single paragraph. She has also been able to draw on multiple sources of information—an interview, some effective quotes from her reading, and her own observations of *Sesame Street*. We sense that the writer is *using* the information, not being used by it.

Handling Quotes.   Avoid the temptation, as Heidi did, to load up your paragraphs with long or full quotes from your sources. I often see what I call "hanging quotes" in research papers. Embedded in a

---

*Used with permission of Heidi R. Dunham.

paragraph is a sentence or two within quotation marks. Though the passage is cited, there's no indication of who said it. Usually, the writer was uncertain about how to summarize or paraphrase or work *part* of the quotation into his own prose.

Use quotations selectively. And if you can, blend them into your own sentences, using a particularly striking or relevant part of the original source. For example, consider how quotes are used in this paragraph:

> Black Elk often spoke of the importance of the circle to American Indian culture. "You may have noticed that everything an Indian does is in a circle, and that is because the Power of the World always works in circles, and everything tries to be round. . . . The sky is round, and I have heard that the earth is round like a ball, and so are all the stars." He couldn't understand why white people lived in square houses. "It is a bad way to live, for there is not power in a square."

The quotes stand out, separate from the writer's own text. A better use of quotes is to work the same material smoothly into your own prose, doing something such as this:

> Black Elk believed the "Power of the World always works in circles," noting the roundness of the sun, the earth, and the stars. He couldn't understand why white people live in square houses: "It is a bad way to live, for there is not power in a square."

Occasionally, however, it may be useful to include a long quotation from one of your sources. A quotation that is longer than four lines should be *blocked,* or set off from the rest of the text by indenting it ten spaces from the left margin. Like the rest of the paper, a blocked quotation is also typed double-spaced. For example:

> According to Robert Karen, shame is a particu-
> larly modern phenomenon. He notes that in
> medieval times, people pretty much let loose, and
> by our modern tastes, it was not a pretty sight:
>
> > Their emotional life appears to have
> > been extraordinarily spontaneous and
> > unrestrained. From Joahn Huizinga's *The*
> > *Waning of the Middle Ages* we learn that the
> > average European town dweller was wildly
> > erratic and inconsistent, murderously
> > violent when enraged, easily plunged into
> > guilt, tears, and pleas for forgiveness,
> > and bursting with psychological eccentrici-
> > ties. He ate with his hands out of a common
> > bowl, blew his nose on his sleeve, defe-
> > cated openly by the side of the road, made
> > love, and mourned with great passion, and
> > was relatively unconcerned about such
> > notions as maladjustment or what others
> > might think. . . . In post-medieval centuries
> > what I've called situational shame spread
> > rapidly. . . . (61)

Note that the quotation marks are dropped around a blocked quotation. In this case, only part of a paragraph was borrowed, but if you quote one or more full paragraphs, indent the first line of each *three* spaces in addition to the ten the block is indented from the left margin.

We'll examine *parenthetical references* more fully in the next section, but notice how the citation in the blocked quotation above is placed *outside* the final period. That's a unique exception to the usual rule that a parenthetical citation is enclosed *within* the period of the borrowed material's final sentence.

Quick Tips for Controlling Quotations

Quotations from your sources can definitely be overused, especially when they seem dumped into the draft, untouched and unexamined, or used as a lazy substitute for paraphrase. But when it works, bringing the voices of others into your own writing can bring the work to life and make readers feel as if there is a genuine conversation going on.

Here are some quick tips for doing this effectively.

Grafting Quotes

Frequently, the best way to use quoted material is to graft it onto your own prose. Sometimes you just use a word or phrase:

Some words for hangover, like ours, refer prosaically to the cause: the Egyptians say they are "still drunk," the Japanese "two days drunk," the Chinese "drunk overnight."*

In other situations, especially when you want to provide a bit more emphasis to what a source has said, you might give over parts of several sentences to a source, like this:

The makers of NoHang, on their Web page, say what your mother would: "It is recommended that you drink moderately and responsibly." At the same time, they tell you that with NoHang "you can drink the night away."

Sandwiching Quotes

A sandwich without the bread isn't a sandwich. Similarly, when you use a quotation, especially one that is a full sentence or more, it should be surrounded by your comments about it. Introduce the quotation: Who said it and why is he or she relevant? When did this person say it and in what context? How does the quote relate to the current discussion in your essay? Followup the quotation: What

*Joan Acocella, "A Few Too Many," *The New Yorker* 26 May 2008: 32–37.

do *you* think is important about what was just said? How does it address an important idea or question? What does the person quoted *fail* to say or fail to see?

Here's an example of what I mean:

> In fact, even back when leeches were held in
> contempt by the medical profession, Sawyer had a
> solid rationale for choosing them as his sub-
> ject. Biology, as taught in the United States
> had left him frustrated: "For sex determination,
> we'd study *Drosophilia,* for physiology we'd study
> frogs, for genetics, bacteria. I thought there
> was more to be learned from studying one organ-
> ism in detail than from parts of many." His
> American professors disdained this approach as a
> throw-back to nineteenth century biology.*

See how the writer here sets up the quotation? He provides background on the significance of what Sawyer, the leech biologist, was about to say. The guy was frustrated with how organisms were studied. The quotation is then sandwiched with a comment about how the quote reflects Sawyer's reputation as an antitraditionalist.

Billboarding Quotes

Another way you can control quotations is adding emphasis to billboard parts of a particular quote. Typically you do this by italicizing the phrase or sentence. It might look something like this:

> For the sake of Millennials—and, through them, the
> future of America—the most urgent adult task is to
> *elevate their expectations.* (Emphasis added)†

Note the parenthetical note that signals the original quote has been altered to give emphasis. In academic writing, this would also include a citation, but more about that later.

---

*Richard Conniff, *Spineless Wonders* (New York: Holt, 1996).
†Neil Howe and William Strauss, *Millennials Rising* (New York: Vintage, 2000).

Splicing Quotes

Sometimes you want to prune away unnecessary information from a quotation to place emphasis on that part that matters most to you or eliminates unnecessary information. Ellipsis points, those three dots (. . .) you sometimes see at the beginning, middle, or end of a sentence signal that some information has been omitted.

Take this passage for example:

> During the Gen-X child era, the American fam-
> ily endured countless new movements and
> trends—feminism, sexual freedom, a divorce
> epidemic, fewer G-rated movies, child-raising
> handbooks telling parents to "consider your-
> self" ahead of a child's needs, gay rights,
> Chappaquiddick, film nudity, a Zero Population
> Growth ethic, *Kramer vs. Kramer,* and *Roe v.*
> *Wade.* A prominent academic in 1969 proclaimed
> in the *Washington Post* that the family needed
> a "decent burial."

That's a pretty long list of movements and trends, and the reader could get a taste without serving up the whole thing. Ellipsis points can help:

> During the Gen-X child era, the American family
> endured countless new movements and trends—
> feminism, sexual freedom, a divorce epidemic . . . ,
> [and a] prominent academic in 1969 proclaimed in
> the *Washington Post* that the family needed a
> "decent burial."

When you have to slightly reword the original text or alter the punctuation for a smoother splice, put the alteration in brackets. In the example, for instance, I turned what was a separate sentence in the original into a compound sentence using the conjunction *and.*

Handling Interview Material

The great quotes you glean from your interviews can be handled like quotations from texts. But there's a dimension to a quote from an interview that's lacking in a quote from a book: Namely, you participated in the quote's creation by asking a question, and in some cases, you were there to observe your subject saying it. This presents some new choices. When you're quoting an interview subject, should you enter your essay as a participant in the conversation, or should you stay out of the way? That is, should you describe yourself asking the question? Should you describe the scene of the interview, your subject's manner of responding, or your immediate reaction to what she said? Or should you merely report what was said and who said it?

Christina's essay, "Crying Real Tears: The History and Psychology of Method Acting," makes good use of interviews. Notice how Christina writes about one of them in the middle of her essay:

> During a phone interview, I asked my acting teacher,
> Ed Claudio, who studied under Stella Adler,
> whether or not he agreed with the ideas behind
> method acting. I could almost see him wrinkle his
> nose at the other end of the connection. He
> described method acting as "self-indulgent,"
> insisting that it encourages "island acting."
> Because of emotional recall, acting became a far
> more personal art, and the actor began to move
> away from the script, often hiding the author's
> purpose and intentions under his own.*

Contrast Christina's handling of the Claudio interview with her treatment of material from an interview with Dave Pierini later in her essay:

> Dave Pierini, a local Sacramento actor, pointed
> out, "You can be a good actor without using
> method, but you cannot be a good actor without
> at least understanding it." Actors are perhaps
> some of the greatest scholars of the human

*Reprinted with permission of Christina B. Kerby.

```
psyche because they devote their lives to the
study and exploration of it. Aspiring artists
are told to "get inside of the character's
head." They are asked, "How would the character
feel? How would the character react?"
```

Do you think Christina's entry into her report of the first interview (with Ed Claudio) is intrusive? Or do you think it adds useful information or even livens it up? What circumstances might make this a good move? On the other hand, what might be some advantages of the writer staying out of the way and simply letting her subject speak, as Christina chooses to do in her treatment of the interview with Dave Pierini?

Trusting Your Memory

One of the best ways to weave references seamlessly into your own writing is to avoid the compulsion to stop and study your sources as you're writing the draft. I remember that writing my research papers in college was typically done in stops and starts. I'd write a paragraph of the draft, then stop and reread a photocopy of an article, then write a few more sentences, and then stop again. Part of the problem was the meager notes I took as I collected information. I hadn't really taken possession of the material before I started writing the draft. But I also didn't trust that I'd remember what was important from my reading.

If, during the course of your research and writing so far, you've found a sense of purpose—for example, you're pretty sure your paper is going to argue for legalization of marijuana or analyze the symbolism on old gravestones on Cape Cod—then you've probably read purposefully, too. You *will* likely know what reference sources you need as you write the draft, without sputtering to a halt to remind yourself of what each says. Consult your notes and sources as you need them; otherwise, push them aside, and immerse yourself in your own writing.

Citing Sources

An Alternative to Colliding Footnotes

Like most people I knew back then, I took a typing class the summer between eighth grade and high school. Our instructional texts were long books with the bindings at the top, and we worked on standard Royal typewriters that were built like tanks. I got up to thirty words a minute, I think, which wasn't very good, but thanks to that class, I can still type without looking at the keyboard. The one thing I never learned, though, was how to turn the typewriter roller up a half space to type a footnote number that would neatly float above the line. In every term paper in high school, my footnotes collided with my sentences.

I'm certain that such technical difficulties were not the reason that most academic writers in the humanities and social sciences have largely abandoned the footnote method of citation for the parenthetical one, but I'm relieved, nonetheless. In the current system, borrowed material is parenthetically cited in the paper by indicating the author of the original work and the page it was taken from or the date it was published. These parenthetical citations are then explained more fully in the "Works Cited" page at the end of your paper where the sources themselves are listed.

By now, your instructor has probably told you which method of citing sources you should use: the Modern Language Association (MLA) style or the American Psychological Association (APA) style. Most English classes use MLA. A complete guide to MLA conventions is provided in Appendix A, and to APA in Appendix B.

Before you begin writing your draft, go to Appendix A and read the section "Citing Sources in Your Essay." This will describe in some detail when and where you should put parenthetical references to borrowed material in the draft of your essay. Don't worry too much about the guidelines for preparing the final manuscript, including how to do the bibliography. You can deal with that next week.

I Hate These Theses to Pieces

Okay, here's a thesis:

```
I hate thesis statements.
```

And you wonder, What is this guy talking about now? What do you mean you hate thesis statements? *All* thesis statements? Why?

You'd be right to wonder for two reasons. First, my thesis statement about thesis statements isn't very good: It is too sweeping, it is overstated (*hate?*), and it deliberately withholds information. Its virtues, if any, are its shock value and the fact that it *is*—as any thesis must be—an assertion, or claim. Second, you're wondering why a teacher of writing would make such a claim in the first place. Doesn't most writing have a thesis, either stated or implied? Isn't writing that lacks a thesis unfocused, unclear? Doesn't a research paper, in particular, need a strong thesis?

Let me try again. Here's a thesis:

```
The thesis statement often discourages inquiry
instead of promoting it.
```

Hmmm . . . This is less overstated, and the claim is qualified in a reasonable way (*often discourages*). This thesis is also a bit more informative because it ever so briefly explains *why* I dislike thesis statements: *They often discourage inquiry.* But how do they do that? For one thing, when you arrive at a thesis statement prematurely, you risk turning the process of exploring your topic into a ritual hunt for examples that simply support what you already think. With this purpose in mind, you may suppress or ignore ideas or evidence that conflicts with the thesis—that threatens to disrupt the orderly march toward proving it is true.

Well, then, you infer, you're not saying you dislike *all* thesis statements, just those that people make up too soon and cling to compulsively.

Yes, I think so. I prefer what I would call the *found thesis,* the idea that you discover or the claim you come to *after* some exploration of a topic. This type of thesis often strikes me as more surprising (or less obvious) and more honest. It suddenly occurs to me, however, that I just discovered the term *found thesis* at this very moment, and I discovered it by starting with a conventional claim: *I hate thesis statements.* Doesn't that undermine my current thesis about thesis statements, that beginning with one can close off inquiry?

Well, yes, come to think of it.

What might we conclude from all of this discussion about the thesis that you can apply to the draft you're writing this week?

1. If you're already committed to a thesis, write it down. Then challenge yourself to write it again, making it somewhat more specific and informative and perhaps even more qualified.

2. At this stage, the most useful thesis may not be one that dictates the structure and arrangement of your draft but one that provides a focus for your thinking. Using the information you've collected, play out the truth of your idea or claim, but also invite questions about it—as I did—that may qualify or even overturn what you initially thought was true. In other words, use your draft to *test* the truthfulness of your thesis about your topic.

3. If you're still struggling to find a tentative thesis, use your draft to discover it. Then use your found thesis as the focus for the revision.

4. Your final draft *does* need to have a strong thesis, or controlling idea, around which the essay is built. The essay may ultimately attempt to *prove* the validity of the thesis, or the final essay may *explore* its implications.

Driving Through the First Draft

You have an opening, a lot of material in your notes—much of it, written in your own words—and maybe an outline. You've considered some general methods of development, looked at ways to write with sources, and completed a quick course in how to cite them. Finish the week by writing through the first draft.

Writing the draft may be difficult. All writing, but especially research writing, is a recursive process. You may find sometimes that you must circle back to a step you took before, discovering a gap in your information, a new idea for a thesis statement, or a better lead or focus. Circling back may be frustrating at times, but it's natural and even a good sign: It means you're letting go of your preconceived ideas and allowing the discoveries you make *through writing* to change your mind.

A Draft Is Something the Wind Blows Through

Remember, too, that a *draft* is something the wind blows through. It's too early to worry about writing a research paper that's airtight, with no problems to solve. Too often, student writers think they have to write a perfect paper in the first draft. You can worry about plugging holes and tightening things up next week. For now, write a draft, and if you must, put a reminder on a piece of paper and post it on the wall next to your thesis statement or research question. Look at this reminder every time you find yourself agonizing over the imperfections of your paper. The reminder should say, "It Doesn't Count."

Keep a few other things in mind while writing your first draft:

1. *Focus on your tentative thesis or your research question.* In the draft consider your thesis a theory you're trying to prove but that you're willing to change. If your paper is more exploratory than argumentative, use your focusing question as a reminder of what you want to know. Remember your question can change, too, as you learn more about your subject.

2. *Vary your sources.* Offer a variety of different sources as evidence to support your assertions. Beware of writing a single page that cites only one source.

3. *Remember your audience.* What do your readers want to know about your topic? What do they need to know to understand what you're trying to say?

4. *Write with your notes.* If you took thoughtful notes during the third week—carefully transforming another author's words into your own, flagging good quotes, and developing your own analysis—then you've already written at least some of your paper. You may only need to finetune the language in your notes and then plug them into your draft.

5. *Be open to surprises.* The act of writing is often full of surprises. In fact, it should be, since *writing* is *thinking* and the more you think about something, the more you're likely to see. You might get halfway through your draft and discover the part of your topic that *really* fascinates you. Should that happen, you may have to change your thesis or throw away your outline. You may even have to reresearch your topic, at least somewhat. It's not necessarily too late to shift the purpose or focus of your paper (though you should consult your instructor before totally abandoning your topic at this point). Let your curiosity remain the engine that drives you forward.

CHAPTER 5

The Fifth Week

Revising for Purpose

My high school girlfriend, Jan, was bright, warm hearted, and fun, and I wasn't at all sure I liked her much, at least at first. Though we had a lot in common—we both loved sunrise over Lake Michigan, bird watching, and Simon and Garfunkel—I found Jan a little intimidating, a little too much in a hurry to anoint us a solid "couple." But we stuck together for three years, and as time passed, I persuaded myself—despite lingering doubts—that I couldn't live without her. There was no way I was going to break my white-knuckled hold on that relationship. After all, I'd invested all that time.

As a writer, I used to have similar relationships with my drafts. I'd work on something very hard, finally finishing the draft. I'd know there were problems, but I'd developed such a tight relationship with my draft that the problems were hard to see. And even when I recognized some problems, the thought of making major changes seemed too risky. Did I dare ruin the things I loved about the draft? These decisions were even harder if the draft took a long time to write.

Revision doesn't necessarily mean you have to sever your relationship with your draft. It's probably too late to make a complete break with the draft and abandon your topic. However, revision does demand finding some way to step back from the draft and change your relationship with it, seeing it from the reader's perspective rather than just the writer's. Revision requires that you loosen your grip. And when you do, you may decide to shift your focus or rearrange the information. At the very least, you may discover gaps in information or sections of the draft that need more development. You will certainly need to prune sentences.

The place to begin is *purpose*. You should determine whether the purpose of your paper is clear and examine how well the information is organized around that purpose.

Presumably, by now you know the purpose of your essay. If you hadn't quite figured it out before you wrote last week's draft, I hope writing the draft helped you clarify your purpose. It did? Great. Then complete the following sentence. Remember that here, you're trying to focus on the *main* purpose of your draft. There are probably quite a few things that you attempt to do in it, but what is the most central purpose?

The main purpose of my essay on _____ is to

(use the appropriate word or words) *explain, argue, explore,*

*describe*_____.

Here's how Christina filled in the blanks for her essay on method acting:

The main purpose of my essay on _____method acting_____ is to

(explain,) argue, explore, describe _the psychological aspects of method_

and its impact on American theater.

Another way of getting at purpose is to clarify your research question, something that you first considered about a month ago. It's likely that your research question has evolved since then. Sometimes, it becomes more narrowly focused and more specific. Say your question began with wondering how social networking sites change the way we think about friendship. Now the question is this: *What is MySpace doing about cyber-bullying, and is it necessary?* On the other hand, sometimes you see that you need to hitch your specific question to a larger idea, one that highlights the importance of your inquiry. For example, Amanda's piece on the trend of teeth whitening began with this research question: *How has cosmetic tooth whitening changed the way Americans feel about their teeth?* As she learned more she considered this question: *How does the tooth whitening trend reflect our culture's quickly changing definitions of beauty, and what does that mean for people who don't fit that definition?*

Go back to the beginning. What was your initial research question? What is it now?

E X E R C I S E   5 . 1

Wrestling with the Draft*

Writing with research is a wrestling match. You're the 120-pound weakling who may not have written many college research essays before trying to take on the heavyweight experts on your topic. You're fighting for your life, trying to use what these authorities say or think *for your own purposes,* without getting slammed to the floor for plagiarizing or meekly submitting a report rather than an essay. The challenge is to get control of the information, to muscle it to the ground using the strength of your own purposes. Establishing this control is one of the hardest parts of drafting research papers. Two extreme responses to this problem are giving up entirely and turning your paper over to your sources, letting them do all the talking, and pretending that you're not really wrestling with anyone and writing a paper that includes only your own opinions. Neither option is what you want.

Who won the wrestling match in your draft? To what extent did you succeed in using other people's ideas and information in the service of your own thoughts and purposes? One way to see who is getting the upper hand in the draft is to mark it up, noting where you've given control to your sources and where you've taken it back. This pattern can say an awful lot about how well you've done drafting a research essay where your own purposes rule.

1. For this exercise you'll use two highlighters, each a different color.

2. Choose a random page of your draft, somewhere in the middle.

3. First mark the parts in which you're a less active author. As you read the page, highlight every sentence, passage, or paragraph that reports facts, quotes sources, or otherwise presents information or ideas that belong to someone else.

4. Now, using the other highlighter, mark the parts in which you're an active author. Read the same page again, but this time highlight every sentence, passage, or paragraph that represents

---

*This exercise is adapted from one I borrowed from my colleague, Dr. Mike Mattison, who borrowed it from his former colleagues at University of Massachusetts–Amherst. Thanks to all.

your ideas, analysis, commentary, interpretation, definition, synthesis, or argument.

   5. Repeat the previous steps with two more pages of your draft.

   Which color dominates? Are you turning over too much of the text to your sources? Are you ignoring them and rattling on too much about what you think? And what do you notice about the pattern of color? Are you taking turns paragraph by paragraph with your sources, or is your own analysis and commentary nicely blended *within* paragraphs, so that the information is always anchored to your own thoughts? Do you surround quoted passages with your own voice and analysis? Who wins the wrestling match? See Figure 5.1 for an example of this exercise.

Our tooth whiteners are safer, and a study by James W. Curtis, DMD, discovered that bleaching through carbamide peroxide actually decreases the amount of plaque on teeth, but we're still doing it for beauty reasons rather than health ones (Nuss 28).

In her article "Bright On," Molly Prior notes that Procter & Gamble and Colgate-Palmolive revolutionized the whitening industry by bringing over-the-counter whiteners to drugstores everywhere at the turn of the twenty-first century (39). No longer did people have to pay high prices for professional whitening—they could do it themselves, at home, for a reasonable cost. In the past, a patient had to eat a bill of $1,000 for a laser whitening treatment, or $10,000 for a full set of veneers; now a package of Crest Whitestrips retails for only $29.99 (Gideonse). Suddenly, whiter teeth were available to everyone. While a shining smile once indicated wealth and the ability to splurge on cosmetic dentistry, it became affordable to the dentally discolored masses eager to emulate the lifestyles of the people they saw in magazines and on television.

Companies didn't create whitening products to fill a demand created by the public for whiter teeth. While Hollywood glitterati did pay high prices for iconic smiles, most people seemed happy with functional teeth. However, companies saw money to be made in creating a whiter norm for teeth, so they barraged the airwaves with advertisements featuring people complaining about the dullness and imperfection of their teeth. Natural teeth were denigrated as ugly. Crest and Colgate-Palmolive

---

FIGURE 5.1   Amanda Wins the Wrestling Match
The text highlighted in light gray is passages from Amanda's sources, and the darker highlights are passages in which she is commenting, clarifying, asserting, or interpreting. Notice the balance between light and dark gray. Clearly Amanda has a strong authorial presence. Also notice how quotations are surrounded by her commentary. By controlling quotations like this she is also using rather than being used by her sources.

wanted to make money, so appealed to the American obsession with beauty to secure a financial reason to smile. As Jonathan Levine, DDS, notes, "It's lately seeming much harder to go broke by overstimating the vanity of the American public" (Walker). The companies succeeded in making mouthfuls of money, netting $450 million dollars, and getting 45 percent of Americans to try some form of whitening (Prior 42). In effect, they appealed to our egos to get to our pocket books.

FIGURE 5.1 (Continued)

The Thesis as a Tool for Revision

Purpose and *thesis* have a tight relationship. When I write an essay, I'm essentially in pursuit of a point, and not infrequently, it playfully eludes me. Just when I think I've figured out exactly what I'm trying to say, I have the nagging feeling that it's not quite right—it's too simplistic or obvious, it doesn't quite account for the evidence I've collected, or it just doesn't capture the spirit of the discoveries I've made. If a thesis is often a slippery fish, then having a strong sense of purpose helps me finally get a grip on it.

Purpose (and its sister *focus*) is a statement of intention—this is what I want to do in this piece of writing. It not only describes how I've limited the territory but what I plan to do when I'm there. That's why the words *explain, argue, explore,* and *describe* are so important. They pinpoint an *action* I'll take in the writing, and they'll move me toward particular assertions about what I see. One of these assertions will seem more important than any other, and that will be my thesis.

Maybe my tendency to see thesis statements as slippery is because I dislike encountering main points in essays that act like schoolyard bullies—they overcompensate for their insecurity by loudly announcing, "Hey, listen to me, bub, *I'm* the main point around here, and whaddya going to do about it, huh?" Essays whose purpose is to argue something and take a broad and unqualified stand in favor of or against a whole category of people/positions/ theories/ideas can be the worst offenders. Things are rarely that simple, and when they are, they usually aren't very interesting to write about.

Just as often, I encounter thesis statements that act more like the kids who get singled out by the bullies for harassment. They are meek or bland assertions that would be easy to pick apart if they weren't so uninteresting. Here's one: *Nuclear bombs are so powerful, so fast, and so deadly that they have become the weapon of today.* There *are* elements of an assertion here; the writer points out that modern nuclear weapons are *fast, powerful,* and *deadly*. But this is such an obvious claim that it probably isn't even worth stating. The phrase *weapon of today* would seem more promising if it was explained a bit. What is it about nations or warfare *today* that makes such weapons so appealing? Is the apparent passion for fast, deadly, and powerful nuclear weapons today analogous to anything—maybe the passion for designer labels, fax machines, and fast food?

EXERCISE 5.2

Dissecting the Fish

The main point in your research essay *may* be a straightforward argument—*Legalization of drugs will not, as some of its supporters claim, reduce violent crime*—or it may be an explanation or description of some aspect of your topic—*Method acting has revolutionized American theater.* But in either case, *use* the main point as a launching place for thinking about what you might do in the revision. Before you do anything else on your draft this week, consider doing the following:

■ In a sentence or two, write down the thesis or controlling idea that emerged in your draft last week. It may have been stated or implied, or perhaps after writing the draft, you have a clearer idea of what you're trying to say. In any case, write down your thesis.

■ Now generate a list of three or more questions that your thesis raises. These questions may directly challenge your assertion, or they may be questions—like those I raised earlier about the thesis about nuclear weapons—that help you further clarify or unpack what you're trying to say.

■ Next, rewrite your thesis statement at least three times. In each subsequent version, play with language or arrangement, add information, or get more specific about exactly what you're saying. For example:

1. Method acting has had a major impact on American theater.

2. The method—which turned Stanislavski's original focus on external actions inward, toward the actor's own feelings—has generated controversy since the beginning.

3. An actor using the method may be crying tears, but whether they're real or not depends on whom you ask: the actor, who is thinking about her dead cat in the midst of a scene about a dying lover, or the writer, who didn't have a dead cat in mind when she wrote it.

If this exercise works for you, several things will happen. Not only will you refine how you express your main point in the next draft, but you will also get guidance about how you might approach the revision—how you might reorganize it, what information you should add or cut, how you can further narrow your focus and even clarify your purpose. For example, the first version of the thesis on method acting provides the writer with little guidance about what information to *exclude* in the next draft. Aren't there lots of ways to show that method acting has had a major impact on American theater? The third version, on the other hand, is not only livelier and more interesting, it points the writer much more directly to what she should emphasize in the next draft: the conflict method acting creates over how theatrical roles are imagined, the license actors have with their material, and the ways that deception may be involved in a powerful performance using this technique.

What I'm suggesting here is this: Once you arrive at the controlling idea for your essay, it need not arrest your thinking about your topic, closing off any further discovery. A thesis is, in fact, a *tool* that will help you reopen the material you've gathered, rearrange it, and understand it in a fresh, new way.

Revision, as the word implies, means "re-seeing" or "reconceiving," trying to see what you failed to notice with the first look. That can be hard. Remember how stuck I was on that one picture of the lighthouse? I planted my feet in the sand, and the longer I stared through the camera lens, the harder it was to see the lighthouse from any other angle. It didn't matter that I didn't particularly like what I was seeing. I just wanted to take the picture.

You've spent more than four weeks researching your topic and the last few days composing your first draft. You may find that you've spent so much time staring through the lens—seeing your topic the way you chose to see it in your first draft—that doing a major revision is about as appealing as eating cold beets. How do you get the perspective to "re-see" the draft and rebuild it into a stronger paper?

Using a Reader

If you wanted to save a relationship, you might ask a friend to intervene. Then you'd get the benefit of a third-party opinion, a fresh view that could help you see what you may be too close to see.

A reader can do the same thing for your research paper draft. She will come to the draft without the entanglements that encumber the writer and provide a fresh pair of eyes through which you can see the work.

What You Need from a Reader

Your instructor may be that reader, or you might exchange drafts with someone else in class. You may already have someone whom you share your writing with—a roommate, a friend. Whomever you choose, try to find a reader who will respond honestly *and* make you want to write again.

What will be most helpful from a reader at this stage? Comments about your spelling and mechanics are not critical right now. You'll deal with those factors later. What the reader needs to point out is if the *purpose* of your paper is clear and if your thesis is convincing. Is it clear what your paper is about, what part of the topic you're focusing on? Does the information presented stay within that focus? Does the information clarify and support what you're trying to say? It would also be helpful for the reader to tell you what parts of the draft are interesting and what parts seem to drag.

EXERCISE 5.3

Directing the Reader's Response

Though you could ask your reader for a completely open-ended reaction to your paper, the following questions might help her focus on providing comments that will help you tackle a revision:

1. After reading the draft, what would you say is the main question the paper is trying to answer or focus on?
2. In your own words, what is the main point?
3. What do you remember from the draft that most convinces you that the ideas in the paper are true? What is least convincing?
4. Where is the paper most interesting? Where does the paper drag?

How your reader responds to the first two questions will tell you a lot about how well you've succeeded in making the purpose and thesis of your paper clear. The answer to the third question may reveal how well you've *used* the information gleaned from research. The reader's response to the fourth question will give you a preliminary reading on how well you engaged her. Did you lose her anywhere? Is the paper interesting?

A reader responding to Jeff's paper titled "The Alcoholic Family" helped him discover some problems that are typical of first drafts. His paper was inspired by his girlfriend's struggles to deal with her alcoholic father. Jeff wondered if he could do anything to help. Jeff's reader was touched by those parts of the paper where he discussed his own observations of the troubled family's behavior; however, the reader was confused about Jeff's purpose. "Your lead seems to say that your paper is going to focus on how family members deal with an alcoholic parent," the reader wrote to Jeff, "but I thought your main idea was that people outside an alcoholic family can help but must be careful about it. I wanted to know more about how you now think you can help your girlfriend. What exactly do you need to be careful about?"

This wasn't an observation Jeff could have made, given how close he is to the topic and the draft. But armed with objective and specific information about what changes were needed, Jeff was ready to attack the draft.

Attacking the Draft

The controlling idea of your paper—that thesis you posted on an index card above your desk a week or more ago—is the heart of your paper and should, in some way, be connected to everything else in the draft.

Though a good reader can suddenly help you see things you've missed, she will likely not give much feedback on what you should do to fix these problems. Physically attacking the draft might help. If you neatly printed your first draft, then doing this may feel sacrilegious—a little like writing in books. One of the difficulties with revision is that writers respect the printed page too much. When the draft is typed up, with all those words marching neatly down the page, it is hard to mess it up again. As pages emerge from the printer, you can almost hear the sound of hardening concrete. Breaking the draft into pieces can free you to clearly see them and how they fit together.

EXERCISE 5.4

Cut-and-Paste Revision

Try this cut-and-paste revision exercise (a useful technique inspired by Peter Elbow and his book *Writing with Power*:*

1. Photocopy or print two copies of your first draft (one-sided pages only). Save the original; you may need it later.

2. Cut apart the copy of your research paper, paragraph by paragraph. (You may cut it into even smaller pieces later.) Once the draft has been completely disassembled, shuffle the paragraphs—get them wildly out of order so the original draft is just a memory.

3. Now go through the shuffled stack and find the *core paragraph*, the most important one in the whole paper. This is probably the paragraph that contains your thesis, or main point. This paragraph is the one that gets to the heart of what you're trying to say. Set it aside.

4. With your core paragraph directly in front of you, work your way through the remaining stack of paragraphs and make two new stacks: one of paragraphs that are relevant to your core and one of paragraphs that don't seem relevant, that don't seem to serve a clear purpose in developing your main idea. Be as tough as a drill sergeant as you scrutinize each scrap of paper. What you are trying to determine is whether each piece of information, each paragraph, is there for a reason. Ask yourself these questions as you examine each paragraph:

- Does it develop my thesis or further the purpose of my paper, or does it seem an unnecessary tangent that could be part of another paper with a different focus?
- Does it provide important *evidence* that supports my main point?
- Does it *explain* something that's key to understanding what I'm trying to say?
- Does it *illustrate* a key concept?
- Does it help establish the *importance* of what I'm trying to say?
- Does it raise (or answer) a *question* that I must explore, given what I'm trying to say?

You might find it helpful to write on the back of each relevant paragraph which of these purposes it serves. You may also discover

*Peter Elbow, *Writing with Power* (New York: Oxford University Press, 1981).

that *some* of the information in a paragraph seems to serve your purpose, while the rest strikes you as unnecessary. Use your scissors to cut away the irrelevant material, pruning back the paragraph to include only what's essential.

5. You now have two stacks of paper scraps: those that seem to serve your purpose and those that don't. For now, set aside your "reject" pile. Put your core paragraph back into the "save" pile, and begin to reassemble a very rough draft, using what you've saved. Play with order. Try new leads, new ends, new middles. As you spread out the pieces of information before you, see if a new structure suddenly emerges. *But especially, look for gaps—places where you should add information.* Jot down ideas for material you might add on a piece of paper; then cut up the paper and splice (with tape) each idea in the appropriate place when you reassemble the draft in the next step. You may rediscover uses for information in your "reject" pile, as well. Mine that pile, if you need to.

6. As a structure begins to emerge, begin taping together the fragments of paper and splicing ideas for new information. Don't worry about transitions; you'll deal with those later. When you're done with the reconstruction, the draft should look drafty—something the wind can blow through—and may be totally unlike the version you started with.

Examining the Wreckage

As you deal with the wreckage your scissors have wrought on your first draft, you might notice other problems with it. For example, you may discover that your draft has no real core paragraph, no part that is central to your point and purpose. Don't panic. Just make sure that you write one in the revision.

To your horror, you may find that your "reject" pile of paragraphs is bigger than your "save" pile. If that's the case, you won't have much left to work with. You may need to reresearch the topic (returning to the library this week to collect more information) or shift the focus of your paper. Perhaps both.

To your satisfaction, you may discover that your reconstructed draft looks familiar. You may have returned to the structure you started with in the first draft. If that's the case, it might mean your first draft worked pretty well; breaking it down and putting it back together simply confirmed that.

When Jeff cut up "The Alcoholic Family," he discovered immediately that his reader was right: Much of his paper did not seem clearly related to his point about the role outsiders can play in helping alcoholic families. His "reject" pile had paragraph after paragraph of information about the roles that alcoholic family members assume when there's a heavy drinker in the house. Jeff asked himself, What does that information have to do with the roles of outsiders? He considered changing his thesis, rewriting his core paragraph to say something about how each family member plays a role in dealing with the drinker. But Jeff's purpose in writing the paper was to discover what *he* could do to help.

As Jeff played with the pieces of his draft, he began to see two things. First of all, he realized that some of the ways members behave in an alcoholic family make them resistant to outside help; this insight allowed him to salvage some information from his "reject" pile by more clearly connecting the information to his main point. Second, Jeff knew he had to go back to the well: He needed to return to the library and recheck his sources to find more information on what family friends can do to help.

When you slice up your draft and play with the pieces, you are experimenting with the basic architecture of your essay. If it is going to hold up, certain fundamentals must be in place (see Figure 5.2). Before you move on to other revision strategies you need to be confident that your purpose—the inquiry question around which your investigation is organized—is stated clearly early in your essay.

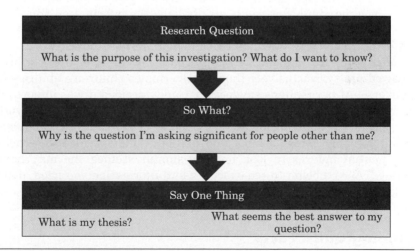

FIGURE 5.2 Three Things the Essay Must Do
As you revise your draft, you can measure your progress by asking whether you've answered these three basic questions: *Is the question I'm asking clear and sufficiently limited? Have I answered the "so what?" question? Is there one most important thing I'm trying to say?* If your draft explicitly answers each of these, then at least the boat will float and have a clear destination.

The significance of this question should be evident, too. Why should anyone care about the extinction of wild horses in the American West, for example? Why does it matter? The answer to this question often leads to the third essential element of your paper: What one thing are you trying to say? To lose wild horses is to diminish the cultural heritage of the West, one that goes beyond the mythical cowboy to include native people and early Spanish colonialists.

Revising for Information

I know. You thought you were done digging. But as I said last week, research is a recursive process. (Remember, the word is *research,* or "look again.") You will often find yourself circling back to the earlier steps as you get a clearer sense of where you want to go.

As you stand back from your draft, looking again at how well your research paper accomplishes your purpose, you'll likely see holes in the information. They may seem more like craters. Jeff discovered he had to reresearch his topic, returning to the library to hunt for new sources to help him develop his point. Since he had enough time, he repeated some of the research steps from the third week. This time, though, he knew exactly what he needed to find.

You may find that you basically have the information you need but that your draft requires more development. Candy's draft on how child abuse affects language included material from some useful studies from the *Journal of Speech and Hearing Disorders,* which showed pretty conclusively that abuse cripples children's abilities to converse. At her reader's suggestion, Candy decided it was important to write more in her revision about what was learned from the studies, since they offered convincing evidence for her thesis. Though she could mine her notes for more information, Candy decided to recheck the journal indexes to look for any similar studies she may have missed. As you begin to see exactly what information you need, don't rule out another trip to the library, even this late in the game.

Finding Quick Facts

The holes of information in your research paper draft may not be large at all. What's missing may be an important but discrete fact that would really help your readers understand the point you're making. For example, in Janabeth's draft on the impact of divorce on father-daughter relationships, she realized she was missing an important fact: the number of marriages that end in divorce in the United States. This single piece of information could help establish the significance of the problem she was writing about. Janabeth could search her sources for the answer, but there's a quicker way: fact books.

One of the Internet's greatest strengths is its usefulness in searching for specific facts. A few days ago, for example, my daughter Julia—who was studying China in the first grade—wanted to know the height of the Great Wall. The answer is thirty feet. We found it in minutes by consulting an online encyclopedia. As always, there are a range of statistical references on the Web. One place to start is the site that claims to be "the single best source for facts on the Net":

www.refdesk.com

I'm inclined to agree. The site has links to encyclopedias, biographical indexes, newspapers and magazines, dictionaries, and government information. Even better, refdesk.com has a convenient "Fast Facts" search engine that will return up-to-date information from a keyword search.

The standard print texts for researchers hunting down facts and statistics are still quite useful. They include the *Statistical Abstracts of the United States,* the *Information Please Alamanac, Facts on File,* and the *World Almanac Book of Facts*—all published annually—but a number of these in abbreviated versions are now available on the Web. The U.S. Census Bureau site for example, is an incredibly rich source of demographic information on all kinds of subjects (see Figure 5.3).

Fact books and online sources can be valuable sources of information that will plug small holes in your draft. These references are especially useful during revision, when you often know exactly what fact you need. But even if you're not sure whether you can glean a useful statistic from one of these sources, they might be worth checking anyway. There's a good chance you'll find something useful.

Revising for Language

Most of my students have the impression that revision begins and ends with concerns about language—about *how* they said it rather than *what* they said. Revising for language is really a tertiary concern (though an important one), to be addressed after the writer has struggled with the purpose and design of a draft.

FIGURE 5.3 Home Page of U.S. Census Bureau

The U.S. Census Bureau offers a wealth of statistical information, including data from the 2000 census. The site, at www.census.gov, includes a search tool called "American Fact Finder" that will help you locate statistics about population, geography, business, housing, and industry. The results can be national statistics all the way down to data about a particular county.

Census Bureau Home Page

http://www.census.gov

RSS | Q Google

U.S. Census Bureau

FAQs | Subjects A to Z | Help   SEARCH:

LATEST
Race, Ethnic
and Age
Estimates

New on the Site
Data Tools
American FactFinder
Jobs@Census
Catalog
Publications
Are You in a Survey?
About the Bureau
Regional Offices
Doing Business with Us
Related Sites

What are the top
industries by state?
business.census.gov

United States
Census
2010

People &
Households

Business &
Industry

Geography

Newsroom

Special
Topics

2010 Census · News
American Community Survey · Census 2000

Estimates · Projections · Housing · Income |
State Median Income · Poverty · Health Insurance
· International · Genealogy · More

Economic Census · Get Help with Your Form
Economic Indicators · NAICS · Survey of Business
Owners · Government · E-Stats
Foreign Trade | Export Codes · Local Employment
Dynamics · More

Maps · TIGER · Gazetteer · More

Releases · Facts For Features · Minority Links ·
Broadcast & Photo Services · Embargo/News
Release Subscription · More

Census Bureau Data and Emergency Preparedness
· Census Calendar · Training · For Teachers &
Students · Statistical Abstract · FedStats
USA.gov

2006

Information & Communication
Technology (ICT) Survey

Data Finders

Population Clocks
U.S. 304,555,285
World 6,708,887,463
16:05 GMT (EST+5) Jul 09, 2008

Population Finder
city/ town, county, or zip
or state
Select a state
GO

Find An Area Profile with QuickFacts
Select a state to begin
Select a state

Latest Economic Indicators
· Quarterly Financial Report – Retail
  Trade
· Monthly Wholesale Trade-Sales and
  Inventories

Economic Indicators
Select an indicator
Select an indicator

U S C E N S U S B U R E A U
Helping You Make Informed Decisions

236

Once you're satisfied that your paper's purpose is clear, that it provides readers with the information they need to understand what you're trying to say, and that it is organized in a logical, interesting way, *then* focus your attention on the fine points of *how* it is written. Begin with voice.

Listening to the Voice

Listen to your paper by reading it aloud to yourself. You may find the experience a little unsettling. Most of us are not used to actively listening to our writing voices. But your readers will be listening.

As you read, ask yourself: Is this the voice you want readers to hear? Does it seem appropriate for this paper? Does it sound flat or wooden or ponderous in any places? Does it sound anything like you?

If revising your writing voice is necessary for any reason, begin at the beginning—the first line, the first paragraph—and rely on your ears. What sounds right?

You may discover that you begin with the right voice but lose it in places. That often happens when you move from anecdotal material to exposition, from telling a story to explaining research findings. To some extent, a shift in voice is inevitable when you move from one method of development to another, especially from personal material to factual material. But examine your word choices in those passages that seem to go flat. Do you sometimes shift to the dry language used by your sources? Can you rewrite that language in your own voice? When you do, you will find yourself cutting away unnecessary, vague, and pretentious language.

Rewriting in your own voice has another effect, too: It brings the writing to life. Readers respond to an individual writing voice. When I read David Quammen, an author whose work you've read in this text, it rises up from the page, like a hologram, and suddenly, I can see him as a distinct individual. I also become interested in how he sees the things he's writing about.

Avoid Sounding Glib

Beware, though, of a voice that calls more attention to itself than the substance of what you're saying. As you've no doubt learned from reading scholarly sources, much academic writing is voiceless, partly because what's important is not *who* the writer is but *what* he has to say.

Sometimes, in an attempt to sound natural, a writer will take on a folksy or overly colloquial voice, which is much worse than sounding lifeless. What impression does the following passage give you?

```
The thing that really blew my mind was that

marijuana use among college students had actually

declined in the past ten years! I was psyched to

learn that.
```

Ugh!

As you search for the right voice in doing your revision, look for a balance between flat, wooden prose, which sounds as if it were manufactured by a machine, and forced, flowery prose, which distracts the reader from what's most important: what you're trying to say.

How to Control Information

One of the basic challenges of writing with sources is integrating them seamlessly. In the past, you may have practiced the "data dump" strategy, or simply dropping factual information into your papers in little or big clumps. Of course, this won't do. Not only does it make the writing horribly dull, but it means that you're not *making use* of the information you worked so hard to find. Surrounding your sources with your own prose and purposes is an important skill you need to learn. Let's see how it might work. Here are three facts from the "Harper's Index," a monthly feature in *Harper's* magazine:

THREE FACTS

1. Percentage of Americans in 1983 who thought it was "possible to start out <u>poor</u> in this country . . . and become rich": 57 [New York Times–CBS News Poll]
2. Percentage who think this today: 80 [New York Times–CBS News Poll]
3. Percentage of U.S. <u>income</u> in 1983 and today, respectively, that went to the top 1 percent of earners: 9, 16 [National Bureau of Economic Research (Cambridge, Mass.)]*

Juxtaposed like this, these three facts tell a story which is merely implied if they stand alone. How might they be integrated smoothly into a paragraph that tells that story? Here's one possibility:

BLAND VERSION 1

```
According to polling data and the National Bureau

of Economic Research, the number of Americans who
```

*"Harper's Index," *Harper's,* September 2006, 13.

believe it is "possible to start out poor . . . and
become rich" has increased by 23 percent since
1983. This growing faith in the rags-to-riches
ideal comes despite the fact that, during the
same period, the top 1 percent of wage earners
nearly doubled their share of total income.

This isn't bad. Version 1 nicely uses the attribution tag,
"According to . . . ," and includes information about the source of the
information. The version is also careful to reword the original text. It
obliquely states a possible implication of the facts, so the writer
offers some analysis or interpretation of the information's significance. Still, it seems lifeless and dry.

LIVELIER VERSION 2

America's enduring belief in the promise of
rising from rags to riches apparently blinds us
to the facts. Surprisingly, while the richest
1 percent in the U.S. have nearly doubled their
share of the nation's income since 1983, according to a New York Times–CBS poll, 23 percent
more Americans since then have more faith in the
proposition that it is "possible to start out
poor . . . and become rich." It's possible that the
success of the richest Americans in getting a
larger slice of the pie inspires other Americans
to believe they can get their piece, even if the
leftovers continue to shrink.

This strikes me as far more lively and interesting, and a more
seamless integration of the three facts. Do you think so? It's not hard
to sense the difference between versions 1 and 2, but what accounts
for them might at first seem pretty subtle. Note how the writer
seems to surround the information with his own voice and purpose.
In particular, consider the following points:

■ *Find your own way of saying things.* While the economic pie metaphor is hardly original, the writer uses it effectively to make the point that Americans can't seem to grasp the simple facts that contradict their beliefs.

■ *Surround factual information with your own analysis.* Version 1 leans on the facts and offers little comment on them. Version 2 begins with the suggestion that the facts imply how strongly Americans want to believe in the American economic success mythology. The passage ends with an alternative explanation for the findings, which is just as quickly dismissed. The writer is working the material.

What else do you notice about the two versions?

Verbal Gestures

Remember Burke's metaphor for the knowledge-making process (see page 132)? He imagined a parlor full of people having an ongoing conversation about what might be true—arguing, agreeing, raising questions, suggesting new ideas, critiquing old ideas, everyone trying to push the conversation along. Any roomful of people in a conversation about things that cause disagreement is also a roomful of gestures. People wave off a point. They nod in assent. They raise a single finger to raise a new question or make a new point. They invite someone to step forward to speak, and ask another to step aside.

Similarly, an essay that is a writer's conversation with others about a question that matters to them also includes verbal gestures. These are words or phrases like the following ones. Some are gestures that invite some people in the room to provide *background* on the question so that everyone understands what has already been said. Other gestures signal *analysis,* or a closer examination and critique of something someone said. Sometimes these verbal gestures signify *speculation;* the writer just isn't quite sure what to think for sure but maybe. . . . Or they might indicate *alignment*—statements in which the writer is taking sides with a particular idea, position, or way of seeing.

Consider whether verbal gestures like these will help you manage the conversation about your topic.

BACKGROUND

Among the most important voices on _____, the most relevant to this inquiry are _____.

Most people _____.

The major sources of controversy are _____.

One idea emerges again and again, and it's _____.

Like most people, I believed that _____.

The unanswered questions are _____.

This much is clear, _____.

_____'s most important contribution is _____.

Most relevant is _____.

ANALYSIS

The most relevant point is _____.

In comparison, . . .

In contrast, . . .

What is most convincing is _____.

What is least convincing is _____.

What's most interesting is _____.

The surprising connection is _____.

Paradoxically, . . .

Actually, . . .

What isn't clear is _____.

SPECULATION

Perhaps . . .

Maybe . . .

It's possible that _____.

ALIGNMENT

Indeed . . .

Obviously . . .

Alternatively . . .

While others have argued that _____, I think _____.

On balance, the most convincing idea is _____.

What _____ has failed to consider is _____.

The more important question is _____.

Based on my research, _____.

A better explanation is _____.

It's hard to argue with _____.

What I understand now that I didn't understand before is _____.

Scrutinizing Paragraphs

How Well Do You Integrate Sources?

Go over your draft, paragraph by paragraph, and look for ways to *use* the information from your research more smoothly. Be especially alert to "hanging quotes" that appear unattached to any source. Attribution is important. To anchor quotes and ideas to people or publications in your paper, use words such as *argues, observes, says, contends, believes,* and *offers* and phrases such as *according to.* Also look for ways to use quotes selectively, lifting key words or phrases and weaving them into your own writing. What can you add that highlights what you believe is significant about the information? How does it relate to your thesis and the purpose of your paper?

Is Each Paragraph Unified?

Each paragraph should be about one idea and organized around it. You probably know that already. But applying this notion is a particular problem in a research paper, where information abounds and paragraphs sometimes approach marathon length.

If any of your paragraphs are similar to that—that is, they seem to run nearly a page or more—look for ways to break them up into shorter paragraphs. Is more than one idea embedded in the long version? Are you explaining or examining more than one thing?

Also take a look at your shorter paragraphs. Do any present minor or tangential ideas that belong somewhere else? Are any of these ideas irrelevant? Should the paragraph be cut? The cut-and-paste exercise (Exercise 5.4) may have helped you with this already.

Scrutinizing Sentences

Using Active Voice

Which of these two sentences seems more passive, more lifeless?

```
Steroids have been used by many high school
athletes.
```

or

```
Many high school athletes use steroids.
```

The first version, written in the passive voice, is clearly the more limp of the two. It's not grammatically incorrect. In fact, you may have found texts written in the passive voice to be pervasive in the reading you've done for your research paper. Research writing is plagued by passive voice, and that's one of the reasons it can be so mind numbing to read.

Passive voice construction is simple: The subject of the sentence—the thing *doing the action*—becomes the thing *acted upon* by the verb. For instance:

```
Clarence kicked the dog.
```

versus

```
The dog was kicked by Clarence.
```

Sometimes, the subject may be missing altogether, as in:

```
The study was released.
```

Who or *what* released it?

Active voice remedies the problem by pushing the subject up front in the sentence or adding the subject if he, she, or it is missing. For example:

```
High school athletes use steroids.
```

Knowing exactly who is using the drugs makes the sentence livelier.

Another telltale sign of passive voice is that it usually requires a *to be* verb: *is, was, are, were, am, be, being, been.* For example:

```
Alcoholism among women has been extensively

studied.
```

Search your draft for *be's,* and see if any sentences are written in the passive voice. (If you write on a computer, some word-processing programs will search for you.) To make a sentence active, replace the missing subject:

```
Researchers have extensively studied alcoholism

among women.
```

See the box, "Active Verbs for Discussing Ideas," which was compiled by a colleague of mine, Cinthia Gannett. If you're desperate for an alternative to *says* or *argues,* check out the 138 alternatives this list offers.

Using Strong Verbs

Though this may seem like nit-picking, you'd be amazed how much writing in the active voice can revitalize research writing. The use of strong verbs can have the same effect.

As you know, verbs make things happen. Some verbs can make the difference between a sentence that crackles and one that merely hums. Instead of this:

```
The study suggested that the widespread assump-

tion that oral sex is common among American

teenagers might be wrong.
```

write this:

```
The study shattered the common belief that

American teens increasingly indulge in oral sex.
```

Varying Sentence Length

Some writers can sustain breathlessly long sentences, with multiple subordinate clauses, and not lose their readers. Joan Didion is one of those writers. Actually, she also knows enough not to do it too often. She carefully varies the lengths of her sentences, going from a breathless one to one that can be quickly inhaled and exhaled. For example, here is how her essay "Dreamers of the Golden Dream" begins. Notice the mix of sentence lengths.

This is the story about love and death in the golden land, and begins with the country. The San Bernadino Valley lies only an hour east of Los Angeles by the San Bernadino Freeway but is in certain ways an alien place: not the coastal California of the subtropical twilights and the soft westerlies off the Pacific but a harsher California, haunted by the Mojave just beyond the mountains, devastated by the hot dry Santa Ana wind that comes down through the passes at 100 miles an hour and

Active Verbs
for Discussing Ideas

accepts	critiques	implies	refutes
acknowledges	declares	infers	regards
adds	defends	informs	rejects
admires	defies	initiates	relinquishes
affirms	demands	insinuates	reminds
allows	denies	insists	repudiates
analyzes	describes	interprets	resolves
announces	determines	intimates	responds
answers	diminishes	judges	retorts
argues	disagrees	lists	reveals
assaults	disconfirms	maintains	reviews
assembles	discusses	marshalls	seeks
asserts	disputes	narrates	sees
assists	disregards	negates	shares
believes	distinguishes	observes	shifts
buttresses	emphasizes	outlines	shows
categorizes	endorses	parses	simplifies
cautions	enumerates	perceives	states
challenges	exaggerates	persists	stresses
claims	experiences	persuades	substitutes
clarifies	experiments	pleads	suggests
compares	explains	points out	summarizes
complicates	exposes	postulates	supplements
concludes	facilitates	praises	supplies
condemns	formulates	proposes	supports
confirms	grants	protects	synthesizes
conflates	guides	provides	tests
confronts	handles	qualifies	toys with
confuses	hesitates	quotes	treats
considers	highlights	ratifies	uncovers
contradicts	hints	rationalizes	urges
contrasts	hypothesizes	reads	verifies
convinces	identifies	reconciles	warns
criticizes	illuminates	reconsiders	

Source: Reproduced with permission of Cinthia Gannett.

whines through the eucalyptus windbreaks and works on the nerves. October is a bad month for the wind, the month when breathing is difficult and the hills blaze up spontaneously. There has been no rain since April. Every voice seems a scream. It is the season of suicide and divorce and prickly dread, wherever the wind blows.*

The second sentence of Didion's lead is a whopper, but it works, especially since it's set among sentences that are more than half its length. Didion makes music here.

Examine your sentences. Are the long ones too long? You can usually tell if, when you read a sentence, there's no sense of emphasis or it seems to die out. Can you break an unnecessarily long sentence into several shorter ones? A more common problem is a string of short, choppy sentences. For example:

```
Babies are born extrasensitive to sounds. This

unique sensitivity to all sounds does not last.

By the end of the first year, they become deaf

to speech sounds not a part of their native

language.
```

This isn't horrible, but with some sentence combining, the passage will be more fluent:

```
Though babies are born extrasensitive to sounds,

this unique sensitivity lasts only through the

end of the first year, when they become deaf

to speech sounds not a part of their native

language.
```

Look for short sentences where you are repeating words or phrases and also for sentences that begin with pronouns. Experiment with sentence combining. The result will be not only more fluent prose but a sense of emphasis, a sense of the relationship between the information and your ideas about it.

*Joan Didion, *Slouching Toward Bethlehem* (New York: Pocket, 1968).

Editing for Simplicity

Thoreau saw simplicity as a virtue, something that's obvious not only by the time he spent beside Walden Pond but also by the prose he penned while living there. Thoreau writes clearly and plainly.

Somewhere, many of us got the idea that simplicity in writing is a vice—that the long word is better than the short word, that the complex phrase is superior to the simple one. The misconception is that to write simply is to be simple minded. Research papers, especially, suffer from this mistaken notion. They are often filled with what writer William Zinsser calls *clutter*.

EXERCISE 5.5

Cutting Clutter

The following passage is an example of cluttered writing at its best (worst?). It contains phrases and words that often appear in college research papers. Read the passage once. Then take a few minutes and rewrite it, cutting as many words as you can without sacrificing the meaning. Look for ways to substitute a shorter word for a longer one and to say in fewer words what is currently said in many. Try to cut the word count by half.

```
The implementation of the revised alcohol policy
in the university community is regrettable at the
present time due to the fact that the administra-
tion has not facilitated sufficient student
input, in spite of the fact that there have been
attempts by the people affected by this policy to
make their objections known in many instances.
(55 words)
```

Stock Phrases in Research Papers

Like many types of writing, the language of the college research paper is littered with words and phrases that find their way to the page the same way drinking root beer prompts my 12-year-old daughter and her friends to hold burping contests. One just seems to inspire the other. Following is a list of stock phrases that I often find in research papers. There is nothing grammatically wrong with these. It's simply that they are old, tired phrases and you can say the same thing more freshly with fewer words. Look for them in your draft and then edit them out.

TIRED PHRASES	FRESHER ALTERNATIVES
Due to the fact that . . .	*Because . . .*
At this point in time . . .	*Now . . .*
In my opinion, . . .	*(Unnecessary. We know it's your opinion)*
A number of . . .	*Many . . .*
A number of studies point to the fact that . . .	*Many researchers conclude (or argue) . . .*
In the event of . . .	*If . . .*
In today's society . . .	*Today we . . .*
In conclusion, . . .	*(Omit. If you're at the end of the paper you're probably concluding)*
Studies have found that . . .	*(Avoid. It's better to mention one or two)*
Until such time as . . .	*Until . . .*
Referred to as . . .	*Called . . .*
It should be pointed out that . . .	*(Omit. You are pointing it out.)*
Is in a position to . . .	*Can*
It is a fact that . . .	*(Omit. Just state the fact, ma'am)*
It may be said that . . .	*(Omit. Just say it)*
There can be little doubt that . . .	*It's likely . . .*
It is possible that . . .	*Perhaps . . .*

Preparing the Final Manuscript

I wanted to title this section "Preparing the Final Draft," but it occurred to me that *draft* doesn't suggest anything final. I always call my work a draft because until it's out of my hands, it never feels finished. You may feel that way, too. You've spent five weeks on this paper—and the last few days, disassembling it and putting it back together again. How do you know when you're finally done?

For many students, the deadline dictates that: The paper is due tomorrow. But you may find that your paper really seems to be coming together in a satisfying way. You may even like it, and you're ready to prepare the final manuscript.

Considering "Reader-Friendly" Design

Later in this section, we'll discuss the format of your final draft. Research papers in some disciplines have prescribed forms. Some papers in the social sciences, for example, require an abstract, an introduction, a discussion of method, a presentation of results, and a discussion of those results. These sections are clearly defined using subheadings, making it easier for readers to examine those parts of the paper they're most interested in. You probably discovered that in your own reading of formal research. You'll likely learn the formats research papers should conform to in various disciplines as you take upper-level courses in those fields.

While you should document this paper properly, you may have some freedom to develop a format that best serves your purpose. As you consider the format of your rewrite, keep readers in mind. How can you make your paper more readable? How can you signal your plan for developing the topic and what's important? Some visual devices might help, including:

- Subheadings
- Graphs, illustrations, tables
- Bulleted lists (like the one you're reading now)
- Block quotes
- Underlining and paragraphing for emphasis
- White space

Long, unbroken pages of text can appear to be a gray, uninviting mass to the reader. All of the devices listed help break up the text, making it more "reader friendly." Subheadings, if not overused, can also cue your reader to significant sections of your paper and how they relate to the whole. Long quotes, those over four lines, should be blocked, or indented ten spaces (rather than the usual five spaces customary for indenting paragraphs), separating them from the rest of the text. (See Chapter 4, "Writing with Sources," for more on blocking quotes.) Bullets—dots or asterisks preceding brief items—can be used to highlight a quick list of important information. Graphs, tables, and illustrations also break up the text, but more importantly, they can help clarify and explain information. (See Section 2.15, "Placement of Tables, Charts, and Illustrations," in Appendix A.)

The format of the book you're reading is intended, in part, to make it accessible to readers. As you revise, consider how the look of your paper can make it more inviting and easily understood.

Following MLA Conventions

I've already mentioned that formal research papers in various disciplines may have prescribed formats. If your instructor expects a certain format, he has probably detailed exactly what that format should be. But in all likelihood, your essay for this class doesn't need to follow a rigid form. It will, however, probably adhere to the basic Modern Language Association (MLA) guidelines, described in detail in Appendix A. There, you'll find methods for formatting your paper and instructions for citing sources on your "Works Cited" page. You'll also find a sample paper in MLA style by Amanda Stewart, "In Search of the Great White". The American Psychological Association (APA) guidelines for research papers, the primary alternative to MLA, are described in Appendix B. Again, you'll also find a sample paper, this one by Jennifer Suittor, titled "What's Love Got to Do with It?"

Proofreading Your Paper

You've spent weeks researching, writing, and revising your paper. You want to stop now. That's understandable, no matter how much you were driven by your curiosity. Before you sign off on your research paper, placing it in someone else's hands, take the time to proofread it.

I was often so glad to be done with a piece of writing that I was careless about proofreading it. That changed about ten years ago, after I submitted a portfolio of writing to complete my master's degree. I was pretty proud of it, especially an essay about dealing with my father's alcoholism. Unfortunately, I misspelled that word—*alcoholism*—every time I used it. Bummer.

Proofreading on a Computer

Proofreading used to involve gobbing on correction fluid to cover up mistakes and then trying to line up the paper and type in the changes. Writing on a computer, you're spared from that ordeal. The text can be easily manipulated on the screen.

Software programs can also help with the job. Most word-processing programs, for example, come with spelling and grammar checkers.

These programs will count the number of words in your sentences, alerting you to particularly long ones, and will even point out uses of passive voice. I find some of these programs irritating because they evaluate writing ability based on factors such as sentence length, which may not be a measure of the quality of your work at all. But for a basic review, these programs can be extremely useful, particularly for flagging passive construction.

Many writers find they need to print out their paper and proofread the hard copy. They argue that they catch more mistakes if they proofread on paper than if they proofread onscreen. It makes sense, especially if you've been staring at the screen for days. A printed copy of your paper *looks* different, and I think you see it differently, maybe with fresher eyes and attitude. You might notice things you didn't notice before. You decide for yourself how and when to proofread.

Looking Closely

You've already edited the manuscript, pruning sentences and tightening things up. Now hunt for the little errors in grammar and mechanics that you missed. Aside from misspellings (usually typos), some pretty common mistakes appear in the papers I see. For practice, see if you can catch some of them in the following exercise.

EXERCISE 5.6

Picking Off the Lint

I have a colleague who compares proofreading to picking the lint off an outfit, which is often your final step before heading out the door. Examine the following excerpt from a student paper. Proofread it, catching as many mechanical errors as possible. Note punctuation mistakes, agreement problems, misspellings, and anything else that seems off.

```
In an important essay, Melody Graulich notes

how "rigid dichotomizing of sex roles" in most

frontier myths have "often handicapped and con-

fused male as well as female writers (187),"
```

she wonders if a "universel mythology" (198)
might emerge that is less confining for both of
them. In Bruce Mason, Wallace Stegner seems to
experiment with this idea; acknowledging the
power of Bo's male fantasies *and* Elsa's ability
to teach her son to feel. It is his strenth. On
the other hand, Bruces brother chet, who dies
young, lost and broken, seems doomed because he
lacked sufficient measure of both the feminine
and masculine. He observes that Chet had
"enough of the old man to spoil him, ebnough of
his mother to soften him, not enough of either
to save him (*Big Rock*, 521)."

If you did this exercise in class, compare your proofreading of
this passage with that of a partner. What did each of you find?

Ten Common Mistakes

The following is a list of the ten most common errors (besides
misspelled words) made in research papers that should be caught in
careful proofreading. A number of these errors occurred in the previous exercise.

1. Beware of commonly confused words, such as *your* instead of
you're. Here's a list of others:

their/there/they're	advice/advise
know/now	lay/lie
accept/except	its/it's
all ready/already	passed/past

2. Watch for possessives. Instead of *my fathers alcoholism,* the
correct style is *my father's alcoholism.* Remember that if a noun ends
in *s*, still add *'s: Tess's laughter.* If a noun is plural, just add the apos-
trophe: *the scientists' studies.*

3. Avoid vague pronoun references. The excerpt in Exercise 5.6
ends with the sentence, *He observes that Chet. . . . Who's he?* The

sentence should read, *Bruce observes that Chet....* Whenever you use the pronouns *he, she, it, they,* and *their,* make sure each clearly refers to someone or something.

4. Subjects and verbs must agree. If the subject is singular, its verb must be, too:

> The perils of climate change are many.

What confuses writers sometimes is the appearance of a noun that is not really the subject near the verb. Exercise 5.6 begins, for example, with this sentence:

> In an important essay, Melody Graulich notes how
> "rigid dichotomizing of sex roles" in most fron-
> tier myths have "often handicapped and confused
> male as well as female writers."

The subject here is not *frontier myths* but *rigid dichotomizing,* a singular subject. The sentence should read:

> In an important essay, Melody Graulich notes how
> "rigid dichotomizing of sex roles" in most fron-
> tier myths has "often handicapped and confused
> male as well as female writers."

The verb *has* may sound funny, but it's correct.

5. Punctuate quotes properly. Note that commas belong inside quotation marks, not outside. Periods belong inside, too. Colons and semicolons are exceptions—they belong *outside* quotation marks. Blocked quotes don't need quotation marks at all unless there is a quote within the quote.

6. Scrutinize use of commas. Could you substitute periods or semicolons instead? If so, you may be looking at *comma splices* or *run-on sentences.* Here's an example:

> Since 1980, the use of marijuana by college
> students has steadily declined, this was
> something of a surprise to me and my friends.

The portion after the comma, *this was . . . ,* is another sentence. The comma should be a period, and *this* should be capitalized.

7. Make sure each parenthetical citation *precedes* the period in the sentence you're citing but *follows* the quotation mark at the end of a sentence. In MLA style, there is no comma between the author's name and page number: (Marks 99).

8. Use dashes correctly. Though they can be overused, dashes are a great way to break the flow of a sentence with a related bit of information. You've probably noticed I like them. In a manuscript, type dashes as *two* hyphens (- -), not one.

9. After mentioning the full name of someone in your paper, normally use her *last name* in subsequent references. For example, this is incorrect:

```
Denise Grady argues that people are genetically

predisposed to obesity. Denise also believes

that some people are "programmed to convert

caloriesto fat."
```

Unless you know Denise or for some other reason want to conceal her last name, change the second sentence to this:

```
Grady also believes that some people are

"programmed to convert calories to fat."
```

One exception to this is when writing about literature. It is often appropriate to refer to characters by their first names, particularly if characters share last names (as in Exercise 5.6).

10. Scrutinize use of colons and semicolons. A colon is usually used to call attention to what follows it: a list, quotation, or appositive. A colon should follow an independent clause. For example, this won't do:

```
The most troubling things about child abuse

are: the effects on self-esteem and language

development.
```

In this case, eliminate the colon. A semicolon is often used as if it were a colon or a comma. In most cases, a semicolon should be used as a period, separating two independent clauses. The semicolon simply implies the clauses are closely related.

Using the "Find" or "Search" Function

If you're writing on a computer, use the "Find" or "Search" function—a feature in most word-processing programs—to help you track down consistent problems. You simply tell the computer what word or punctuation to look for, and it will locate all occurrences in the text. For example, if you want to check for comma splices, search for commas. The cursor will stop on every comma, and you can verify if it is correct. You can also search for pronouns to locate vague references or for words (like those listed in item 1) you commonly misuse.

Avoiding Sexist Language

One last proofreading task is to do a *man* and *he* check. Until recently, sexism wasn't an issue in language. Use of words such as *mankind* and *chairman* was acceptable; the implication was that the terms applied to both genders. At least, that's how use of the terms was defended when challenged. Critics argued that words such as *mailman* and *businessman* reinforced ideas that only men could fill these roles. Bias in language is subtle but powerful. And it's often unintentional. To avoid sending the wrong message, it's worth making the effort to avoid sexist language.

If you need to use a word with a *man* suffix, check to see if there is an alternative. *Congressperson* sounds pretty clunky, but *representative* works fine. Instead of *mankind,* why not *humanity?* Substitute *camera operator* for *cameraman.*

Also check use of pronouns. Do you use *he* or *his* in places where you mean both genders? For example:

```
The writer who cares about his topic will bring
it to life for his readers.
```

Since a lot of writers are women, this doesn't seem right. How do you solve this problem?

1. Use *his or her, he or she,* or that mutation *s/he.* For example:

```
The writer who cares about his or her topic will
bring it to life for his or her readers.
```

This is an acceptable solution, but using *his or her* repeatedly can be awkward.

2. Change the singular subject to plural. For example:

```
Writers who care about their topics will bring
them to life for their readers.
```

This version is much better and avoids discriminatory language altogether.

3. Alternate *he* and *she, his* and *hers* whenever you encounter an indefinite person. If you have referred to a writer as *he* on one page, make the writer *she* on the next page, as long as you are not talking about the same person. Alternate throughout.

Looking Back and Moving On

This book began with your writing, and it also will end with it. Before you close your research notebook on this project, open it one last time and fastwrite your response to the following questions. Keep your pen moving for seven minutes.

How was your experience writing this research paper different from writing others? How was it the same?

When students share their fastwrites, this comment is typical: "It was easier to sit down and write this research paper than others I've written." One student last semester added, "I think it was easier because before writing the paper, I got to research something I wanted to know about and learn the answers to questions that mattered to me." If this research project was successful, you took charge of your own learning, as that student did.

Your research paper wasn't necessarily fun. Research takes time, and writing is work. Every week, you had new problems to solve. But if the questions you asked about your topic mattered, then you undoubtedly had moments, perhaps late at night in the library, when you encountered something that suddenly cracked your topic open and let the light come pouring out. The experience can be dazzling. It's even great when it's merely interesting.

What might you take away from this research paper that will prepare you for doing the next one? At the very least, I hope you've cultivated basic research skills: how to find information efficiently, how to document, how to avoid plagiarism, and how to take notes. But I also hope that you've learned more. Perhaps you've recovered a part of you that may have been left behind when you turned eleven or twelve—the curiosity that drove you to put bugs in mayonnaise jars, read about China, disassemble a transistor radio, and wonder about Mars. Curiosity is a handy thing in college. It gets you thinking. And that's the idea.

Guide to MLA Style

This section contains guidelines for preparing your essay in the format recommended by the Modern Language Association, or MLA. Part One, "Citing Sources in Your Essay," will be particularly useful as you write your draft; it provides guidance on how to parenthetically cite the sources you use in the text of your essay. Part Two, "How the Essay Should Look," will help you with formatting the manuscript after you've revised it, including guidelines for margins, tables, and pagination. Part Three, "Preparing the 'Works Cited' Page," offers detailed instructions on how to prepare your bibliography at the end of your essay; this is usually one of the last steps in preparing the final manuscript. Finally, Part Four presents a sample research essay in MLA style, which will show you how it all comes together.

Checklist before Handing in a Paper in MLA Style

- My name, instructor's name, course, and date are in the upper left-hand corner of the first page (see pages 270–271).
- All my pages are numbered using my last name next to the appropriate page number (see pages 271–272).
- My "Works Cited" page begins on a new page, not at the bottom of the last page of text.
- Everything, including my "Works Cited" page(s), is double-spaced.
- Because my printer cartridge has enough ink, every page of the paper's text is readable.
- There are no commas in my parenthetical citations between the author's name and the page number (see page 260).
- All my parenthetical citations are *inside* the periods at the ends of sentences, unless the citation appears at the end of a "blocked" quote (see pages 260 and 274–275).
- Parenthetical citations of Web sources *don't* include the URLs (see pages 297–306).
- My paper has a title but no separate title page (unless my instructor says otherwise).
- The entries in my "Works Cited" page(s) are listed alphabetically, and every line after the first one in an entry is indented five spaces.

Directory of MLA Style

Part One: Citing Sources in Your Essay
1.1 When to Cite

Before examining the details of how to use parenthetical citations, remember when you must cite sources in your paper:

1. Whenever you quote from an original source
2. Whenever you borrow ideas from an original source, even when you express them in your own words by paraphrasing or summarizing
3. Whenever you borrow factual information from a source that is *not common knowledge*

The Common Knowledge Exception.   The business about *common knowledge* causes much confusion. Just what does this term mean? Basically, *common knowledge* means facts that are widely known and about which there is no controversy.

Sometimes, it's really obvious whether something is common knowledge. The fact that the Super Bowl occurs in late January or early February and pits the winning teams from the American and National Football Conferences is common knowledge. The fact that former president Ronald Reagan was once an actor and starred in a movie with a chimpanzee is common knowledge, too. And the fact that most Americans get most of their news from television is also common knowledge, though this information is getting close to leaving the domain of common knowledge.

But what about Carolyn's assertion that most dreaming occurs during rapid eye movement (REM) sleep? This is an idea about which all of her sources seem to agree. Does that make it common knowledge?

It's useful to ask next, How common to whom? Experts in the topic at hand or the rest of us? As a rule, consider the knowledge of your readers. What information will not be familiar to most of your readers or may even surprise them? Which ideas might even raise skepticism? In this case, the fact about REM sleep and dreaming goes slightly beyond the knowledge of most readers, so to be safe, it should be cited. Use common sense, but when in doubt, cite.

1.2 The MLA Author/Page System

Starting in 1984, the Modern Language Association (MLA), a body that, among other things, decides documentation conventions for papers in the humanities, switched from footnotes to the author/page parenthetical citation system. The American Psychological Association (APA), a similar body for the social sciences, promotes use of the author/ date system.

You will find it fairly easy to switch from one system to the other once you've learned both. Since MLA conventions are appropriate for English classes, we will focus on the author/page system in the following sections. APA standards are explained more fully in Appendix B, which also includes a sample paper. (For a comparison of the basic features of APA and MLA see Table 1.)

The Basics of Using Parenthetical Citation.   The MLA method of in-text citation is fairly simple: As close as possible to the borrowed material, you indicate in parentheses the original source (usually, the author's name) and the page number in the work that material came from. For example, here's how you'd cite a book or article with a single author using the author/page system:

> From the very beginning of *Sesame Street* in
> 1969, kindergarten teachers discovered that
> incoming students who had watched the program
> already knew their ABCs (Chira 13).*

The parenthetical citation here tells readers two things: (1) This information about the success of *Sesame Street* does not originate with the writer but with someone named *Chira,* and (2) readers can consult the original source for further information by looking on page 13

---

*This and the following "Works Cited" example are used with permission of Heidi R. Dunham.

Table 1   Key Differences between MLA and APA Formats

MLA	APA
Capitalizes most words in book and article titles on works cited page	Only capitalizes the first letter of titles and proper nouns on reference page
Uses author's full first and last name on works cited page	Uses author's last name along with first and middle initials on reference page
Uses the word "and" to combine authors' names in in-text citations and on works cited page if there is more than one author for a source	Uses an ampersand (&) to combine authors' names in in-text citations and on reference page if a source has more than one author
In-text citations use author's last name and pages cited	In-text citations use author's last name and date; page numbers aren't required
In-text citations use no punctuation between author's name and page number	In-text citations use a comma between author's last name and date
Page numbers are listed simply as a number in in-text citations	Page numbers are denoted with a "p." or "pp." in in-text citations
No cover sheet	Cover sheet, with running head
Uses page number on first page	Uses page number on first page— usually the cover sheet
Running head contains author's last name and the page number	Running head contains the first words of the paper's title and the page number
No subheadings within the paper	Uses subheadings within the paper; often begins with an abstract
Tables and figures integrated into the body of the paper	Tables and figures kept separate from the main text

of Chira's book or article, which is cited fully at the back of the paper in the "Works Cited." Here is what readers would find there:

```
             Works Cited
   Chira, Susan. "Sesame Street at 20: Taking
        Stock." New York Times 15 Nov. 1989: 13.
        Print.
```

Here's another example of parenthetical author/page citation from another research paper. Note the differences from the previous example:

> "One thing is clear," writes Thomas Mallon,
> "plagiarism didn't become a truly sore point
> with writers until they thought of writing as
> their trade. . . . Suddenly his capital and
> identity were at stake" (3-4).

The first thing you may have noticed is that the author's last name—Mallon—was omitted from the parenthetical citation. It didn't need to be included, since it had already been mentioned in the text. *If you mention the author's name in the text of your paper, then you only need to parenthetically cite the relevant page number(s).* This citation also tells us that the quoted passage comes from two pages rather than one.

1.2.1 PLACEMENT OF CITATIONS

Place the citation as close as you can to the borrowed material, trying to avoid breaking the flow of the sentences, if possible. To avoid confusion about what's borrowed and what's not—particularly in passages longer than a sentence—mention the name of the original author *in your paper*. Note that in the next example the writer simply cites the source at the end of the paragraph, not naming the source in the text. Doing so makes it hard for the reader to figure out whether Blager is the source of the information in the entire paragraph or just part of it:

> Though children who have been sexually abused
> seem to be disadvantaged in many areas,
> including the inability to forge lasting
> relationships, low self-esteem, and crippling
> shame, they seem advantaged in other areas.
> Sexually abused children seem to be more
> socially mature than other children of their
> same age group. It's a distinctly mixed
> blessing (Blager 994).

In the following example, notice how the ambiguity about what's borrowed and what's not is resolved by careful placement of the author's name and parenthetical citation in the text:

> Though children who have been sexually abused seem to be disadvantaged in many areas, including the inability to forge lasting relationships, low self-esteem, and crippling shame, they seem advantaged in other areas. According to Blager, sexually abused children seem to be more socially mature than other children of their same age group (994). It's a distinctly mixed blessing.

Citations That Go with the Flow

There's no getting around it—parenthetical citations can be like stones on the sidewalk. Readers stride through a sentence in your essay and then have to step around the citation at the end before they resume their walk. Yet citations are important in academic writing because they help readers know who you read or heard that shaped your thinking.

However, you can minimize citations that trip up readers and make your essay more readable.

- Avoid lengthy parenthetical citations by mentioning the name of the author in your essay. That way, you usually only have to include a page number in the citation.
- Try to place citations where readers are likely to pause anyway—for example, the end of the sentence, or right before a comma.
- Remember you *don't* need a citation when you're citing common knowledge or referring to an entire work by an author.
- If you're borrowing from only one source in a paragraph of your essay, and all of the borrowed material comes from a single page of that source, don't bother repeating the citation over and over again with each new bit of information. Just put the citation at the end of the paragraph.

In this latter version, it's clear that Blager is the source for one sentence in the paragraph, and the writer is responsible for the rest. Generally, use an authority's last name, rather than a formal title or first name, when mentioning her in your text. Also note that the citation is placed *inside* the period of the sentence (or last sentence) that it documents. That's almost always the case, except at the end of a blocked quotation, where the parenthetical reference is placed after the period of the last sentence. The citation can also be placed near the author's name, rather than at the end of the sentence, if it doesn't unnecessarily break the flow of the sentence. For example:

```
Blager (994) observes that sexually abused
children tend to be more socially mature than
other children of their same age group.
```

1.2.2 WHEN YOU MENTION THE AUTHOR'S NAME

It's generally good practice in research writing to identify who said what. The familiar convention of using attribution tags such as "According to Fletcher . . . " or "Fletcher argues . . . " and so on helps readers attach a name with a voice, or an individual with certain claims or findings. When you do mention the author of a source, then you can drop his or her name for the parenthetical citation and just list the page number. For example,

```
Robert Harris believes that there is "widespread
uncertainty" among students about what consti-
tutes plagiarism (2).
```

You may also list the page number directly after the author's name.

```
Robert Harris (2) believes that there is
"widespread uncertainty" among students about
what constitutes plagiarism.
```

1.2.3 WHEN THERE IS NO AUTHOR

Occasionally, you may encounter a source in which the author is anonymous—the article doesn't have a byline, or for some reason the author hasn't been identified. This isn't unusual with pamphlets, editorials, government documents, some newspaper articles, online sources, and short filler articles in magazines. If you can't parenthetically name the author, what do you cite?

Most often, cite the title (or an abbreviated version, if the title is long) and the page number. If you choose to abbreviate the title, begin with the word under which it is alphabetized in the "Works Cited" list. For example:

> Simply put, public relations is "doing good and getting credit" for it (*Getting Yours* 3).

Here is how the publication cited above would be listed at the back of the paper:

> Works Cited
>
> *Getting Yours: A Publicity and Funding Primer*
>
> *for Nonprofit and Voluntary Organizations*.
>
> Lincoln: Contact Center, 2008. Print.

For clarity, it's helpful to mention the original source of the borrowed material in the text of your paper. When there is no author's name, refer to the publication (or institution) you're citing or make a more general reference to the source. For example:

> An article in *Cuisine* magazine argues that the best way to kill a lobster is to plunge a knife between its eyes ("How to Kill" 56).

> *or*

> According to one government report, with the current minimum size limit, most lobsters end up on dinner plates before they've had a chance to reproduce ("Size" 3-4).

1.2.4 WORKS BY THE SAME AUTHOR

Suppose you end up using several books or articles by the same author. Obviously, a parenthetical citation that merely lists the author's name and page number won't do, since it won't be clear *which* of several works the citation refers to. In this case, include the author's name, an abbreviated title (if the original is too long), and the page number. For example:

> The thing that distinguishes the amateur from
> the experienced writer is focus; one "rides off
> in all directions at once," and the other finds
> one meaning around which everything revolves
> (Murray, *Write to Learn* 92).

The "Works Cited" list would show multiple works by one author as follows:

Works Cited

Murray, Donald M. *Write to Learn*. 8th ed.

    Boston: Heinle, 2004. Print.

---. *A Writer Teaches Writing*. Boston:

    Heinle, 2004. Print.

It's obvious from the parenthetical citation which of the two Murray books is the source of the information. Note that in the parenthetical reference, no punctuation separates the title and the page number, but a comma follows the author's name. If Murray had been mentioned in the text of the paper, his name could have been dropped from the citation.

How to handle the "Works Cited" list is explained more fully later in this appendix, but for now, notice that the three hyphens used in the second entry are meant to signal that the author's name in this source is the same as in the preceding entry.

1.2.5 INDIRECT SOURCES

Whenever you can, cite the original source for material you use. For example, if an article on television violence quotes the author of a book and you want to use the quote, try to hunt down the book. That way, you'll be certain of the accuracy of the quote and you may find some more usable information.

Sometimes, however, finding the original source is not possible. In those cases, use the term *qtd. in* to signal that you've quoted or paraphrased a quotation from a book or article that initially appeared elsewhere. In the following example, the citation signals that Bacon's quote was culled from an article by Guibroy, not Bacon's original work:

> Francis Bacon also weighed in on the dangers of
> imitation, observing that "it is hardly possible
> at once to admire an author and to go beyond
> him" (qtd. in Guibroy 113).

1.2.6 PERSONAL INTERVIEWS

If you mention the name of your interview subject in your text, no parenthetical citation is necessary. On the other hand, if you don't mention the subject's name, cite it in parentheses after the quote:

> Instead, the recognizable environment gave some-
> thing to kids they could relate to. "And it had
> a lot more real quality to it than, say, *Mister*
> *Rogers* . . . ," says one educator. "Kids say the
> reason they don't like *Mister Rogers* is that
> it's unbelievable" (Diamonti).

Regardless of whether you mention your subject's name, you should include a reference to the interview in the "Works Cited." In this case, the reference would look like this:

> Works Cited
>
> Diamonti, Nancy. Personal Interview. 5 Nov. 1999.

1.2.7 SEVERAL SOURCES IN A SINGLE CITATION

Suppose two sources both contributed the same information in a paragraph of your essay? Or perhaps even more common is when you're summarizing the findings of several authors on a certain topic—a fairly common move when you're trying to establish a context for your own research question. How do you cite multiple authors in a single citation? In the usual fashion, using author name and page number, but separating each with a semicolon. For example,

> A whole range of studies have looked closely
> at the intellectual development of college

```
students, finding that they generally
assume "stages" or "perspectives" that
differ from subject to subject (Perry 122;
Belenky et al. 12).
```

If you can, however, avoid long citations because they can be cumbersome for readers.

Sample Parenthetical References for Other Sources. MLA format is pretty simple, and we've already covered some of the basic variations. You should also know five additional variations, as follow:

1.2.8 AN ENTIRE WORK

If you mention the author's name in the text, no citation is necessary. The work should, however, be listed in the "Works Cited."

```
Leon Edel's Henry James is considered by many to
be a model biography.
```

1.2.9 A VOLUME OF A MULTIVOLUME WORK

If you're working with one volume of a multivolume work, it's a good idea to mention which volume in the parenthetical reference. The citation below attributes the passage to the second volume, page 3, of a work by Baym and three or more other authors. The volume number always precedes the colon, which is followed by the page number:

```
By the turn of the century, three authors
dominated American literature: Mark Twain,
Henry James, and William Dean Howells (Baym
et al. 2: 3).
```

1.2.10 SEVERAL SOURCES FOR A SINGLE PASSAGE

Occasionally, a number of sources may contribute to a single passage. List them all in one parenthetical reference, separated by semicolons:

```
American soccer may never achieve the popu-
larity it enjoys in the rest of the world, an
unfortunate fact that is integrally related to
```

```
the nature of the game itself (Gardner 12;
"Selling Soccer" 30).*
```

1.2.11 A LITERARY WORK

Because so many literary works, particularly classics, have been reprinted in so many editions, it's useful to give readers more information about where a passage can be found in one of these editions. List the page number and then the chapter number (and any other relevant information, such as the section or volume), separated by a semicolon. Use arabic rather than roman numerals, unless your teacher instructs you otherwise:

```
Izaak Walton warns that "no direction can be
given to make a man of a dull capacity able to
make a Flie well" (130; ch. 5).
```

When citing classic poems or plays, instead of page numbers, cite line numbers and other appropriate divisions (book, section, act, scene, part, etc.). Separate the information with periods. For example, (*Othello* 2.3.286) indicates act 2, scene 3, line 286 of Shakespeare's work.

1.2.12 AN ONLINE SOURCE

In most cases, online documents don't have page numbers, though you may find that when you print out the material, the printer assigns page numbers, usually beginning with "1." The key question to ask yourself is this: Are these numbers *permanent?* This is usually not the case. Different printers might give electronic documents different page numbers.

When a document or Web page lacks permanent page numbers you don't need to include them in your parenthetical citation. For example, here's a passage from an authorless article from the Web that lacks page numbers. The citation would therefore just include the title of the page in quotation marks.

```
Many women who wait to begin a family may
wonder if prior birth control choices nega-
tively affect their fertility. It's not
uncommon, for instance, for a woman to take
```

---

*Jason Pulsifer, University of New Hampshire, 1991. Used with permission.

oral contraceptives for 10 years or longer. The
birth control pill itself doesn't affect long-
term fertility ("Infertility: Key Q and A").

On the other hand, PDF files frequently have permanent pagination, particularly if the document is a copy of the original article.
In that case, the page numbers should be used in your citation.

Part Two: Format

2.1 The Layout

There is, well, a certain fussiness associated with the look of academic papers. The reason for it is quite simple—academic disciplines
generally aim for consistency in format so that readers of scholarship
know exactly where to look to find what they want to know. It's a matter
of efficiency. How closely you must follow the MLA's requirements for
the layout of your essay is up to your instructor, but it's really not that
complicated. A lot of what you need to know is featured in Figure A1.

2.1.1 PRINTING

Print your paper on white, $8\frac{1}{2}$" × 11" paper. Make sure the
printer has sufficient ink or toner.

2.1.2 MARGINS AND SPACING

The old high school trick is to have big margins. That way, you
can get the length without the information. Don't try that trick with
this paper. Leave one-inch margins at the top, bottom, and sides of
your pages. Indent the first line of each paragraph five spaces and
blocked quotes ten spaces. Double-space all of the text, including
blocked quotes and "Works Cited."

2.1.3 TITLE PAGE

Your paper doesn't need a separate title page. Begin with the
first page of text. One inch below the top of the page, type your name,

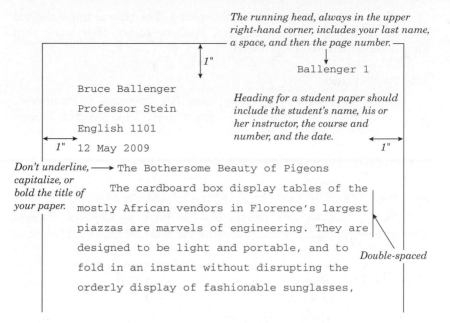

The running head, always in the upper right-hand corner, includes your last name, a space, and then the page number.

Ballenger 1

1"

Bruce Ballenger

Professor Stein

English 1101

12 May 2009

1"

1"

Heading for a student paper should include the student's name, his or her instructor, the course and number, and the date.

Don't underline, capitalize, or bold the title of your paper.

The Bothersome Beauty of Pigeons

The cardboard box display tables of the mostly African vendors in Florence's largest piazzas are marvels of engineering. They are designed to be light and portable, and to fold in an instant without disrupting the orderly display of fashionable sunglasses,

Double-spaced

FIGURE A1 **The Basic Look of an MLA-Style Paper**

your instructor's name, the course number, and the date (see following). Below that, type the title, centered on the page. Begin the text of the paper below the title.

Karoline Ann Fox

Professor Dethier

English 401

15 December 2008

Metamorphosis, the Exorcist,

and Oedipus

Ernst Pawel has said that Franz Kafka's *The Metamorphosis* . . . *

---

*Reprinted with permission of Karoline A. Fox.

Note that every line is double-spaced. The title is not italicized (unless it includes the name of a book or some other work that should be italicized) or boldfaced.

2.1.4 PAGINATION

Make sure that every page after the first one is numbered. That's especially important with long papers. Type your last name and the page number in the upper-righthand corner, flush with the right margin: Ballenger 3. Don't use the abbreviation *p.* or a hyphen between your name and the number.

2.1.5 PLACEMENT OF TABLES, CHARTS, AND ILLUSTRATIONS

With MLA format, papers do not have appendixes. Tables, charts, and illustrations are placed in the body of the paper, close to the text that refers to them. Number illustrations consecutively (Table 1 or Figure 3), and indicate sources below them (see Figure A2). If you use a chart or illustration from another text, give the full citation. Place any table caption above the table, flush left. Captions for illustrations or diagrams are usually placed below them.

2.1.6 HANDLING TITLES

The MLA guidelines about handling titles are, as the most recent *Handbook* observes, "strict." The general rule is that the writer should capitalize the first letters of all principal words in a title, including any that follow hyphens. The exceptions include

Table 1   Percentage of Students Who Self-Report Acts of Plagiarism

Acts of Plagiarism	Never/ Rarely	Some- times	Often/ Very Freq.
Copy text without citation	71	19	10
Copy paper without citation	91	5	3
Request paper to hand in	90	5	2
Purchase paper to hand in	91	6	3

Source: Scanlon, Patrick M., and David R. Neumann; "Internet Plagiarism among College Students," *Journal of College Student Development* 43.3 (2002): 379; print.

FIGURE A2   Example of Format for a Table

articles (*a, an,* and *the*), prepositions (*for, of, in, to*), coordinating conjunctions (*and, or, but, for*), and the use of *to* in infinitives. These exceptions apply *only if the words appear in the middle of a title;* capitalize them if they appear at the beginning or end.

In May 2008, the MLA updated its citation style, and among the changes is a no-brainer in this era of word processing: a shift to *italicizing* titles of works rather than <u>underlining</u> them. The APA figured this out about a decade ago.

The new rules for deciding whether to italicize a title or place it in quotation marks (the usual alternative) makes this distinction:

1. If the work is "published independently," italicize it. These works are typically books, Web sites, online databases, TV broadcasts, plays, periodicals, and so on.
2. If the title is part of a larger work—say, an article in a periodical or an episode of a TV program—then place it in quotation marks.

Here are some examples:

The Curious Researcher (book)

A Streetcar Named Desire (play)

"Once More to the Lake" (essay in a collection)

New York Times (newspaper)

"Psychotherapy" (encyclopedia article)

2.1.7 LANGUAGE AND STYLE

Names. Though it may seem as if you're on familiar terms with some of the authors you cite by the end of your research project, it's not a good idea to call them by their first names. Typically, initially give the full names of people you cite, and then only their last names if you mention them again in your essay.

Ellipsis Points. Those are the three (always three) dots that indicate you've left out a word, phrase, or even whole section of a quoted passage. It's often wise to do this since you want to emphasize only certain parts of a quotation rather than burden your reader with unnecessary information, but be careful to preserve the basic intention and idea of the author's original statement. Ellipsis points can come at the beginning of a quotation, in the middle, or at the end, depending where it is you've omitted material. For example,

> "After the publication of a controversial
> picture that shows, for example, either dead
> or grieving victims . . . , readers in telephone
> calls and in letters to the editor, often attack
> the photographer for being tasteless . . . "

Quotations. Quotations that run more than four lines long should be blocked, or indented ten spaces from the left margin. The quotation should be double-spaced and quotation marks should be omitted. In an exception from the usual convention, the parenthetical citation is placed *outside* the period at the end of the quotation. A colon is a customary way to introduce a blocked quotation. For example,

> Chris Sherman and Gary Price, in *The Invisible
> Web*, contend that much of the Internet, possibly
> most, is beyond the reach of researchers who use
> conventional search engines:
>
> > The problem is that vast expanses of the Web
> > are completely invisible to general-purpose
> > search engines like AltaVista, HotBot, and
> > Google. Even worse, this "Invisible Web" is
> > in all likelihood growing significantly
> > faster than the visible Web that you're
> > familiar with. It's not that search engines
> > and Web directories are "stupid" or even
> > badly engineered. Rather, they simply can't
> > "see" millions of high quality resources
> > that are available exclusively on the Invis-
> > ible Web. So what is this Invisible Web and

```
why aren't search engines doing anything
about it to make it visible? (xxi)
```

Part Three:
Preparing the "Works Cited" Page

The "Works Cited" page ends the paper. (This may also be called the "References Cited" or "Sources Cited" page, depending on the nature of your sources or the preferences of your instructor.) In the old footnote system (which, by the way, is still used in some humanities disciplines), this section used to be called "Endnotes" or "Bibliography." There are also several other lists of sources that may appear at the end of a research paper. An "Annotated List of Works Cited" not only lists the sources used in the paper but also includes a brief description of each. A "Works Consulted" list includes sources that may or may not have been cited in the paper but shaped your thinking. A "Content Notes" page, keyed to superscript numbers in the text of the paper, lists short commentaries or asides that are significant but not central enough to the discussion to be included in the text of the paper.

The "Works Cited" page is the workhorse of most college papers. The other source lists are used less often. "Works Cited" is essentially an alphabetical listing of all the sources you quoted, paraphrased, or summarized in your paper. If you have used MLA format for citing sources, your paper has numerous parenthetical references to authors and page numbers. The "Works Cited" page provides complete information on each source cited in the text for the reader who wants to know. (In APA format, this page is called "References" and is only slightly different in how items are listed. See Appendix B for APA guidelines.)

In March 2009, the Modern Language Association (MLA) changed the citation rules for "Works Cited" pages. A groan issued from classrooms across America. But it's not so bad. Really. The changes actually make sense. Here are the highlights:

1. **Italics good, underlining bad.** From now on the titles of independent works (i.e., books, periodicals, Web sites, and so on) in citations are to be italicized rather than underlined. Welcome to the 21st century.

2. **Adios to long and ugly Web addresses.** Unless your online source can't be found any other way, you no longer have to include the URL for the source in your citation.

3. **Provide a medium.** Every source citation now indicates the "medium of publication." The most common are the following: Print, Web, Film, CD, Performance, Interview, Video, and Audio.

3.1 Format

Alphabetizing the List. "Works Cited" follows the text of your paper on a separate page. After you've assembled complete information about each source you've cited, put the sources in alphabetical order by the last name of the author. If the work has multiple authors, use the last name of the first listed. If the source has no author, then alphabetize it by the first key word of the title. If you're citing more than one source by a single author, you don't need to repeat the name for each source; simply place three dashes followed by a period (---.) for the author's name in subsequent listings.

Indenting and Spacing. Type the first line of each entry flush left, and indent subsequent lines of that entry (if any) five spaces. Double-space between each line and each entry. For example:

Hall 10

Works Cited

Biernacki, Patrick. *Pathways from Heroin*
    Addiction. Philadelphia: Temple UP, 1986.
    Print.

Brill, Leon. *The De-Addiction Process*. Springfield:
    Thomas, 1972. Print.

Epstein, Joan F., and Joseph C. Gfroerer. "Heroin
    Abuse in the United States." *National Clear-*
    inghouse for Alcohol and Drug Information. US
    Dept. of Health and Human Services, Aug.
    1997. Web. 24 Nov. 2008.

Hall, Lonny. Personal interview. 1 Mar. 2009.

Kaplan, John. *The Hardest Drug: Heroin and Public*
    Policy. Chicago: U of Chicago P, 1983. Print.

"Methadone." *Encyclopaedia Britannica*. 1999 ed.
    1999. CD-ROM.

Shaffner, Nicholas. *Saucerful of Secrets: The Pink Floyd Odyssey*. New York: Dell, 1992. Print.

Strang, John, and Michael Gossop. *Heroin Addiction and Drug Policy: The British System*. New York: Oxford UP, 1994. Print.

Swift, Wendy, et al. "Transitions between Routes of Heroin Administration: A Study of Caucasian and Indochinese Users in South-Western Sydney, Australia." *Addiction* (1999): 71-82. Print.

3.2 Citing Nonperiodical Publications (Books)

You usually need three pieces of information to cite a book: the name of the author or authors, the title, and the publication information. Occasionally, other information is required. The *MLA Handbook** lists this additional information in the order it would appear in the citation. Remember, any single entry will include a few of these things, not all of them. Use whichever are relevant to the source you're citing.

1. Name of the author
2. Title of the book (or part of it)
3. Number of edition used
4. Number of volume used
5. Where published, by whom, and the date
6. Page numbers used
7. Medium of publication (*Print*)
8. Name of the series
9. Any annotation you'd like to add.

Each piece of information in a citation is followed by a period and one space (not two).

Title. As a rule, the titles of books are italicized, with the first letters of all principal words capitalized, including those in any subtitles. Titles that are not italicized are usually those of pieces found

---

*Modern Language Association, *MLA Handbook for Writers of Research Papers*, 7th ed. (New York: MLA, 2009). Print.

within larger works, such as poems and short stories in anthologies. These titles are set off by quotation marks. Titles of religious works (the Bible, the Koran) are neither italicized nor enclosed within quotation marks. (See the guidelines in "Handling Titles," in Part Two.)

Edition.   If a book doesn't indicate any edition number, then it's probably a first edition, a fact you don't need to cite. Look on the title page. Signal an edition like this: *2nd ed., 3rd ed.,* and so on.

Publication Place, Publisher, and Date.   Look on the title page to find out who published the book. Publishers' names are usually shortened in the "Works Cited" list: for example, *St. Martin's Press, Inc.,* is shortened to *St. Martin's.*

It's sometimes confusing to know what to cite about the publication place, since several cities are often listed on the title page. Cite the first. For books published outside the United States, add the country name along with the city to avoid confusion.

The date a book is published is usually indicated on the copyright page. If several dates or several printings by the same publisher are listed, cite the original publication date. However, if the book is a revised edition, give the date of that edition. One final variation: If you're citing a book that's a reprint of an original edition, give both dates. For example:

> Stegner, Wallace. *Recapitulation.* 1979. Lincoln:
>
> U of Nebraska P, 1986. Print.

This book was first published in 1979 and then republished in 1986 by the University of Nebraska Press.

Page Numbers.   Normally, you don't list page numbers of a book. The parenthetical reference in your paper specifies that. But if you use only part of a book—an introduction or an essay—list the appropriate page numbers following the publication date. Use periods to set off the page numbers. If the author or editor of the entire work is also the author of the introduction or essay you're citing, list her by last name only in subsequent citations. For example:

> Lee, L. L., and Merrill Lewis. Preface. *Women,*
>
> *Women Writers, and the West.* Ed. Lee and
>
> Lewis. Troy: Whitston, 1980. v-ix. Print.

Sample Book Citations

3.2.1 A BOOK BY ONE AUTHOR

> Armstrong, Karen. *The Spiral Staircase*. New
>   York: Knopf, 2004. Print.

In-Text Citation: (Armstrong 22)

3.2.2 A BOOK BY TWO AUTHORS

> Ballenger, Bruce, and Michelle Payne. *The Curious*
>   *Reader*. New York: Longman, 2006. Print.

In-Text Citation: (Ballenger and Payne 14)

3.2.3 A BOOK WITH MORE THAN THREE AUTHORS

If a book has more than three authors, list the first and substitute the term *et al.* for the others.

> Jones, Hillary, et al. *The Unmasking of Adam*.
>   Highland Park: Pegasus, 1992. Print.

In-Text Citation: (Jones et al. 21–30)

3.2.4 SEVERAL BOOKS BY THE SAME AUTHOR

> Baldwin, James. *Tell Me How Long the Train's Been*
>   *Gone*. New York: Dell-Doubleday, 1968. Print.

> ---. *Going to Meet the Man*. New York: Dell-
>   Doubleday, 1948. Print.

In-Text Citation: (Baldwin, *Going* 34)

3.2.5 AN ENTIRE COLLECTION OR ANTHOLOGY

> Crane, R. S., ed. *Critics and Criticism:*
>   *Ancient and Modern*. Chicago: U of
>   Chicago P, 1952. Print.

In-Text Citation: (Crane xx)

3.2.6 A WORK IN A COLLECTION OR ANTHOLOGY

The title of a work that is part of a collection but was originally published as a book should be underlined. Otherwise, the title of a work in a collection should be enclosed in quotation marks.

Bahktin, Mikhail. *Marxism and the Philosophy of Language*. *The Rhetorical Tradition*. Ed. Patricia Bizzell and Bruce Herzberg. New York: St. Martin's, 1990. 928-44. Print.

In-Text Citation: (Bahktin 929-31)

Jones, Robert F. "Welcome to Muskie Country." *The Ultimate Fishing Book*. Ed. Lee Eisenberg and DeCourcy Taylor. Boston: Houghton, 1981. 122-34. Print.

In-Text Citation: (Jones 131)

3.2.7 AN INTRODUCTION, PREFACE, FOREWORD, OR PROLOGUE

Scott, Jerie Cobb. Foreword. *Writing Groups: History, Theory, and Implications*. By Ann Ruggles Gere. Carbondale: Southern Illinois UP, 1987. ix-xi. Print.

In-Text Citation: (Scott x-xi)

Rich, Adrienne. Introduction. *On Lies, Secrets, and Silence*. By Rich. New York: Norton, 1979. 9-18. Print.

In-Text Citation: (Rich 12)

3.2.8 A BOOK WITH NO AUTHOR

American Heritage Dictionary. 4th ed. Boston: Houghton, 2000. Print.

In-Text Citation: (*American Heritage Dictionary* 444)

3.2.9 AN ENCYLOPEDIA

"City of Chicago." *Encyclopaedia Britannica*.
1999 ed. Print.

In-Text Citation: ("City of Chicago" 397)

Citing online encyclopedias is a bit different from citing paper ones. Online versions should include the name of the publisher or sponsor of the Web site and the date you accessed the site. It's also common that online encyclopedias lack page numbers.

"Diarrhea." *Columbia Encyclopedia Online*.
Columbia UP, 2008. Web. 10 June 2008.

In-Text Citation: ("Diarrhea")

Wikipedia raises eyebrows among many academics who don't consider it a particularly authoritative source, but should you need to cite it, include the date and time of the latest revision of the page you're citing.

"Social Networking Services." *Wikipedia*.
Wikimedia Foundation, 7 June 2008. Web.
11 June 2008.

In-Text Ciation: ("Social Networking")

3.2.10 A BOOK WITH AN INSTITUTIONAL AUTHOR

Hospital Corporation of America. *Employee Benefits Handbook*. Nashville: HCA, 2004.
Print.

In-Text Citation: (Hospital Corporation of America 5-7)

3.2.11 A BOOK WITH MULTIPLE VOLUMES
Include the number of volumes in the work between the title and publication information.

Baym, Nina, ed. *The Norton Anthology of American Literature*. 6th ed. 2 vols. New York: Norton, 2002. Print.

In-Text Citation: (Baym 2: 3)

If you use one volume of a multivolume work, indicate which one along with the page numbers, adding the total number of volumes in the work as supplementary information.

Anderson, Sherwood. "Mother." *The Norton Anthology of American Literature*. Ed. Nina Baym 6th ed. Vol 2. New York: Norton, 2002. 1115–31. Print. 2 vols.

In-Text Citation: (Anderson 1115)

3.2.12 A BOOK THAT IS NOT A FIRST EDITION
Check the title page to determine whether the book is *not* a first edition (2nd, 3rd, 4th, etc.); if no edition number is mentioned, assume it's the first. Put the edition number right after the title.

Ballenger, Bruce. *The Curious Researcher*. 5th ed. Boston: Longman, 2007. Print.

In-Text Citation: (Ballenger 194)

Citing the edition is necessary only for books that are *not* first editions. This includes revised editions (*Rev. ed.*) and abridged editions (*Abr. ed.*).

3.2.13 A BOOK PUBLISHED BEFORE 1900
For a book this old, it's usually unnecessary to list the publisher.

Hitchcock, Edward. *Religion of Geology*. Glasgow, 1851. Print.

In-Text Citation: (Hitchcock 48)

3.2.14 A TRANSLATION

Montaigne, Michel de. *Essays*. Trans. J. M. Cohen.

Middlesex: Penguin, 1958. Print.

In-Text Citation: (Montaigne 638)

3.2.15 GOVERNMENT DOCUMENTS

Because of the enormous variety of government documents, citing them properly can be a challenge. Since most government documents do not name authors, begin an entry for such a source with the level of government (U.S. Government, State of Illinois, etc., unless it is obvious from the title), followed by the sponsoring agency, the title of the work, and the publication information. Look on the title page to determine the publisher. If it's a federal document, then the *Government Printing Office* (abbreviated *GPO*) is usually the publisher.

United States. Bureau of the Census. *Statistical*

Abstract of the United States. Washington:

GPO, 1990. Print.

In-Text Citation: (United States, Bureau of the

Census 79-83)

3.2.16 A BOOK THAT WAS REPUBLISHED

A fairly common occurrence, particularly in literary study, is to find a book that was republished, sometimes many years after the original publication date. In addition, some books first appear in hard cover and then are republished in paperback. To cite, put the original date of publication immediately after the book's title, and then include the more current publication date, as usual, at the end of the citation. Do it like so:

Ballenger, Bruce, and Barry Lane. *Discovering*

the Writer Within: 40 Days to More

Imaginative Writing. 1989. Shoreham:

Discover Writing P, 2008. Print.

In-Text Citation: (Ballenger and Lane 31)

3.2.17 AN ONLINE BOOK

Citing a book you found online requires more information than the usual citation for a book you can hold in your hands. As usual, include the author's name (if listed), an italicized title, and publication information. What you include in publication information depends on whether the text was published exclusively online or is also based on a print version. If only a digital book, include the date of electronic publication and the group or organization that sponsored it. If the book also appeared on paper, add the usual information (if provided) about the print version (city of publication, publisher, and date). The citation ends, finally, with the medium of publication (*Web*) and the date you accessed the title. For example,

> Badke, William. *Research Strategies: Finding Your*
>
> *Way through the Information Fog.* Lincoln:
>
> Writers Club P, 2000. *iUniverse.* Web.
>
> 12 July 2008.

In-Text Citation: (Badke)

3.3 Citing Periodical Print Publications

Periodicals—magazines, newspapers, journals, and similar publications that appear regularly—are cited similarly to books but sometimes involve different information, such as date, volume, and page numbers. Online articles have their own special requirement (see Section 3.5). The *MLA Handbook* lists the information to include in a periodical citation in the order in which it should appear:

1. Name of the author
2. Article title
3. Periodical title
4. Series number or name
5. Volume number
6. Issue number
7. Date
8. Page numbers
9. Medium of publication (*Print*)

Author's Name.   List the author(s) as you would for a book citation.

Article Title.   Unlike book titles, article titles are usually enclosed in quotation marks.

Periodical Title.   Italicize periodical titles, dropping introductory articles (*Aegis,* not *The Aegis*). If you're citing a newspaper your readers may not be familiar with, include in the title—enclosed in brackets but not underlined—the city in which it was published. For example:

```
MacDonald, Mary. "Local Hiker Freezes to
    Death." Foster's Daily Democrat [Dover, NH]
    28 Jan. 1992: 1. Print.
```

Volume Number.   Most academic journals are numbered as volumes (or occasionally feature series numbers); the volume number should be included in the citation. Popular periodicals sometimes have volume numbers, too, but these are not included in the citations. Indicate the volume number immediately after the journal's name. Omit the tag *vol.* before the number.

Issue Number. Most scholarly journals have issue numbers as well as volume numbers. Include the issue number in your citation if one is given. Cite the volume number, then a period, followed by the issue number, with no space between the period and the issue number. Volume 12, issue 1, would appear in your citation as "12.1."

Date.   When citing popular periodicals, include the day, month, and year of the issue you're citing—in that order—following the periodical name. Academic journals are a little different. Since the issue number indicates when the journal was published within a given year, just indicate that year. Put it in parentheses following the volume number and before the page numbers (see examples following).

Page Numbers.   Include the page numbers of the article at the end of the citation, followed by a period. Just list the pages of the entire article, omitting abbreviations such as *p.* or *pp.* It's common for articles in newspapers and popular magazines *not* to run on consecutive pages. In that case, indicate the page on which the article begins, followed by a "+" (*12+*).

Newspaper pagination can be peculiar. Some papers wed the section (usually a letter) with the page number (*A4*); other papers simply begin numbering anew in each section. Most, however, paginate continuously. See the following sample citations for newspapers for how to deal with these peculiarities.

Online sources, which often have no pagination at all, present special problems. For guidance on how to handle them, see the section "Citing Web Publications" later in this part of the appendix.

Sample Periodical Citations

3.3.1 A MAGAZINE ARTICLE

> Oppenheimer, Todd. "The Computer Delusion."
>   *Atlantic Monthly* July 1997: 47–60.
>   Print.

In-Text Citation: (Oppenheimer 48)

> Zimmer, Marc. "How to Find Students' Inner
>   Geek." *Chronicle of Higher Education*
>   12 Aug. 2005: B5. Print.

In-Text Citation: (Zimmer B5)

3.3.2 A JOURNAL ARTICLE

For articles in scholarly journals, include both the volume and issue numbers (unless there is no issue number).

> Allen, Rebecca E., and J. M. Oliver.
>   "The Effects of Child Maltreatment
>   on Language Development." *Child Abuse
>   and Neglect* 6.2 (1982): 299–305.
>   Print.

In-Text Citation: (Allen and Oliver 299–300)

> Goody, Michelle M., and Andrew S. Levine.
>   "Health-Care Workers and Occupational
>   Exposure to AIDS." *Nursing Management*
>   23.1 (1992): 59–60. Print.

In-Text Citation: (Goody and Levine 59)

Increasingly, researchers turn to online library databases to search for journal articles. A fuller discussion of how to cite articles from academic databases follows in Section 3.5, but here is the basic format: Cite the article as you would a print periodical, then add the title of the database in italics, the medium of publication (*Web*), and the date you accessed the article.

> Boettger, Suzaan. "Global Warnings." *Art in*
> *America* June–July 2008: 154-60. *Academic*
> *OneFile*. Web. 10 June 2008.

In-Text Citation: (Boettger 154)

3.3.3 A NEWSPAPER ARTICLE

Some newspapers have several editions (morning edition, late edition, national edition), and each may contain different articles. If an edition is listed on the masthead, include it in the citation.

> Mendels, Pamela. "Internet Access
> Spreads to More Classrooms." *New York*
> *Times* 1 Dec. 1999, late ed.: C1+.
> Print.

In-Text Citation: (Mendels C1)

Some papers begin numbering pages anew in each section. In that case, include the section number if it's not part of pagination.

> Brooks, James. "Lobsters on the Brink."
> *Portland Press* 29 Nov. 1999, sec. 2: 4.
> Print.

In-Text Citation: (Brooks 4)

Increasingly, full-text newspaper articles are available online using library databases such as Newspaper Source or through the newspapers themselves. Citing newspaper articles from library databases involves adding information about the name of the database in italics (e.g., *Newspaper Source*), the medium of publication (*Web*), and the date you accessed the article.

Here's what the citation would look like:

```
"Lobsterman Hunts for Perfect Bait."
    AP Online 7 July 2002. Newspaper
    Source. Web. 13 July 2008.
```

In-Text Citation: ("Lobsterman")

Here's an example of a citation for an article I found on the newspaper's own Web site:

```
Sterngold, James. "Lessons from '92 Keep
    Angry City Calm." New York Times.
    New York Times, 10 July 2002. Web.
    12 July 2008.
```

In-Text Citation: (Sterngold)

3.3.4 AN ARTICLE WITH NO AUTHOR

```
"The Understanding." New Yorker 2 Dec.
    1991: 34-35. Print.
```

In-Text Citation: ("Understanding" 35)

3.3.5 AN EDITORIAL

```
"Paid Leave for Parents." Editorial.
    New York Times 1 Dec. 1999: 31.
    Print.
```

In-Text Citation: ("Paid Leave" 31)

Opinion articles harvested from online newspapers include date of publication, the name of the site's publisher, medium of publication (*Web*), and the date of access.

```
McGurn, William. "Obama, Religion, and
    the Public Square." Wall Street
```

Journal. Dow Jones, 8 June 2008. Web.
10 June 2008.

In-Text Citation: (McGurn)

3.3.6 A LETTER TO THE EDITOR

Ault, Gary Owen. "A Suspicious Stench."
Letter. *Idaho Statesman* 18 Aug. 2005:
14. Print.

In-Text Citation: (Avlt 14)

3.3.7 A REVIEW

Page, Barbara. Rev. of *Allegories of Cinema:*
American Film in the Sixties, by David
E. James. *College English* 54 (1992):
945-54. Print.

In-Text Citation: (Page 945-46)

3.3.8 AN ABSTRACT

It's usually better to have the full text of an article for research purposes, but sometimes all you can come up with is an abstract, or short summary of the article that highlights its findings or summarizes its argument. Online databases frequently offer abstracts when they don't feature full-text versions of an article.

To cite an abstract, begin with information about the full version, and then include the information about the source from which you got the abstract. If the title of the source fails to make it obvious that what you are citing is an abstract (i.e., it's not called something such as *Psychological Abstracts*), include the word "abstract" after the original publication information, but don't underline it or put it in quotation marks. In this example, the source of the abstract is a periodical database called MasterFILE Premier. In addition, I include the medium of publication (*Web*) and the date I accessed the abstract online.

Edwards, Rob. "Air-raid Warning." *New*
Scientist 14 Aug. 1999: 48-49.

```
Abstract. MasterFILE Premier. Web.

1 May 2009.
```

In-Text Citation: (Edwards)

The following citation is from another useful source of abstracts, the *Dissertation Abstracts International*. In this case, the citation is from the print version of the index.

```
McDonald, James C. "Imitation of Models in the

    History of Rhetoric: Classical, Belletris-

    tic, and Current-Traditional." U of Texas,

    Austin. DAI 48 (1988): 2613A. Print.
```

In-Text Citation: (McDonald 2613A)

3.4 Citing Other Sources

3.4.1 AN INTERVIEW

If you conducted the interview yourself, list your subject's name first, indicate what kind of interview it was (telephone interview, e-mail interview, or personal interview), and provide the date.

```
Hall, Lonny. Personal interview. 1 Mar. 2005.
```

In-Text Citation: (Hall)

Or avoid parenthethical reference altogether by mentioning the subject's name in the text: According to Lonny Hall, . . .

If you're citing an interview done by someone else (perhaps from a book or article) and the title does not indicate that it was an interview, you should, after the subject's name. Always begin the citation with the subject's name.

```
Stegner, Wallace. Interview. Conversations

    with Wallace Stegner. By Richard Eutlain

    and Wallace Stegner. Salt Lake: U of

    Utah P, 1990. Print.
```

In-Text Citation: (Stegner 22)

Or if there are other works by Stegner on the "Works Cited" page:

(Stegner, *Conversations* 22)

As radio and TV interview programs are increasingly archived on the Web, these can be a great source of material for a research essay. In the example below, the interview was on a transcript I ordered from the *Fresh Air* Web site. Note that the national network, National Public Radio, *and* the local affiliate that produced the program, WHYY, are included in the citation along with the air date.

Mairs, Nancy. Interview. *Fresh Air*. Natl. Public

Radio. WHYY, Philadelphia, 7 June 1993.

Web. 15 Apr. 2009.

In-Text Citation: (Mairs)

The following citation is for an interview published on the Web. The second date listed is the date of access.

Messner, Tammy Faye Bakker. Interview. *The Well*

Rounded Interview. Well Rounded Entertain-

ment, Aug. 2000. Web. 14 July 2008.

In-Text Citation: (Messner)

3.4.2 SURVEYS, QUESTIONNAIRES, AND CASE STUDIES

If you conducted the survey or case study, list it under your name and give it an appropriate title.

Ball, Helen. "Internet Survey." Boise State U,

1999. Print.

In-Text Citation: (Ball)

3.4.3 RECORDINGS

Generally, list a recording by the name of the performer and italicize the title. Also include the recording company, catalog number, and year. (If you don't know the year, use the abbreviation *n.d.*) Include the medium (*CD*, *Audiocassette*, *LP*, etc.).

```
Orff, Carl. Carmina Burana. Cond. Seiji Ozawa.

     Boston Symphony. RCA, 6533-2-RG, n.d. CD.
```

In-Text Citation: (Orff)

When citing a single song from a recording, put it in quotation marks:

```
Larkin, Tom. "Emergence." Oceans. Enso, 1997.

     CD.
```

In-Text Citation: (Larkin)

3.4.4 TELEVISION AND RADIO PROGRAMS

List the title of the program (italicized), the station, and the date. If the episode has a title, list that first in quotation marks. You may also want to include the name of the narrator or producer after the title.

```
All Things Considered. Interview with Andre

     Dubus. Natl. Public Radio. WBUR, Boston,

     12 Dec. 1990. Radio.
```

In-Text Citation: (*All Things Considered*)

```
"U.S. to Limit Sales Related to Amphetamine

     Scourge." All Things Considered. Natl.

     Public Radio. WBUR, Boston, 18 Aug. 2005.

     Radio.
```

In-Text Citation: ("U.S. to Limit")

3.4.5 FILMS, VIDEOTAPES, AND DVDS

Begin with the title (italicized), followed by the director, the distributor, and the year. You may also include names of writers, performers, or producers. End with the date and any other specifics about the characteristics of the film or videotape that may be relevant (length and size).

```
Saving Private Ryan. Dir. Steven Spielberg.

     Perf. Tom Hanks, Tom Sizemore, and Matt

     Damon. Paramount, 1998. Videocassette.
```

In-Text Citation: (*Saving*)

You can also list a video or film by the name of a contributor you'd like to emphasize.

Capra, Frank, dir. *It's a Wonderful Life*.

Perf. Jimmy Stewart and Donna Reed. RKO

Pictures, 1946. Film.

In-Text Citation: (Capra)

3.4.6 ARTWORK

List each work by artist. Then cite the title of the work (italicized), the year of its creation, and where it's located (institution and city). If you've reproduced the work from a published source, include that information as well.

Homer, Winslow. *Casting for a Rise*. 1889.

Hirschl and Adler Galleries, New York.

Ultimate Fishing Book. Ed. Lee Eisenberg

and DeCourcy Taylor. Boston: Houghton,

1981. Print.

In-Text Citation: (Homer 113)

3.4.7 AN ADVERTISEMENT

Citing an advertisement in a periodical is straightforward. First list the company behind the ad, then include the word *Advertisement,* followed by publication information.

Volkswagen. Advertisement. *Men's Health*

August 2005: 115. Print.

In-Text Citation: (Volkswagen)

3.4.8 LECTURES AND SPEECHES

List each by the name of the speaker, followed by the title of the address (if any) in quotation marks, the name of the sponsoring organization, the location, and the date. Also indicate what kind of address it was (lecture, speech, etc.).

Naynaha, Siskanna. "Emily Dickinson's Last

Poems." Sigma Tau Delta, Boise, 15 Nov.

1999. Lecture.

Avoid the need for parenthetical citation by mentioning the speaker's name in your text.

3.4.9 PAMPHLETS

Cite a pamphlet as you would a book.

`New Challenges for Wilderness Conservationists.`
    `Washington: Wilderness Society, 1973.`
    `Print.`

In-Text Citation: (`New Challenges`)

3.5 Citing Publications on CD-ROM or DVD-ROM

While the encyclopedia is the most familiar *portable* database on CD-ROM, there are many others, including full-text versions of literary classics, journal article abstracts, indexes, and periodicals. These databases on disk are less common because much of the same information has migrated online, but you will still encounter them. Citation of these materials requires much of the usual information and in the usual order. But it will also include the name of the *vendor,* or company that distributed it (for example, SilverPlatter or UMI-Proquest), and the *date of electronic publication* (or the release date of the disk or tape).

There are two categories of portable databases: (1) those that are issued periodically, like magazines and journals, and (2) those that are not routinely updated, like books. Citing a source in each category requires some slightly different information.

3.5.1 A NONPERIODICAL PUBLICATION ON CD-ROM OR DVD-ROM

This is cited much like a book, with the medium of publication added.

- Author. If no author is given, list the editor or translator, followed by the appropriate abbreviation (*ed., trans.*).
- Publication title (italicized) or title of the portion of the work you're using (if relevant)
- Name of editor, compiler, or translator (if relevant)
- Edition or release or version (if relevant)
- Place of publication
- Name of publisher and date of publication
- Medium of publication (*CD-ROM, DVD-ROM*, etc.)

For example:

> Shakespeare, William. *Romeo and Juliet*. Vers.
>
>   1.5. New York: CMI, 1995. Diskette.

In-Text Citation: (Shakespeare)

> "Psychotherapy." *Microsoft Encarta*. 2005 ed.
>
>   Everett: Microsoft, 2006. CD-ROM.

In-Text Citation: ("Psychotherapy")

3.5.2 MATERIAL FROM A PERIODICALLY PUBLISHED DATABASE ON CD-ROM OR DVD-ROM

Frequently a periodical database is a computer version—or an analogue—of a printed publication. For example, *The New York Times* has a disk version, as does *Dissertation Abstracts*. Both databases refer to articles also published in print; therefore, the citation often includes two dates: the original publication date and the electronic publication date. Note the location of each in the citations below.

> Haden, Catherine Ann. "Talking about the Past
>
>   with Preschool Siblings." *DAI* 56 (1996).
>
>   Emory U, 1995. CD-ROM. *Dissertation*
>
>   *Abstracts Ondisc*. UMI-ProQuest. Mar. 1996.

> Kolata, Gina. "Research Links Writing Style to
>
>   the Risk of Alzheimer's." *New York Times*
>
>   21 Feb. 1996: A1. CD-ROM. *Newspaper*
>
>   *Abstracts*. UMI-ProQuest. 1996.*

In-Text Citation: (Kolata)

Frequently, a periodically issued electronic source doesn't have a printed analogue. In that case, obviously, you can't include publication information about the printed version.

---

*Sometimes information about an electronic source is unavailable. In that case, include what information you have. For example, in this example, I was unable to find the month of publication for the *Newspaper Abstracts* and had to omit that piece of information from the citation.

3.6 Citing Web Publications

So much has changed since I wrote the first edition of *The Curious Researcher* in the early nineties, and I'm not a bit nostalgic. Internet access to academic databases and full-text articles that you can print out at home have made research dramatically more convenient. In addition, Google Scholar has opened up a universe of online information. Academic organizations like the Modern Language Association (MLA), folks who decide the intricacies of citing these online sources, have struggled to keep up with the changes. This edition of *The Curious Researcher* includes the latest citation information as of this writing, but to stay current, always check the latest edition of the *MLA Handbook for Writers of Research Papers* or the *MLA Style Manual*. Multiple copies are usually stashed somewhere in your library's reference room, though you may have to talk to an actual human being to find out where they are.

Electronic-source citations usually include at least two dates: the *date of electronic publication* and the *date of access* (when you visited the site and retrieved the document). There is a good reason for listing both dates: Online documents are changed and updated frequently—when you retrieve the material matters. If the online document you are using originally appeared in print, it might be necessary to include three dates: the print publication date, the online publication date, and your access date.

The most recent MLA style guidelines have streamlined the way sources found on the Web and through online databases are cited. In most cases, you do not need to include a URL or Internet address for your source unless that's the only way a reader would be able to find it.

It's important to remember that you cannot simply copy and paste a URL or bookmark into your list of works cited. Web publications are cited much like print sources are, but you sometimes need to include additional information to tell your readers where and when you accessed an online source.

For a work cited only on the Web, your citation needs to include these elements:

1. The author's name

2. The title of the work

3. The title of the Web site (in italics)

4. The version or edition used (if necessary)

5. The publisher or sponsor of the Web site

6. The date of publication (day, month, year; use *n.d.* if no date is listed)

7. The medium of publication (*Web*)

8. The date you accessed the site (day, month, year)

For example:

> Coates, Ta-Nehisi. "Sensitive Thugs, Y'all All
> Need Hugs." *The Atlantic.com*. Atlantic
> Monthly Group, 5 Feb. 2009. Web. 6 Feb.
> 2009.

Note: If you cannot find a publisher or sponsor listed for the Web site, use *N.p.*

To cite articles you find through an online database, begin by giving the information for the article as you would for a print source (see Section 3.3 above) and then add the following:

1. The title of the database (in italics)

2. The medium of publication (*Web*)

3. The date you accessed the article (day, month, year)

For example:

> Liu, Eric Zhi Feng, and Chun Hung Liu.
> "Developing Evaluative Indicators for
> Educational Computer Games." *British
> Journal of Educational Technology* 40.1

```
            (2009): 174-78. Academic Search Complete.

            Web. 5 Feb. 2009.
```

Note: If no page numbers are listed, use *n. pag.*

Is It Also in Print?   Databases from computer services or networks feature information available in printed form (like a newspaper or magazine) and online, or information available exclusively online. This distinction is important. If the online source has a printed version, include information about it in the citation. For example:

```
    Worth, Robert W. "Sunnis Protest Charter

            as Leaders Struggle to Finalize It."

            New York Times 26 Aug. 2005: A1.

            NYTimes.com. Web. 27 Aug. 2005.
```

In-Text Citation: (Worth)

Note that the first date lists when the print version appeared, the second date when the researcher accessed the document.

Material that appeared online only is somewhat simpler to cite since you'll only need to include information about the electronic version.

```
    Beyea, Suzanne C. "Best Practices of

            Safe Medicine Administration."

            Aorn Journal. Apr. 2005. Web. 26

            Aug. 2005.
```

In-Text Citation: No page or paragraph numbers were used in this document, so simply list the author's last name: (Beyea). Or avoid parenthetical citation altogether by mentioning the name of the source in your essay (for example: "According to Suzanne Beyea, medications are . . . ").

You may be missing citation information on some Internet material—like page numbers and publication dates—that are easy to find in printed texts. Use the information that you have. Keep in mind that the relevant information for a citation varies with the type of electronic source.

Sample Online Citations

3.6.1 AN ARTICLE

Ketcham, Christopher. "They Shoot Buffalo,
    Don't They?" *Harper's Magazine*. Harper's
    Magazine Foundation, June 2008. Web.
    10 June 2008.

In-Text Citation: (Ketcham 72)

"Freeman Trial Delayed over Illness."
    USA Today. Gannett, 26 May 2008. Web.
    26 May 2008.

In-Text Citation: ("Freeman")

Dvorak, John C. "Worst Case Scenarios."
    PC Magazine Online. Ziff Davis Media,
    26 May 2008. Web. 1 June 2008.

In-Text Citation: (Dvorak 2)

3.6.2 AN ARTICLE OR ABSTRACT IN A LIBRARY DATABASE

One of the great boons to researchers in recent years is the publication of full-text versions of articles as part of the online databases available on your campus library's Web pages. Quite a few databases, such as MasterFILE or Newspaper Source, offer this service, and more are adding it every year. Some that don't offer full-text versions of articles offer abstracts, and even these can be useful. Citing articles or abstracts from library databases requires some information beyond what is usually required for citing other online articles. Specifically, you need

- The name of the database (e.g., Newspaper Source)
- The date you accessed the database to get the article

All of this information is pretty easy to come up with. Figure A3 lists the Web addresses of some of the most popular of these providers, along with some of the databases each features. Note in the following example that information on the print version of the article is provided first, and then information about the database and its provider is shown.

Database Provider	Databases	Web Address
Britannica Online	Encyclopaedia Britannica	http://www.britannica.com
EBSCOhost	Academic Search Elite, Academic Search Premier, Business Source Elite, Computer Source, Health Source, MasterFile Elite, MasterFile Premier, Newspaper Source, Nursing and Allied Health Collection, World Magazine Bank	http://www.epnet.com
Gale Group Databases	Contemporary Authors, Biography Index, Expanded Academic ASAP, General Business File ASAP, General Reference Center, Health Reference Center, Info Trac, Literary Index	http://www.infotrac. galegroup.com

FIGURE A3   URLs of Popular Databases
The table lists the Web addresses for most of the major companies that provide databases for libraries. Usually a database has a specific name, such as *Expanded Academic ASAP*, as shown in the second column, and then a service that provides it, a name that you can usually find somewhere on the search page of the database. For Expanded Academic ASAP, for example, it's a provider called *Gale Group*, shown in the first column.

FIGURE A3　(Continued)

LexisNexis	Academic Universe, Government Periodicals Universe, History Universe, Statistical Universe	http://www.lexisnexis.com/
OCLC First Search	Art Index, Book Review, Contemporary Women's Issues, EconLit, Essay and General Literature Index, Reader's Guide Abstracts, Social Science Index, WorldCat	http://newfirstsearch.oclc.org
ProQuest	ABI/INFORM, Academic Research Library, Magazine Index, National Newspapers, Wall Street Journal	http://www.bellhowell.infolearning.om/proquest
SilverPlatter/ Web SPIRS	Agricola, Biological Abstracts, CINHAL, EconLit, Essay and General Literature Index, Philosopher's Index, PsychINFO	http://webspirs.silverplatter.com
Wilson Web	Applied Science and Technology Abstracts, Art Index, Bibliographic Index, Biography Index, Book Review Digest, Education Index, General Science Index, Reader's Guide, Humanities Index, Social Science Index, World Authors	http://hwwilsonweb.com/

Winbush, Raymond A. "Back to the Future:

　　　Campus Racism in the 21st Century."

　　　Black Collegian Oct. 2001: 102–03.

　　　Expanded Academic ASAP. Web.

　　　12 Apr. 2002.

In-Text Citation: (Winbush)

When citing an abstract from a library database, include the word "abstract" in the citation. For example,

> Erskine, Ruth. "Exposing Racism, Exploring
> Race." *Journal of Family Therapy*
> 24 (2002): 282-97. Abstract. *EBSCO*
> *Online Citations*. Web. 3 Dec. 2002.

In-Text Citation: (Erskine)

3.6.3 AN ONLINE BOOK

I can't imagine why anyone would read the *Adventures of Huckleberry Finn* online, but it's available, along with thousands of other books and historical documents in electronic form. If you use an online book, remember to include publication information (if available) about the printed version in the citation.

> Twain, Mark. *Adventures of Huckleberry Finn*.
> New York: Harper, 1912. *Google Book Search*.
> Web. 10 Feb. 2008.

In-Text Citation: (Twain)   Or better yet, since there are no
page numbers, mention the author in the text rather
than citing him parenthetically: In the *Adventures*
of Huckleberry Finn, Twain recreates
southern dialect . . .

When citing part of a larger work, include the title of that smaller part in quotation marks before the title of the work. Also notice that the text cited below is part of an online scholarly project. Include the name of the project, the editor and compiler of the work if listed, and its location.

> Service, Robert. "The Mourners." *Rhymes*
> *of a Red Cross Man*. 1916. Ed. A. Light.
> Aug. 1995. *Project Gutenberg*. Web.
> 1 July 2008.

In-Text Citation: (Service)

3.6.4 A WEB SITE OR PAGE FROM A WEB SITE

If you're citing a Web site, you're referring to either the entire site or a particular page on it. This distinction is important. A citation for an entire Web site includes its name, when it was posted or revised, the sponsoring organization, date of access, and medium of publication. For example,

> *Son of Citation Machine*. Landmark Project, 2009.
>
>   Web. 12 Feb. 2009.

> *In-Text Citation:* (*Son of Citation Machine*)

More commonly, though, you'll be citing a page on a larger Web site, and this must include not just the title of the Web site but the title of the Web *page* from which you're getting information.

> Rogers, Scott. "The Stupid Vote." *The*
>
>   *Conservative Voice*. Salem Web Network,
>
>   7 June 2008. Web. 10 June 2008
>
>   <http://www.theconservativevoice.com/
>
>   article/32556.html>.

> *In-Text Citation:* (Rogers)

3.6.5 AN ONLINE POSTING

An online post can be a contribution to an e-mail discussion group like a listserv, a post to a bulletin board or usenet group, or a WWW forum. The description *Online posting* is included after the title of the message (usually drawn from the subject line). List the date the material was posted, the access date, and the online address as you would for any other online citation.

> Alvoeiro, Jorge. "Neurological Effects of
>
>   Music." Online posting. *sci.psychology.misc*
>
>   *Newsgroup*. 20 June 1996. Web. 10 Aug. 1996.

> *In-Text Citation:* (Alvoeiro)

The following example is from an e-mail discussion group. The address at the end of the citation is from the group's archives, available on the Web. If you don't have an Internet address for the post you want to cite, include the e-mail address of the group's moderator or supervisor.

> Ledgerberg, Joshua. "Re: You Shall Know
>
>   Them." Online posting. 2 May 1997.
>
>   Darwin Discussion Group. Web. 27 May 2008.

In-Text Citation: (Ledgerberg)

3.6.6 AN E-MAIL MESSAGE

> Kriebel, David. "Environmental Address."
>
>   E-mail to the author. 8 June 2008.

In-Text Citation: (Kriebel)

3.6.7 A SOUND CLIP OR PODCAST

> Gonzales, Richard. "Asian American Political
>
>   Strength." Natl. Public Radio. 27 May 2008.
>
>   Web. 12 July 2008.

In-Text Citation: (Gonzales)

> Mondello, Bob. "Charlton Heston, Old-School
>
>   Gentleman, Dies at 84." 8 May 2008.
>
>   Podcast. "NPR Movies." Natl. Public Radio.
>
>   10 April 2008.

In-Text Citation: (Mondello)

3.6.8 AN ONLINE VIDEO

> "Daughter Turns Dad In." Online video clip.
>
>   *CNN.com*. Cable News Network, 4 Apr. 2008.
>
>   Web. 10 Apr. 2008.

In-Text Citation: ("Daughter Turns")

Shimabukuro, Jake. "Ukelele Weeps by
      Jake Shimabukuro." Online video clip.
      YouTube. You Tube, 4 Apr. 2008. Web.
      6 Apr. 2008.

In-Text Citation: (Shimabukuro)

3.6.9 AN INTERVIEW

Boukreev, Anatoli. Interview. *Outside*.
      Mariah Media, 14 Nov. 2007. Web.
      27 May 2008.

In-Text Citation: (Boukreev)

3.6.10 A BLOG ENTRY OR BLOG COMMENT

For a blog entry, include the author's name, title of the entry, the phrase "Weblog entry," name of the blog, sponsoring organization (if any), date of update, your date of access, and the entry's URL.

Dent, Shirley. "Written on the Body: Literary
      Tattoos." Weblog entry. *The Blog: Books*.
      Guardian News and Media, 9 June 2008.
      Web. 10 June 2008.

In-Text Citation: (Dent)

If you want to cite a comment on a blog—and sometimes they're pretty interesting—then include the author's name (or screen name), a title, if there is one, and, if not, the first few words of the post, "[Weblog comment]," and the date it was posted. Then include the information on the blog, which is the subject of the comment.

MargotBlackSheep. "Tattoos Exist in Every
      Culture." Weblog comment. 10 June 2008.

Dent, Shirley. "Written on the Body:

Literary Tattoos." *The Blog: Books*.

Guardian News and Media, 9 June 2008.

Web. 10 June 2008.

In-Text Citation: (MargotBlackSheep)

3.6.11 AN ONLINE IMAGE

Online images often don't give you much to go on. If there is a name of the artist and title of the image, include them. If not, at least describe the image, and include the name of the sponsoring organization or site, and when you downloaded it.

"China Town Engulfed." Online image. 12 May

2008. *BBC News*. BBC, 8 June 2008. Web.

10 June 2008.

Part Four:
Student Essay in MLA Style

Throughout *The Curious Researcher* you've followed Amanda Stewart's progress on her research essay, reading excerpts from her research notebook as she tried many of the exercises in the book. Her investigation of the cultural phenomenon of teeth whitening proves, once again, that there are no boring topics, only bad questions. Teeth whitening, at first blush, hardly seems a subject worthy of academic study. But as you will see in the essay that follows, "In Search of the Great White," Amanda manages to take something as ordinary as the American obsession with white teeth and draws out its larger implications. Are standards of beauty moving targets that we all must chase? And at what cost?

Amanda Stewart

Prof. Ballenger

English 101

20 April 2008

In Search of the Great White

Lately I haven't felt much like
smiling. It's not that I broke up with
my boyfriend or failed a class—it's that
my teeth are dingy brown. As part of the
"great un-whitened masses," I feel self-
conscious every time I go to grin. While
my teeth have been the same color my
entire life, I've never felt bad about
showing them in public before. Until the
1990s, most people's teeth pretty much
looked like mine, but since then they've
steadily been getting whiter. White teeth
are now as important as plucked eyebrows
or brushed hair. In fact, in 2002 Americans increased the amount they had spent
on whitening from the previous year by
90 percent, apparently it isn't just my
imagination— smiles have gone from just
white to fluorescent. Now that it's standard to have a blazing smile, I feel like
a mottled eggshell in a sea of pearly
whites. The tooth-whitening phenomenon
gives insight into broader social phe-
nomena: why do standards for physical
appearance keep changing, and why do we

Stewart 2

rush to stay in style? How does this
change the way we feel about our natural
appearances? The microcosm of tooth
whitening shows the greater sphere of
beauty is about meeting the expectations
around us rather than feeling secure in
our natural appearances.

Despite the recent boom in tooth
whitening, people have been concerned
about the appearance of their teeth for
a while. In the Middle Ages, barbers
began trimming out excess teeth along
with hair, and started cleaning them as
well. They also applied nitric acid to
whiten teeth, though it ate through the
enamel and ushered in rapid tooth decay.
Despite the pain and destruction of
nitric acid, people continued to use it
until Italians discovered the value of
fluoride in the 1800s. Even by then,
white teeth were a status symbol for the
upper class to flaunt. Thankfully, our
tooth whiteners *are* safer. A study by
James W. Curtis, DMD, discovered that
bleaching through carbamide peroxide
actually decreases the amount of plaque
on teeth; but we're still doing it
for beauty reasons rather than health
ones (Nuss 28).

This well-crafted lead starts with the personal—what it is at stake for the writer in exploring the topic—and then moves to the more universal—how the phenomenon raises larger questions that matter to all of us. We want to follow this lead because the writer has given us a reason to.

Stewart 3

In her article "Bright On," Molly
Prior notes that Procter & Gamble and
Colgate-Palmolive revolutionized the
whitening industry by bringing over-the-
counter whiteners to drugstores everywhere
at the turn of the twenty-first century
(39). No longer did people have to pay
high prices for professional whitening—
they could do it themselves, at home, for
a reasonable cost. In the past, a patient
had to eat a bill of $1,000 for a laser
whitening treatment, or $10,000 for a
full set of veneers; now a package of
Crest Whitestrips retails for only
$29.99 (Gideonse). Suddenly, whiter
teeth were available to everyone. While
a shining smile once indicated wealth
and the ability to splurge on cosmetic
dentistry, it became affordable to the
dentally discolored masses eager to emu-
late the lifestyles of the people they
saw in magazines and on television.

Companies didn't create whitening
products to fill a demand created by the
public for whiter teeth. While Hollywood
glitterati did pay high prices for iconic
smiles, most people seemed happy with
functional teeth. However, companies saw
money to be made in creating a whiter norm

*Amanda has
spent the last few
paragraphs pro-
viding back-
ground on her
research question,
and in a key
move, offers a
comment on the
significance of
what she has cov-
ered so far. This
sentence tacks
down the infor-
mation, attaching
it to the writer's
purpose.*

for teeth, so they barraged the airwaves
with advertisements featuring people
complaining about the dullness and imperfection of their teeth. Natural teeth were
denigrated as ugly. Crest and Colgate-
Palmolive wanted to make money, so they
appealed to the American obsession with
beauty to secure a financial reason to
smile. As Jonathan Levine, DDS, notes,
"It's lately seeming much harder to go
broke by overestimating the vanity of the
American public" (Walker). The companies
succeeded in making mouthfuls of money,
netting $450 million dollars, and getting
45 percent of Americans to try some form
of whitening (Prior 42). In effect, they
appealed to our egos to get to our
pocket books.

　　When selling whiter smiles, retailers
typically appeal to our need for approval.
Our mouths are no longer simply havens for
gingivitis and halitosis, but self-esteem
as well. Procter & Gamble's marketing
director, David Dintenfass, says, "Today,
beauty and confidence have a lot to do
with having a white smile. And isn't confidence what beauty is all about?" (Prior
42). Obviously Dintenfass has a desire for
all of us to want whiter teeth; that's his

Stewart 5

paycheck. But notice how he's no longer selling whiter teeth to us. He is selling confidence. The mouth has changed from first being a masticatory portal, to an important aspect of physical appearance, to a status symbol. We are now being judged as people based on the appearance of our teeth. The trend towards making the perfect smile a commodity is more disturbing than other movements to change beauty standards, however, because changing our smiles changes the way we express a basic emotion. We are now modifying the way a feeling is expressed, which can change the way we actually feel. Smiles are now as much about making a statement as displaying a feeling.

This paragraph is a great example of how a writer can surround fact with commentary. Note how Amanda provides a layer of commentary to begin the paragraph, provides a quote, and then adds another layer of commentary teasing out its significance to her project.

Last winter I went out for coffee on a date, and over the course of the evening I started to loosen up and laugh. Halfway through the flirting, I realized I had been flashing my dingy teeth at my date, and I clammed up out of self-consciousness. I was afraid he wouldn't want to be around a girl with such nasty teeth: I felt ugly. After I stopped smiling, though, I felt awkward and uncomfortable. With my lips sealed to my teeth, pantomiming my enjoyment, I felt inhibited and

Stewart 6

confined. In squelching my smile I squashed my joy, and made the evening much less fun than it could have been. In retrospect I shouldn't have cared what a near stranger thought about my teeth, but it's hard to ignore others' perceptions and feel secure that my beauty can be as unique to me as my fingerprints.

Julie Beatty, a mining executive in San Francisco, is much like me in her discomfort with her natural teeth. She epitomizes the type of consumer Procter & Gamble's Dintenfass is marketing directly to—an upper-class woman (Ives). She has spent $12,500 to make-over her smile by straightening, enlarging, and whitening her teeth. She hopes to appear aggressive and masculine with her new smile, because her naturally small and rounded teeth conveyed her to be "easygoing, kind of a pushover," according to Dr. Joe Carrick, president of the American Academy of Cosmetic Dentistry (Gideonse). The fact that changing Julie's teeth changes the way other people treat her—and she feels about herself—is disturbing. Society's increasing shift towards encapsulating a person into certain specific aspects of

Here Amanda uses a case study to anchor her information to a particular person affected by it. By giving the issue a "face" it becomes less abstract.

appearance like their teeth shows both
an over-reliance on looks and an under-
reliance on character.

Propelling people to whiten and
change their teeth is dentist to the
stars Jonathan Levine. He created GoS-
mile, a portable whitening system, after
his wife convinced him people believed
it was a "real lifestyle opportunity"
(Walker). Levine started marketing his
product to the general public not to
just create whiter teeth, but to convey
an image of a whole, healthy lifestyle.
Levine believes that using his product,
and improving one's image helps to
"ameliorate deficiencies in pulchri-
tude," or, more simply, to move a
person higher up the social ladder
(Walker). That explains why 72 percent
of consumers want whiter teeth (Ives).
Collier Strong, an LA makeup artist,
believes "now public awareness has risen
to the point where if you don't have
nice teeth, people look at you and ask
themselves, why not? . . . How primitive!"
(Walker). We are no longer just a
normal-looking people with healthy,
natural teeth—we are backwards Ludites
hanging far behind the times.

Stewart 8

People whitening their teeth aren't having an easy time, either. Sona Balanian, a publicist in LA, spent $500 on getting her teeth whitened at the dentist-run clinic BriteSmile. "I'm embarrassed to admit I spent that much," she says, "but I live in Hollywood and everyone has perfect teeth" (Prior 41). Unfortunately, she will probably run into the same problem that Laurie Hardjowirogo has. Laurie has been using bleaching trays from her dentist once a month for the past five years. "Now my much whiter teeth seem like they're the way they're supposed to be. But I don't know if I have a fair assessment anymore because so many people are doing it. I don't know where the bar is anymore" (Naversen Geraghty 158). She obviously believes cosmetic dentist Clifford Williams, who preaches, "White is not white enough. Everyone wants 'TV teeth'" (Prior 42). There is no way to gauge what is a little too white or too perfect anymore; it's hard to hit the moving target of beauty standards.

It would be hard to make up a quote that drives the writer's point about the standards of beauty being a "moving target" better than this one.

I still don't want to whiten my teeth to follow the trend and step into the trap created by conglomerates and dentists looking only to line their pocketbooks,

Stewart 9

but I'm having a hard time feeling judged
as dirty and poor simply because my teeth
don't sparkle. I wish the standards of
beauty relied more on what was natural and
less on what was being promoted by groups
with vested interests. It's hard to fight
back against social standards, because
it's a battle one must undergo alone. I
can't stop people from judging me by my
teeth, and I can't make others stop using
whitening products. I can, however, become
confident enough in myself and my value as
a person to eschew whatever beauty trends
come down the pipeline, and steel myself
in the fact that my value doesn't change
when standards do. I'm going to look away
from the whitening strips and toothpastes,
and into myself to find my smile.

Stewart 10

Works Cited

Gideonse, Ted. "Move Over, Mona Lisa." *Newsweek*.

Newsweek, 14 Dec. 1998. Web. 20 May 2008.

Ives, Nat. "The Giants of Tooth Whitening See

Spinoff Products Expanding a Fast-growing

Market." *New York Times*. New York Times,

10 May 2008. Web. 23 Apr. 2003.

Naversen Geraghty, Laurel. "Great White Hope."

Prevention 58.6 (2006): 152-60. Print.

Nuss, Ellen. "How Safe Is Tooth Bleaching?"

Dental Assistant 73.3 (2004): 26-29. Print.

Prior, Molly. "Bright on: Americans' Insatiable

Appetite for Whiter-Than-White Teeth Is

Giving Retailers Something to Smile About."

Beauty Biz 1 Sept. 2005: 36-43. Print.

Walker, Rob. "Consumed; Unstained Masses." *New

York Times*. New York Times, 2 May 2004.

Web. 19 Apr. 2008.

"Works Cited" always begins a new page.

Guide to APA Style

The Modern Language Association (MLA) author/page number system for citing borrowed material, described in Appendix A, is the standard for most papers written in the humanities, though some disciplines in the fine arts as well as history and philosophy may still use the footnote system. Confirm with your instructor that the MLA system is the one to use for your paper.

Another popular documentation style is the American Psychological Association (APA) author/date system. APA style is the standard for papers in the social sciences as well as biology, earth science, education, and business. In those disciplines, the currency of the material cited is often important.

I think you'll find APA style easy to use, especially if you've had some practice with MLA. Converting from one style to the other is easy. Basically, the APA author/date style cites the author of the borrowed material and the year it was published. A more complete citation is listed in the "References" (the APA version of MLA's "Works Cited") at the back of the paper. (See the sample APA-style paper in Part Four of this appendix.)

The *Publication Manual of the American Psychological Association** is the authoritative reference on APA style, and the sixth edition, published in 2010, features updates on citing electronic sources, among other things. The APA web site (http://www.apastyle.org/) now includes some helpful tutorials on mastering the citation style.

**Publication Manual of the American Psychological Association,* 6th ed. Washington, DC: APA, 2010.

Directory of APA Style

Checklist before Handing in a Paper in APA Style

- The text and references page of my paper are double-spaced (see pages 322 and 326).
- I have a running head (see page 324) on each page in the upper right-hand corner with a page number.
- The references begin on a new page.
- I've cited page numbers in my paper whenever I've quoted a source.
- I've "blocked" every quotation that is longer than forty words (see pages 325–326).
- Whenever possible, I've mentioned the names of authors I cite in my paper and put the date of the appropriate publication next to their names.
- I've doubled-checked the accuracy of URLs of Web pages or databases that I included in my "References" page.
- My references are organized alphabetically by the authors' last names.
- The first words in article and book titles are capitalized in citations and the remaining words are not capitalized unless they are proper nouns.

Recent APA Style Changes

- There are new suggestions for avoiding gender bias in your writing.
- Hold on to your hats: APA now suggests two spaces, rather than one, when beginning a sentence after a period!
- In the absence of page or paragraph numbers in an online document, include the number of the paragraph by your own count of the specific material you're citing. Include a heading in the citation if the relevant section includes one (e.g. Introduction, para. 5).
- Use serif typeface in text, and san serif in figures, tables, and illustrations.

(continued)

> - If an electronic journal article has a Digital Object Identifier (DOI), cite that instead of the document's URL.
> - With a few exceptions, it's no longer necessary to include the database name in a citation for an article.
>
> *Source*: APA *Publication Manual*, 6th. ed.

Part One: How the Essay Should Look

1.1 The Layout

1.1.1 PAGE FORMAT

Papers should be double-spaced, with at least 1-inch margins on all sides. Times-Roman is the preferred font. Number all pages consecutively, beginning with the title page; put the page number in the upper right-hand corner and the "running head" or abbreviated title of your paper flush left. As a rule, the first line of all paragraphs of text should be indented five spaces.

1.1.2 TITLE PAGE

Unlike a paper in MLA style, an APA-style paper often has a separate title page, containing the following information: the title of the paper, the author, and the author's affiliation (e.g., what university she is from). See Figure B1. At the top of the title page, in upper-case letters, you may also include a *running head*, or an abbreviation of the title (fifty characters or less, including spaces). A page header, which uses the first two or three words of the title followed by the page number, begins on the title page, too. This is different from the running head, which tends to be longer and appears only on the title page. Each line of information should be centered and double-spaced.

1.1.3 ABSTRACT

Though it's not always required, many APA-style papers include a short abstract (often no longer than 120 words) following the title page. See Figure B2. An abstract is essentially a short summary of the paper's contents. This is a key feature, since it's usually the first thing a reader encounters. The abstract should include statements about what problem or question the paper examines and what approach it follows; the abstract should also cite the thesis and significant findings. Type the title "Abstract" at the top of the page. Type the abstract text in a single block, without indenting.

1

Running head: DEPRESSION AND PATTERNS OF

INTERNET USE

A "running head," flush left,
is the abbreviated title that could
be used in a published article.

Depression and Patterns of Internet Use

Among Adolescents

Double-space the title
and set centered on the
upper half of the page.

Christopher Weber

Florida State University

FIGURE B1 **Title Page in APA Style**

An abstract usually follows the title page.
This is a concise (no longer than 120 words)
summary of the article and its thesis,
purpose, or findings.

DEPRESSION AND PATTERNS   2

Abstract

Continue the
page header.

With the growth of the Internet as both a

source of information and entertainment,

researchers have turned their attention to

the psychology of Internet use, particularly

focusing on the emotional states of high

Internet users. This project focuses on the

relationship between patterns of Internet

use and depression in adolescent users,

arguing that

FIGURE B2 **The Abstract Page**

1.1.4 BODY OF THE PAPER

The body of the paper begins with the center title, followed by a double space and then the text. A page number (usually an abbreviated title and "3" if the paper has a title page and abstract) should appear at the top of each page. See Figure B3.

You may find that you want to use headings within your paper. If your paper is fairly formal, some headings might be prescribed, such as "Introduction," "Method," "Results," and "Discussion." Or create your own heads to clarify the organization of your paper.

If you use headings, the APA recommends a hierarchy like this:

Centered, Boldface, UPPERCASE and

Lowercase Heading (Level 1)

Flush Left, Boldface, UPPERCASE and   *Five levels*
                                                          of headings
Lowercase Heading (Level 2)

   Indented, Boldface, lowercase paragraph

   heading ending with a period. (Level 3)

   Indented, boldface, italicized, lowercase

   paragraph heading ending with a period.

   (Level 4)

   Indented, italicized, lowercase paragraph

   heading ending with a period. (Level 5)[1]

A paper, particularly a short one, will rarely use all five levels of headings. In fact, it's much more common for a student paper to use just two or possibly three. For example, a common mix would be Level 1 and Level 3 headings:

The Reactions of Felines to Pictures of Bearded Men

Introduction

Another common combination in student papers would be Levels 1, 3, and 4. Check with your instructor about her preferences.

1.1.5 HANDLING QUOTED MATERIAL

Whenever you borrow words, phrases, or passages from another author they must be contained in quotation marks (". . ."). Usually, this material is smoothly integrated, typically with attribution

---

[1] From Publication Manual of the APA, Sixth Edition, Section 3.03

DEPRESSION AND PATTERNS   3

Depression and Patterns of Internet Use Among

Adolescents

   Before Johnny Beale's family got a new

computer in August 2008, the sixteen-year-old

high school student estimated that he spent

about twenty minutes a day online, mostly

checking his e-mail. Within months, however,

Beale's time at the computer tripled, and he

admitted that he spent most of his time

playing games. At first, his family noticed

Center the title of the paper and double-space to begin the body of the text.

FIGURE B3   The Body of the Paper in APA Style

(*According to Ballenger, . . .*), into your own sentences and para-graphs. But if the quoted material is longer than forty words, then it should be "blocked." Indent the entire quoted passage, and omit the quotation marks. For example,

According to Perfiti's (2003) book on medieval

women and laughter,

> Laughter is both a defense mechanism and a
> weapon of attack, essential to groups strug-
> gling to be taken seriously by the rest of
> society. But it is perhaps women, more than
> any other group, who have had the most com-
> plicated relationship with humor in Western
> culture. People of every religion, national-
> ity, ethnicity, class, and occupation have at
> some time found themselves the butt of an
> offensive joke and told to lighten up because
> "it's just a joke." But it is women who have
> been told that their refusal to laugh at

> jokes made at their expense shows that they
> don't have a sense of humor at all. So a
> woman has to assert her right not to laugh at
> offensive jokes but simultaneously prove that
> she is capable of laughter or risk being seen
> as a humorless spoilsport: a balancing act
> requiring a quick wit. (p. viii)

Notice that when citing a blocked quotation, the parenthetical reference is placed *outside* of the period rather than inside it.

If you omit material from an original source—a common method of using just the relevant information in a sentence or passage—use *ellipsis points* (. . .) to signal where you've left something out.

1.1.6 REFERENCES PAGE

All sources cited in the body of the paper are listed alphabetically by author (or title, if anonymous) on the page titled "References." See Figure B4. This list should begin a new page. Each entry is double-spaced; begin each first line flush left, and indent subsequent lines five to seven spaces. Explanation of how to cite various sources in the references follows (see "Part Three: Preparing the 'References' List").

DEPRESSION AND PATTERNS   10

References

Sanders C., Tiffany, M., & Diego, M. (2000).

    The relationship of Internet use to   *Always start*
the "References"
    depression and social isolation among *on a new page.*

    adolescents. *Adolescence, 35,* 237–242.

Waestlund, E., Norlander, T., & Archer, T.

Create a   (2001). Internet blues revisited:
five-space
"hanging   Replication and extension of an
indent."
    Internet paradox study. *CyberPsychology*

    & Behavior, 4, 385–391.

FIGURE B4   **The References Page**

1.1.7 APPENDIX

This is a seldom-used feature of an APA-style paper, though you might find it helpful for presenting specific or tangential material that isn't central to the discussion in the body of your paper: a detailed description of a device described in the paper, a copy of a blank survey, or the like. Each item should begin on a separate page and be labeled "Appendix" followed by "A," "B," and so on, consecutively, if there is more than one page.

1.1.8 NOTES

Several kinds of notes might be included in a paper. The most common is *content notes*, or brief commentaries by the writer keyed to superscript numbers in the body of the text. These notes are useful for discussion of key points that are relevant but might be distracting if explored in the text of your paper. Present all notes, numbered consecutively, on a page titled "Footnotes." Each note should be double-spaced. Begin each note with the appropriate superscript number, keyed to the text. Indent each first line five to seven spaces; consecutive lines run the full page measure.

1.1.9 TABLES AND FIGURES

The final section of an APA-style paper features tables and figures mentioned in the text. Tables should all be double-spaced. Type a table number at the top of the page, flush left. Number tables "Table 1," "Table 2," and so on, corresponding to the order they are mentioned in the text. A table may also include a title. Each table should begin on a separate page.

Figures (illustrations, graphs, charts, photographs, drawings) are handled similarly to tables. Each should be titled "Figure" and numbered consecutively. Captions may be included, but all should be typed on a separate page, clearly labeled "Figure Captions," and listed in order. For example:

Figure Captions

Figure 1: A photograph taken in the 1930s

by Dorthea Lange.

Figure 2: Edward Weston took a series of green

pepper photographs like this. This is titled

"No. 35."

1.1.10 LANGUAGE AND STYLE

The APA is comfortable with the italics and bold functions of modern word processors, and underlining may soon be a thing of the past. The guidelines for *italicizing* call for its use when writing the following:

- The titles of books, periodicals, and publications that appear on microfilm.
- When using new or specialized terms, but only the first time you use them (e.g., the authors' *paradox study* of Internet users . . .)
- When citing a phrase, letter, or word as an example (e.g., the second *a* in *separate* can be remembered by remembering the word *rat*).

The APA calls for quotation marks around the title of an article or book chapter when mentioned in your essay.

Been nagged all your life by the question of whether to spell out numbers or use numerals in APA style? Here, finally, is the answer: Numbers less than 10 that aren't precise measurements should be spelled out, and numbers 10 or more should be numeric. Feel better now?

Part Two: Citing Sources in Your Essay

2.1 The APA Author/Page System

2.1.1 WHEN THE AUTHOR IS MENTIONED IN THE TEXT

The author/date system is pretty uncomplicated. If you mention the name of the author in text, simply place the year her work was published in parentheses immediately after her name. For example:

```
Herrick (2006) argued that college testing was
biased against minorities.
```

2.1.2 WHEN THE AUTHOR ISN'T MENTIONED IN THE TEXT

If you don't mention the author's name in the text, then include that information parenthetically. For example:

```
A New Hampshire political scientist (Bloom, 2008)
recently studied the state's presidential primary.
```

Note that the author's name and the year of her work are separated by a comma.

2.1.3 WHEN TO CITE PAGE NUMBERS

If the information you're citing came from specific pages (or chapters or sections) of a source, that information may also be included in the parenthetical citation. Including page numbers is essential when quoting a source. For example:

> The first stage of language acquisition is
> called *caretaker speech* (Moskowitz, 1985,
> pp. 50—51), in which children model their
> parents' language.

The same passage might also be cited this way if the authority's name is mentioned in the text:

> Moskowitz (1985) observed that the first stage
> of language acquisition is called *caretaker*
> *speech* (pp. 50-51), in which children model
> their parents' language.

2.1.4 A SINGLE WORK BY TWO OR MORE AUTHORS

When a work has two authors, always mention them both whenever you cite their work in your paper. For example:

> Allen and Oliver (2008) observed many cases of
> child abuse and concluded that maltreatment
> inhibited language development.

If a source has more than two authors but less than six, mention them all the first time you refer to their work. However, any subsequent references can include the surname of the first author followed by the abbreviation *et al*. When citing works with six or more authors, *always* use the first author's surname and *et al*.

2.1.5 A WORK WITH NO AUTHOR

When a work has no author, cite an abbreviated title and the year. Place article or chapter titles in quotation marks, and italicize book titles. For example:

```
The editorial ("Sinking," 2007) concluded that

the EPA was mired in bureaucratic muck.
```

2.1.6 TWO OR MORE WORKS BY THE SAME AUTHOR

Works by the same author are usually distinguished by the date; these would rarely be published in the same year. But if they are, distinguish among works by adding an *a* or *b* immediately following the year in the parenthetical citation. The reference list will also have these suffixes. For example:

```
Douglas's studies (1986a) on the mating habits of

lobsters revealed that the females are dominant.

He also found that the female lobsters have the

uncanny ability to smell a loser (1986b).
```

This citation alerts readers that the information came from two studies by Douglas, both published in 1986.

2.1.7 AN INSTITUTIONAL AUTHOR

When citing a corporation or agency as a source, simply list the year of the study in parentheses if you mention the institution in the text:

```
The Environmental Protection Agency (2007)

issued an alarming report on global warming.
```

If you don't mention the institutional source in the text, spell it out in its entirety, along with the year. In subsequent parenthetical citations, abbreviate the name. For example:

```
A study (Environmental Protection Agency [EPA],

2007) predicted dire consequences from continued

global warming.
```

And later:

```
Continued ozone depletion may
result in widespread skin cancers
(EPA, 2007).
```

2.1.8 MULTIPLE WORKS IN THE SAME PARENTHESES

Occasionally, you'll want to cite several works at once that speak to a topic you're writing about in your essay. Probably the most common instance is when you refer to the findings of several relevant studies, something that is a good idea as you try to establish a context for what has already been said about your research topic. For example,

```
A number of researchers have explored the con-
nection between Internet use and depression
(Sanders, Field, & Diego, 2000; Waestlund,
Norlander, & Archer, 2001).
```

When listing multiple authors within the same parentheses, order them as they appear in the references. Semicolons separate each entry.

2.1.9 INTERVIEWS, E-MAIL, AND LETTERS

Interviews and other personal communications are not listed in the references at the back of the paper, since they are not *recoverable data,* but they are parenthetically cited in the text. Provide the initials and surname of the subject (if not mentioned in the text), the nature of the communication, and the complete date, if possible.

```
In a recent e-mail, Michelle Payne (personal
communication, January 4, 2008)
complained that. . . .
```

2.1.10 NEW EDITIONS OF OLD WORKS

For reprints of older works, include both the year of the original publication and that of the reprint edition (or the translation).

```
Pragmatism as a philosophy sought connection
between scientific study and real people's lives
(James, 1906/1978).
```

2.1.11 A WEB SITE

When referring to an *entire* Web site (see example below), cite the address parenthetically in your essay. Like e-mail, it isn't necessary to include a citation for an entire Web site in your references list.

```
The Google Scholar search engine
(http://scholar.google.com) is very good for
academic research.
```

Part Three: Preparing the "References" List

All parenthetical citations in the body of the paper correspond to a complete listing of sources on the "References" page. The format for this section was described earlier in this appendix (see "References Page").

3.1 Order of Sources

List the references alphabetically by author or by the first key word of the title if there is no author. The only complication may be if you have several articles or books by the same author. If the sources weren't published in the same year, list them in chronological order, the earliest first. If the sources were published in the *same* year, include a lowercase letter to distinguish them. For example:

```
Lane, B. (2007a). Verbal medicine . . .
Lane, B. (2007b). Writing . . .
```

While the alphabetical principle—listing authors according to the alphabetical placement of their last names—works in most cases, there are a few variations you should be aware of.

- If you have several entries by the same author, list them by year of publication, beginning with the earliest.
- Since scholars and writers often collaborate, you may have several references in which an author is listed with several *different* collaborators. List these alphabetically using the second author's last name. For example,

```
Brown, M., Nelson, A. (2002)

Brown, M., Payne, M. (1999)
```

- Sources with the same authors are listed chronologically.

3.2 Order of Information

A reference to a periodical or book in APA style includes this information, in order: author, date of publication, article title, periodical title, and publication information.

Author. List all authors—last name, comma, and then initials. Invert all authors' names. Use commas to separate authors' names; add an *ampersand* (&) before the last author's name. When citing an edited book, list the editor(s) in place of the author, and add the abbreviation Ed. or Eds. in parentheses following the last name. End the list of names with a period.

Date. List the year the work was published, along with the date if it's a magazine or newspaper (see "3.3 Sample References," following), in parentheses, immediately after the last author's name. Add a period after the closing parenthesis.

Article or Book Title. APA style departs from MLA, at least with respect to periodicals. In APA style, only the first word of the article title is capitalized, and it is not underlined or quoted. Book titles, on the other hand, are italicized; capitalize only the first word of the title and any subtitle. End all titles with periods.

Periodical Title and Publication Information. Italicize the complete periodical title; type it using both uppercase and lowercase letters. Add the volume number (if any), also italicized. Separate the title and volume number with a comma (e.g., *Journal of Mass Communication, 10*, 138–150). If each issue of the periodical starts with page 1, then also include the issue number in parentheses immediately after the volume number (see examples following). End the entry with the page numbers of the article. Use the abbreviation *p.* (for one page) or *pp.* (for more than one page), if you are citing a newspaper. Other APA-style abbreviations include:

Chap.	p. (pp.)
Ed. (Eds.)	Vol.
Rev. ed.	No.
2nd ed.	Pt.
Trans.	Suppl.

For books, list the city and state or country of publication (use postal abbreviations) and the name of the publisher; separate the city and publisher with a colon. End the citation with a period. Cities that do not require state or country abbreviations include:

Baltimore	Amsterdam
Boston	Jerusalem
Chicago	London
Los Angeles	Milan
New York	Moscow
Philadelphia	Paris
San Francisco	Rome
	Stockholm
	Tokyo
	Vienna

Remember that the first line of each citation should begin flush left and all subsequent lines should be indented five to seven spaces. Double-space all entries.

3.3 Sample References

3.3.1 A JOURNAL ARTICLE

Cite a print journal article like this:

Blager, F. B. (1979). The effect of intervention on the speech and language of children. *Child Abuse and Neglect*, 5, 91—96.

In-Text Citations: (Blager, 1979)
If the author is mentioned in the text, just parenthetically cite
the year: Blager (1979) stated that . . .
If the author is quoted, include the page number(s):
(Blager, 1979, p. 92)

3.3.2 A JOURNAL ARTICLE NOT PAGINATED CONTINUOUSLY

Most journals begin on page 1 with the first issue of the year
and continue paginating consecutively for subsequent issues. A few
journals, however, start on page 1 with each issue. For these, include
the issue number in parentheses following the volume number:

Williams, J., Post, A. T., & Stunk, F. (1991).

The rhetoric of inequality. *Attwanata*,

12(3),54-67.

First In-Text Citation: (Williams, Post, & Stunk, 1991)
Subsequent citations would use *et al.*: (Williams et al.,
1991)
If quoting material, include the page number(s): (Williams
et al., 1991, pp. 55-60)

3.3.3 A MAGAZINE ARTICLE

Moore, Peter. (2003, August). Your heart will

stop. *Men's Health*. 142-151.

In-Text Citations: (Kelly, 2005)
Kelly (2005) observed that . . .
If quoting, include the page number(s): (Kelly, 2005, p. 58)

3.3.4 A NEWSPAPER ARTICLE

Honan, W. (1991, January 24). The war affects

Broadway. *New York Times*, pp. C15-16.

In-Text Citations: (Honan, 1991)
Honan (1991) argued that . . .

Honan (1991) said that "Broadway is
abattleground" (p. C15).

If there is no author, a common situation with newspaper
articles, alphabetize using the first "significant word" in the article

title. The parenthetical citation would use an abbreviation of the title in quotation marks, then the year.

3.3.5 A BOOK

Barry, J. M. (2004). *The great influenza: The epic story of the deadliest plague in history*. New York, NY: Viking.

In-Text Citations: (Barry, 2004)
According to Barry (2004), . . .
If quoting, include the page number(s).

Burnheim, J. (2006). *Is democracy possible: The alternative to electoral politics.* Retrieved from http://setis.library .usyd.edu.au/democracy/index.html.

In-Text Citation: (Burnheim, 2006)

3.3.6 A BOOK OR ARTICLE WITH MORE THAN ONE AUTHOR

Rosenbaum, A., & O'Leary, D. (1978). Children: The unintended victims of marital violence. *American Journal of Orthopsychiatry, 4,* 692–699.

In-Text Citations: (Rosenbaum & O'Leary, 1978)
Rosenbaum and O'Leary (1978) believed that . . .
If quoting, include the page number(s).

3.3.7 A BOOK OR ARTICLE WITH AN UNKNOWN AUTHOR

New Hampshire loud and clear. (2008, February 19). *The Boston Globe*, p. 22.

In-Text Citations: ("New Hampshire," 2008)
Or mention the source in text: In the article "New Hampshire loud and clear" (2008), . . .

If quoting, provide the page number(s) as well.

A manual of style (14th ed.). (1993). Chicago:
>   University of Chicago Press.

In-Text Citations: (*Manual of Style*, 1993)
According to the *Manual of Style* (1993), . . .
If quoting, include the page number(s).

3.3.8 AN ENCYCLOPEDIA ENTRY

Hansen, T. S. (2003). Depression. In *The New Ency-*
>   *clopaedia Britannica* (Vol. 12, pp.408-412).
>   Chicago: Encyclopaedia Britannica.

In-Text Citations: (*Encyclopaedia Britannica*, 2003)
Or mention the source in the text: *The Encyclopaedia*
Britannica (2003) defines depression as . . .

Diarrhea. (2008). In Columbia encyclopedia
>   [Web]. New York: Columbia. Retrieved June
>   23, 2008, from http://www.encyclopedia.com/
>   doc/1E1-diarrhea.html

In-Text Citation: ("Diarrhea," 2008)
According to the Columbia Encyclopedia (2008),
diarrhea . . .

3.3.9 A DICTIONARY

Mathews, R. H. (2000). *Mathews' Chinese-*
>   *English dictionary.* (19th ed.). Cambridge:
>   Harvard.

In-Text Citation: (Mathews, 2000)
In Mathews's (2000) Chinese dictionary, . . .

Capacious. (n.d.). In Dictionary.com. Retrieved
June 23, 2008, from http://dictionary.reference.
com/browse/capacious.

In-Text Citation: (Dictionary.com,n.d.)
"Capacious," according to *Dictionary.com,* . . .

3.3.10 A BOOK WITH AN INSTITUTIONAL AUTHOR

American Red Cross. (2007). *Advanced first aid*
and emergency care. New York: Doubleday.

In-Text Citation: (*Advanced First Aid*, 2007)
The book *Advanced First Aid and Emergency Care*
(2007) stated that . . .
If quoting, include the page number(s).

3.3.11 A BOOK WITH AN EDITOR

Crane, R. S. (Ed.). (1952). *Critics and criti-*
cism. Chicago: University of Chicago Press.

In-Text Citations: (Crane, 1952)
In his preface, Crane (1952) observed that . . .
If quoting, include the page number(s).

3.3.12 A SELECTION IN A BOOK WITH AN EDITOR

McKeon, R. (1952). Rhetoric in the Middle Ages.
In R. S. Crane (Ed.), *Critics and criticism*
(pp. 260–289). Chicago: University of
Chicago Press.

In-Text Citations: (McKeon, 1952)
McKeon (1952) argued that . . .
If quoting, include the page number(s).

3.3.13 A REPUBLISHED WORK

James, W. (1978). *Pragmatism.* Cambridge,
MA:Harvard University Press. (Original
work published 1907)

In-Text Citations: (James, 1907/1978)
According to William James (1907/1978), . . .
If quoting, include the page number(s).

3.3.14 AN ABSTRACT

The growth of online databases for articles has increased the availability of full-text versions or abstracts of articles. While the full article is almost always best, sometimes an abstract alone contains some useful information. To cite, use the term *Abstract* in brackets following the title and before the period. If the abstract was retrieved from a database or some other secondary source, include information about it. Aside from the name of the source, this information might involve the date, if different from the year of publication of the original article, an abstract number, or a page number. In the following example, the abstract was used from an online database, *Biological Abstracts*.

> Garcia, R. G. (2002). Evolutionary speed of
>
> species invasions. *Evolution*, 56, 661–668.
>
> Abstract retrieved from
>
> *Biological Abstracts*.

In-Text Citations: (Garcia, 2002), *or* Garcia (2002) argues that . . .

3.3.15 A SOURCE MENTIONED BY ANOTHER SOURCE

Frequently, you'll read an article that mentions another article you haven't read. Whenever possible, track down that original article and read it in its entirety. But when that's not possible, you need to make it clear that you know of the article and its findings or arguments indirectly. The APA convention for this is to use the expression *as cited in* parenthetically, followed by the author and date of the indirect source. For example, suppose you want to use some information from Eric Weiser's piece that you read about in Charlotte Jones's book. In your essay, you would write something like:

> Weiser argues (as cited in Jones,
>
> 2002) that . . .

It isn't necessary to include information about the Weiser article in your references. Just cite the indirect source; in this case, that would be the Jones book.

3.3.16 A BOOK REVIEW

> Dentan, R. K. (1989). A new look at the brain
>
>   [Review of the book *The dreaming*
>
>   *brain].Psychiatric Journal, 13*, 51.

In-Text Citations: (Dentan, 1989)
Dentan (1989) argued that . . .
If quoting, include the page number(s).

> Benfey, C. (2008). Why implausibility sells
>
>   [Review of the book *Painter in a savage*
>
>   *land]. Slate.* Retrieved from
>
>   http://www.slate.com/id/2193254/

In-Text Citations: (Benfey, 2008)
Benfey (2008), in a review of the book,
argues that . . .

3.3.17 A GOVERNMENT DOCUMENT

> U.S. Bureau of the Census. (1991). *Statistical*
>
>   *abstract of the United States* (111th ed.).
>
>   Washington, DC: U.S. Government Printing
>
>   Office.

In-Text Citations: (U.S. Bureau, 1991)
According to the U.S. Census Bureau (1991), . . .
If quoting, include the page number(s).

3.3.18 A LETTER TO THE EDITOR

> Hill, A. C. (1992, February 19). A flawed
>
>   history of blacks in Boston [Letter to the
>
>   editor]. *The Boston Globe*, p. 22.

In-Text Citations: (Hill, 1992)
Hill (1992) complained that . . .
If quoting, include page number(s).

3.3.19 A PUBLISHED INTERVIEW

Personal interviews are usually not cited in an APA-style paper, unlike published interviews. Here is what such a citation might look like, however:

> Cotton, P. (1982, April). [Interview with Jake
>
>   Tule, psychic]. *Chronicles Magazine*,
>
>   pp. 24—28.

In-Text Citations: (Cotton, 1982)
Cotton (1982) noted that . . .
If quoting, include the page number(s).

3.3.20 A FILM, VIDEOTAPE, OR ONLINE VIDEO

> Hitchcock, A. (Producer & Director). (1954).
>
>   *Rear window* [Film]. Los Angeles: MGM.

In-Text Citations: (Hitchcock, 1954)
In *Rear Window*, Hitchcock (1954) . . .

> *Slate Online.* (2008). California gay marriage
>
>   rush [Video file]. Video posted to
>
>   http://link.brightcove.com/services/link/
>
>   bcpid988092926/bctid1616709116

In-Text Citations: ("California Gay Marriage," 2008)
Slate's video (2008) on gay marriage . . .

3.3.21 A TELEVISION PROGRAM

> Burns, K. (Executive Producer). (1996). *The West*
>
>   [Television broadcast]. New York and
>
>   Washington, DC: Public Broadcasting Service.

In-Text Citations: (Burns, 1996)
In Ken Burns's (1996) film, . . .

For an episode of a television series, use the scriptwriter as the author, and provide the director's name after the scriptwriter. List the producer's name after the episode.

In-Text Citations: (Duncan, 1996)
In the second episode, Duncan (1996) explores . . .

3.3.22 A MUSICAL RECORDING

Wolf, K. (1986). Muddy roads [Recorded by

    E. Clapton]. *On Gold in California* [CD].

    Santa Monica, CA: Rhino Records. (1990)

In-Text Citations: (Wolf, 1986, track 5)
In Wolf's (1986) song, . . .

3.3.23 A COMPUTER PROGRAM

TLP.EXE (Version 1.0) [Computer software].

    (1991). Hollis, NH: Transparent Language.

In-Text Citations: (TLP.EXE Version 1.0, 1991)
In TLP.EXE Version 1.0 (1991), a pop-up
window . . .

3.4 Citing Electronic Sources

The ever-changing Internet is forcing continual change on professional organizations such as the APA. The sixth edition of the group's *Publication Manual* significantly expanded instructions on how to cite electronic sources, largely reflecting the growth in the variety of documents on the Web. The APA's Web page, www.apastyle.org, includes some excerpted information from the *Publication Manual* and is a good source for any new changes in documentation methods. But much of what you need to know can be found here. The key in any citation is to help readers find the original sources if they want to, and for Web-based documents, that means the Internet address, or URL, has to be accurate. The copy-and-paste function of your word-processing program will be your ally in this.

The essential information when citing an electronic source, in order, includes the following:

- The author(s), if indicated
- The title of the document, Web page, or newsgroup
- A date of publication, update, or retrieval
- The URL or Digital Object Identifier (DOI)

Things change on the Internet—articles appear and disappear, move to different sites or may be updated—and this is a headache for academic researchers. Since one of the purposes of citing something is to help readers find it, the changeability of a document's location is a problem. Recently, some scholarly publishers offered one solution: Give a document a Digital Object Identifier, a code that will forever be associated with the article. Because of the stability of the DOI, APA guidelines now instruct writers to use the DOI, if available, instead of the URL. (That's three sets of initials in a single sentence, some indication of how arcane this can all seem).

3.4.1 AN ELECTRONIC VERSION OF AN ARTICLE ALSO IN PRINT

Because so much scholarly information on the Web is simply an electronic version of an article published in print, some of what you cite will simply list the conventional bibliographic information for any periodical article. But if you only viewed an electronic version, you must indicate that in your citation. For example,

> Codrescu, A. (March, 2002). Curious? Untouchable
>
>   porcelain meets fluttering pigeons
>
>   [Electronic version]. *Smithsonian*, 104.

In-Text Citations: (Codrescu, 2002), *or* Codrescu(2002) believes that . . .

If you suspect that the electronic version of an article that also appeared in print has been changed in any way, then you should include the date you retrieved the article from the Web and the URL of the document. For example,

> Ballenger, B. (1999). Befriending the Internet.
>
>   *The Curious Researcher*, 59–76. Retrieved
>
>   July 18, 2002, from http://english
>
>   .boisestate.edu/bballenger

In-Text Citations: (Ballenger, 1999) *or* Ballenger (1999) features an exercise . . .

3.4.2 AN ARTICLE ONLY ON THE INTERNET

> O'Hehir, A. (2008). Beyond the multiplex.
>
>   *Salon.com*. Retrieved June 23, 2008, from
>
>   http://www.salon.com/ent/movies/btm/

In-Text Citations: (O'Hehir, 2008)
According to O'Hehir (2008), . . .
If quoting, include page numbers, if available.

3.4.3 AN ELECTRONIC TEXT

Encyclopedia Mythica. (1996). Retrieved from

http://www.pantheon.org/myth

In-Text Citations: (*Encyclopedia Mythica*, 1996)
The *Encyclopedia Mythica* (1996) presents . . .

If the text is an electronic version of a book published in print earlier, include the original publication date in parentheses following the title: (Orig. pub. 1908)

3.4.4 AN ARTICLE OR ABSTRACT FROM A LIBRARY DATABASE

As mentioned earlier, library databases, often accessed online, increasingly offer not just citations of articles, but full-text versions or abstracts, too. This wonderful service can make a trip to the library superfluous. The 2010 update to citing electronic sources dropped the requirement that the name of the database needs to be included at the end of the citation if there is a DOI number for the document. For example,

Lizardi, D., Dervic, K., Grunebaum, M. F., Burke,

A. K., Mann, J. J., & Oquendo, M. A. (2008).

The role of moral objections to suicide in

the assessment of suicidal patients.

(Report). *Journal of Psychiatric Research*,

42, 10. p.815(7). doi: http://dx.doi.org/

10.1016/j.jpsychires.2007.09.007

In-Text Citations: (Lizardi, Dervic, Grunebaum,
Burke, Mann, & Oquendo, 2008)

Not all journal articles include a DOI, and therefore your citation should include the URL where the document can be located, or the URL of the journal's home page, if a subscription is required to access the article. A retrieval date isn't necessary since this is the final version of the document.

Kaveshar, J. (2008). Kicking the rock and the
hard place to the curb: An alternative and
integrated approach to suicidal students in
higher education. *Emory Law Journal,*
57(3), 651-693. Retrieved from http://
find.galegroup.com/itx/start.do?prodId=AONE

In-Text Citations: (Kaveshar, 2008) According to
Kaveshar (2008), . . .
Don't forget to include page numbers if quoting.

3.4.5 A PART OF A WORK

Hunter, J. (n.d.). Achilles. In
EncyclopediaMythica. Retrieved from
http://www.pantheon.org/myth/achill

In-Text Citations: (Hunter, n.d.)
According to Hunter (no date), Achilles was . . .
If quoting, include the page or paragraph number(s), if any.

3.4.6 AN ONLINE JOURNAL

Smith, C. G. (2008). Braddock revisited: The fre-
quency and placement of topic sentences in
academic writing. *The Reading Matrix: An*
International Online Journal, 8(1), 78-95.
Retrieved from http://www.readingmatrix.com/

In-Text Citations: (Smith, 2008)
Smith (2008) recently noted that . . .
If quoting, include page or paragraph numbers, if any.

3.4.7 A NEWSPAPER ARTICLE

It's not hard anymore to find articles online from all the major
American and even international newspapers. Like other nonscholarly periodicals, include more specific information about date of
publication in the parenthesis following the author's name, and as
usual, include the date retrieved and the URL.

Broad, J. W. (2002, July 18). Piece by piece a
Civil War battleship is pulled from the
sea. *New York Times*. Retrieved from
http://www.nytimes.com

In-Text Citations: (Broad, 2002) *or* Broad (2002)
reports that . . .

3.4.8 AN ENTIRE WEB PAGE

If you're referring to an entire Web site in the text of your
essay, include the address parenthetically. However, there is no need
to include it in the reference list. For example:

The Google Scholar search engine
(http://scholar.google.com) is considered
good for academic research.

3.4.9 AN ARTICLE ON A WEB SITE

Note that this citation includes the retrieval date since this
article may, at some point, be updated or changed.

Lopez, M. (n.d.). Intellectual development of
toddlers. *National Network for Childcare*.
Retrieved June 30, 2008, from http://
www.nncc.org/Child.Dev/intel.dev.todd.html

In-Text Citations: (Lopez, n.d.)
According to Lopez (n.d.), . . .

3.4.10 AN AUDIO PODCAST

Kermode, M. (2008, June 20). The edge of love.
*Mark Kermode and Simon Mayo's Movie
Reviews*. Podcast retrieved from http://
www.bbc.co.uk/fivelive/entertainment/
kermode.shtml

In-Text Citations: (Kermode, 2008)
In his latest review, Kermode (2008) decried . . .

3.4.11 A BLOG

Shen, H. (2008, June 4). Does your password meet

the test? Message posted to http://

googleblog.blogspot.com/2008/06/does-your-

password-pass-test.html

In-Text Citations: (Shen, 2008)
Our passwords are vulnerable, says Shen (2008),
because . . .

3.4.12 A WIKI

How to use Audacity for podcasting. (n.d.).

Retrieved June 30, 2008, from the Podcast-

ing Team Wiki: https://sites.google.com/

a/biosestate.edu/podcasting-team/Home

In-Text Citations: ("Audacity," n.d.)

3.4.13 DISCUSSION LISTS

Discussion lists abound on the Internet. They range from groups of flirtatious teenagers to those with a serious academic purpose. Though virtually all of these discussion lists are based on e-mail, they do vary a bit. The most useful lists for academic research tend to be e-mail discussion lists called listservs. Newsgroups, or usenet groups, are extremely popular among more general Internet users. There are various search engines that will help you find these discussion groups on your topic. You can join or monitor the current discussion or, in some cases, search the archives for contributions that interest you. Google is a great search tool for newsgroups and includes an archive for many of them. *If there are no archives, don't include the citation in your references since the information isn't recoverable.* However, you may still cite these in your essay as a personal communication (see Part Two, Section 2.9).

The method of citation varies slightly if it's a newsgroup, an online forum, or a listserv. For example,

Hord, J. (2002, July 11). Why do pigeons lift

one wing up in the air? [Msg 5]. Message

posted to rec://pets.birds.pigeons

In-Text Citations: (Hord), *or* Hord asks (2002) . . .

Note that the citation includes the subject line of the message as the title, and the message number of the "thread" (the particular discussion topic). The protocol for this newsgroup is *rec*, which indicates the list is hobby oriented.

Listservs, or electronic mailing lists, would be cited this way:

```
Cook, D. (2002, July 19). Grammar and the teach-

     ing of writing. Message posted to the

     CompTalk electronic mailing list, archived

     at http://listserv.comptalk.boisestate.edu
```

In-Text Citations: (Cook, 2002), *or* According to Cook (2002) . . .

3.4.14 E-MAIL

E-mail is not cited in the list of references. But you should cite e-mail in the text of your essay. It should look like this:

In-Text Citations: Michelle Payne (personal communication, January 4, 2000) believes that PDAs are silly . . .

Part Four: Sample Paper in APA Style

Riffing on a phrase from Tina Turner's song, "What's Love Got to Do with It," Jennifer Suittor concludes, not much, really. In this lively and interesting argumentative essay, Jennifer asserts that the key to a lasting relationship isn't love at all but compatibility. Read her research essay to find out the compatibility factors that might make or break a relationship.

What I like about this informal research essay is not only its appealing conversational style and focused argument. I love the topic and the way in which Jennifer challenges the conventional wisdom about the power of love to keep lovers together. Ultimately, Jennifer's research essay is not only an argument that compatibility factors are far more important than love in sustaining relationship; her paper is also a critique of our culture's delusional ideas about love and how they can get us into trouble.

This brief research essay could easily be expanded into a much longer work. As you read it, imagine that this is an early draft. What exactly would you suggest might be developed more? Where in the draft do you want more information? Can you imagine how Jennifer could have used interviews to great effect in this paper?

WHAT'S LOVE GOT TO DO WITH IT?   1

What's Love Got to Do with It? Compatibility
and Marital Success

Jennifer Suittor

English 102

Professor Marian Thomas

9 December 2005

A running head is an abbreviated title. This will appear, along with page numbers, on every page, including the title page.

WHAT'S LOVE GOT TO DO WITH IT?   2

What's Love Got to Do with It: Compatibil-

ity and Marital Success

"So, why aren't you married?" This is

a question often thrown at me with reck-

less disregard. Sometimes daily. What

people really want to know is "so what the

hell is wrong with you?" That something is

"wrong" is a common assumption of everyone

who encounters a man or woman in their

late 20's or early 30's who isn't married

with 2.4 children. What's the big deal?

Why is it social standard that everyone

must be in a committed relationship by the

time they reach that magical age X?

The truth is the rush to marriage

often has unhappy results. Warren (2003,

quoted in Mulrine) notes that "43 percent

of married couples are not together within

15 years and of those who do stay

together, 4 in 10 say they are not happy

[and] that three-quarters of marriages are

in trouble the day they get started" (p.

56). These are very disturbing statistics

for a society which focuses so much on

whether or not you are in a relationship.

And just what does it all mean? It

means that we don't pay enough attention

to basic compatibilities. Warren (2003)

states,

This is the convention when you use a quote from someone who is not the author of the source you're citing.

By the beginning of the third paragraph, Jennifer states the thesis or central claim of her essay. Notice how the preceding paragraphs build toward her main point.

WHAT'S LOVE GOT TO DO WITH IT?   3

"In this culture, if we like a person's looks, if they have the ability to chatter at a cocktail party, and a little hint of status, we're halfway to marriage. We're such suckers" (p. 24). If superficial things don't make for a successful relationship, what makes two people compatible? How do you ever know you've found that special someone you won't get tired of and toss aside seven (or less) years later? Just what is love and what does it have to do with it?

The very idea that love alone can keep two people together is not only silly and outdated but also dangerously misleading. "Happily ever after love" is implanted into our brains at a very young and impressionable age. We are led to believe that love is a fairy tale from beginning to end, "true love conquers all," and "all you need is love." Our ideas about love are so delusional that many poor souls in unhappy relationships never realize that they probably weren't even compatible in the first place and blame it on the same old, "I'm just not in love with him/her anymore."

If love isn't the cement that holds relationships together, what is? Put simply, it's finding someone with whom we're

WHAT'S LOVE GOT TO DO WITH IT?   4

compatible. Whipple and Whittle (1976) are among researchers who study compatibility, and they argue that a successful relationship depends on acknowledging the importance of compatibility. They state that "a high percentage of divorces could be prevented by compatibility matching, more careful selection of mates, a better understanding of each other, and premarital instruction or study" (p. 6). They add that, "marital success must be based on something more than 'I love him (or her)'" (p. 7).

Whenever you directly quote a source, always include the page number.

  I remember quite vividly a bridal shower I attended a few years ago. The ecstatic bride-to-be was gushing over her new presents and answering questions as they were thrown at her left and right about the ceremony, the colors she had picked out, the shape of her dress, and her honeymoon destination ideas. Then the sister of the groom asked her, "Why do you want to marry my brother?" I do not believe the question was intended to embarrass her, but the bride looked completely stumped, and the silence that followed was so awkward that it visibly made everyone squirm in their chiffon draped seats. Finally, after what seemed

More formal research papers might not include a personal digression like this one. But in this essay, it nicely supports Jennifer's claim that people are deluded by the idea of love.

WHAT'S LOVE GOT TO DO WITH IT?   5

like an eternity, the bride slowly opened
her mouth and said, "Because I love him
and I will love him forever." The last I
heard, their marriage lasted 9 months.

Whipple and Whittle (1976) argue that
certain compatibilities must exist between
two individuals before a healthy relationship (love) can evolve. They are grouped
into three categories. The first is an
overall "goodness of fit." Partners should
share basic ideas about social needs, domi-
nance, intellect, sexuality, and basic
human dynamics. Yet we hear over and over
that opposites attract. Balance is achieved
with the pairing of yin and yang. One seeks
out a specific mate because of a deficiency
that the other fulfills. This is a fallacy,
according to Whipple and Whittle. Opposites
may attract, but are rarely enough to sustain.

The second compatibility factor
uncovers our "dowry" or what we bring
to the table in a relationship. Whipple
and Whittle (1976) argue that, "It is
hard, if not impossible, to walk hand-
in-hand . . . day in and day out if
one does not share the same attitudes,
interests, cultural background, education, and outlook on life" (p. 122).
Indeed, these are fundamental ways of

*The date of
publication is
important
information in
the social
sciences.*

thinking that are formed even before we
meet our future partner.

The key to a lasting relationship,
according to Goleman (1997), author of
Emotional Intelligence, is to "know thyself." There is an old saying that before
you can truly love someone else, you must
love yourself, and realizing who we are
is revealed to us through a series of
epiphanies that blossom with age and
self-discovery. This is something that
occurs partly as we mature as humans and
is partly something we are born with.
Someone with high "emotional intelligence," according to Goleman, has at least
five abilities, including an awareness of
one's own feelings and an ability to handle them as well as recognizing emotions
in others, or empathy. "Social competence
and incompetence" in "handling relationships" is also key (p. 43).

There is much to be said about the
ways that two people's emotional intelligence impact compatibility, and
emotional intelligence remains the major
component of all compatibility "must
have" lists. In fact, emotional intelligence is a dominant factor in determin-
ing if a relationship will last because
it governs how well we communicate with

*These attribu-
tion "tags"—
brief phrases
that identify
the source of a
quote or
idea—are
important con-
ventions in
academic writ-
ing. Use them
regularly.*

WHAT'S LOVE GOT TO DO WITH IT?   7

our partners. Coincidently, if we are
unable to communicate with our partners,
we aren't going to have much to stand on.
"Communication necessitates similar levels
of intelligence" (Whipple & Whittle, 1976,
p. 42). Respected communication expert
Dr. John Gray, the author of *Men Are from
Mars. Women Are from Venus* reiterates the
importance of knowing thyself before
entering into a healthy relationship.
"When the student is ready, the teacher
appears. When the question is asked, the
answer is heard. When we are truly ready
to receive, what we need will become
available" (Gray, 1992, p. 55).

*The APA
italicizes book
titles.*

   Make no mistake, there is no perfect relationship (and never has been)
just like there are no perfect people in
this world. Rough spots and disagree-
ments will always be a very normal piece
of human interaction. The key lies in
knowing how to overcome these and carry
on that is conducive to a lasting relationship. According to Goleman (1997),
"The presence or absence of ways to
repair a rift is a crucial difference
between the fights of couples who
have a healthy marriage and those
of couples who eventually end up
divorcing" (p. 143). Without this

WHAT'S LOVE GOT TO DO WITH IT?   8

compatibility factor-a shared willingness to thoughtfully manage conflict-a
relationship may be doomed, particularly
if the partners persist in believing
that love will somehow ultimately squeak
them through.

There are so many other compatibility
factors that it would be impossible to
mention them all here. Where Whipple &
Whittle (1976) listed three major groups
of compatibility traits, Shedd (1978)
lists ten, and Warren (2003) lists
twenty-nine. Having all or even most of
these compatibility factors are major
indicators of whether or not a relationship will be healthy and successful.

Love by itself is nowhere on any of
these lists of compatibility factors. So,
what does love have to do with anything?
The truth is, not much! At least not initially. Love in the healthy relationship
sense will grow as a result of being two
very compatible individuals. Whipple &
Whittle (1976) conclude that "most marriages
would turn out more satisfactorily if
the contracting parties gave less thought
to love and more to mental and emotional
compatibilities" (p. 256). A slap in the
face to hopeless romantics everywhere
who believe that true love conquers all?

WHAT'S LOVE GOT TO DO WITH IT?   9

Perhaps, but more importantly, it is a testament to the seemingly unattainable and rare healthy relationship with another individual.

Now that we know how we must be matched up with our life partners, just where do we go to find him or her? Hundreds of online matching services are springing up everyday. Do they work? The "scientific matching service" Eharmony.com makes all participants take a lengthy online personality test before one can even start browsing your potential mates. After it has gathered all information, it matches a person up with prospects based upon mutual ideas and compatibility factors. Does it work? That is, again, a different argument altogether. Online dating is not for the faint of heart, and it certainly isn't for everybody, however, Eharmony.com credits over 1,500 marriages since its inception in 2000 (Mulrine, 2003, p. 58). Check with them in seven years.

WHAT'S LOVE GOT TO DO WITH IT?   10

References

Goleman, D. (1997). *Emotional
    intelligence: Why it can matter more
    than IQ.* New York, NY: Bantam 1997.

Gray, J. (1992) *Men are from Mars, Women are
    from Venus: A practical guide for improv-
    ing communication and getting what you
    want from relationships.* New York, NY:
    HarperCollins.

Mulrine, A. (2003, September 29). "Love.com."
    U.S. News and World Report, 52–58.

Shedd, C. (1978). *How to know if you're
    really in love.* Mission, KS: Universal
    Press.

Warren, N.C. (2003). "Why eharmony's
    scientific matching works."
    Retrieved October 23, 2003
    from http://www.eharmony.com/core/
    eharmony?cmd=scientific-matching.

Whipple, C., & Whittle, D. (1976). *The
    compatibility test.* Englewood
    Cliffs, NJ: Prentice Hall.

*The "Refer-
ences" section
always begins
on a new page.*

*With online
sources that
don't include a
DOI, include
not only the
complete URL.
Include the
retrieval date
if the source is
unstable.*

APPENDIX C

Understanding Research Assignments

About fifteen years ago, in a dark, dimly lit basement floor of the University of New Hampshire library, I discovered the textbook that may have had the very first research paper assignment for undergraduates. Charles Baldwin's 1906 *A College Manual of Rhetoric* encouraged students to write essays based on reading that emphasized "originally" compiling facts so that the writer gives "already known" information his or her "own grouping and interpretation." In an article that year, Baldwin noted that "from the beginning a student should learn that his use of the library will be a very practical measure of his culture."

In the century since then, the college research paper is probably the most common genre of student writing in the university. It is a fixture in composition classes and many other courses that require a "term paper." Naturally, this is why there are books like *The Curious Researcher*—to help students understand these assignments and give them guidance in the process of writing them. As you know, a major thrust of this book is the research *essay* rather than the formal research paper. My argument is that this more exploratory, possibly less formal, researched piece is the best way to introduce you to the spirit of inquiry that drives most academic research. The habits of mind that come from essaying, along with the research and writing skills that accompany them, should help you whenever you're asked to write a paper that involves research.

There's another skill that's invaluable when you encounter a research paper assignment in another class: Knowing how to interpret what exactly you're being asked to do. This involves reading your writing assignment rhetorically. In other words, analyze the *situation* for each assignment: How does it fit into other writing projects in the course? What particular purpose does this assignment have? What do you know about the instructor's particular attitudes about research and about writing? How do you figure out the best approaches to the research project? Apparently, students' struggle to do this well is a huge problem. In one study, for example, 92 percent of students said that the most frustrating part of doing research was figuring out what their professor wanted.*

Instructors aren't trying to be obtuse. They want you to understand the assignment, and most have made an effort to be clear. While there's not much you can do about *how* the assignment is conceived or described, you can be savvier at analyzing the assignment's purpose and guidelines.

I've recently conducted a review of research paper assignments from courses across the disciplines, and actually there are striking similarities between them. I tried to read them as a student would, actively looking for guidance about how to approach the assignment and also alert to subtleties that students might miss.

Analyzing the Purpose of the Assignment

One of the things I hear most often from my students who have research assignments in other classes is that the instructor "doesn't want my opinion in the paper." Frankly, I'm often skeptical of this. College writing assignments typically are about what or how you think. But because research papers involve considerable time collecting and considering the ideas of others, it's easy to assume that you're supposed to be a bystander.

Actually, even some instructors seem to equate the term "research paper" with merely reporting information. "This is not a research paper," said one assignment. "The idea here is not to pack in as much information as you can, but instead to present a thoughtful and clearly written analysis." Another noted that "although this is a research paper, the focus is fundamentally on your own analysis and interpretation. . . ."

What these instructors are at pains to point out is that, contrary to what you might think, they are actively interested in what you think. They want students to *do* something with the information they collect. But merely having an opinion isn't enough. As one assignment put it, "You are not being graded on your opinion, but your ability to communicate and support a point of view (your thesis)."

*Alison Head, "Beyond Google: How Do Students Conduct Academic Research?" *First Monday* 12.8 (2007). 30 March 2008 <http://www.firstmonday.org/issues/issue12_8/head/>.

However, the ability to write a convincing paper still begs the question of the larger purposes of the assignment. The assignments I reviewed sometimes talk about encouraging "critical thinking" or helping students enter "a scholarly conversation." A few talk about "advancing your knowledge" about a topic or learning the conventions of research writing in a particular discipline. But many, unfortunately, don't talk about a purpose for the assignment at all. Instead, these frequently focus on the method of inquiry, and most often it is the requirement that your paper make an argument.

Argumentative Research: Open or Closed?

The language that research assignments use to emphasize argument is quite often very explicit: "You are to write a research paper on a subject related to Southeast Asia. *Make an argument* about the overall significance of your topic to some aspect of life in Southeast Asia." Not much ambiguity there. Similarly, some assignments ask that you "take a position" on a topic. Argumentative research papers are most often organized around a thesis, and some assignment descriptions go to great lengths to explain what makes a strong one (usually sufficiently narrow, addressing a significant question, and explicitly stated).

What may not be obvious, however, is how much latitude you have in letting your research revise your thesis or even dramatically change your initial point of view. Most often, instructors *expect* the research to change your thinking, and they often use the term "working thesis" to describe your initial position. These are the more open-ended assignments that might specify that the crafting of a final thesis can occur late rather than early in the research process. These are also assignments that emphasize a focus on a *research question* much like we've discussed in this book.

More rarely, an assignment will imply a closed approach: First identify a thesis and then seek evidence from your research that will support it. This is the conventional thesis-support model in which the expectation is that you will use your thesis, and not your research question, to dictate not just the structure of your paper but the goal of your research. These kinds of assignments tend to not mention that a thesis might be revised and are silent on how it arises from a research question or problem.

Always ask your instructor about whether your reading of the assignment as more closed-ended is accurate. The key questions are these:

- Where should the thesis in this assignment come from?
- What process do you suggest for arriving at it?
- Finally, might it be revised—even substantially—later in the process?

In a more open-ended research paper, the inquiry-based methods of *The Curious Researcher* directly apply. For example, crafting a researchable question is an important route to coming up with a strong working thesis, and the dialogue or double-entry journal can help you think through how your research might develop or revise that thesis. The strict thesis-example paper seems to have little opportunity for inquiry. Indeed, the emphasis in these assignments is frequently on the formal qualities of the paper—how well it's organized around a thesis, the proper use of citations, and mechanical correctness. Developing an outline at the front end of the project is usually helpful. However, there's no reason that after developing working knowledge of your topic you can't use exercises like "Reclaiming Your Topic" (Exercise 4.2) in Chapter 4, or "Dissecting the Fish" (Exercise 5.2) in Chapter 5 to help you come up with a strong thesis, especially since that's such an important part of a thesis-example paper.

Audience

For whom are you writing? So much hinges on the answer to this question: the tone of the paper, how specialized its language might be, the emphasis you give on providing background on the research question, and the degree to which you stress reader interest. Despite the importance of audience, research paper assignments frequently fail to mention it at all. This omission can often mean one thing: You are writing for your instructor. It actually might surprise you how often this isn't the case. If your assignment includes peer review of drafts or class presentations, then you may be writing for a more generalized audience. Sometimes this is explicit: "Your paper should be understood by a broader audience than scholars in your field. You will have to explain concepts and not expect your audience to understand in-housing jargon." If the audience for your paper isn't clear, ask your instructor this simple question:

■ Who is the audience for this assignment—readers like the instructor who are knowledgeable about the topic or readers who are not?

Emphasis on Formal Qualities

An essay like Amanda Stewart's "In Search of the Great White" in Appendix A of this book is relatively informal: It's casual in tone, has a strong individual voice, and is structured to explore a question—*to find out* rather than *to prove*. It certainly has a thesis, but it is a delayed thesis, appearing not in the introduction but toward the end of the essay. The writer's questions are the organizing principles of the essay rather than the exercise of making a point and logically providing evidence to support it. It does, however, have some formal qualities, including careful citation and attribution, the marshalling of appropriate evidence to explore the topic, and a sensible organization that moves from question to answers.

Research paper assignments in other classes are likely to put considerably more emphasis on a structure based on logic and reasoning. Put another way, these papers, unlike an essay such as Amanda's, report the *products* of the process of researching the question rather than follow the thinking that led to them. The chief product, of course, is your thesis—the thing you are trying to say—and typically you're expected to place this in the introduction of your paper. Fairly often research paper assignments instruct you to state your thesis or position explicity in a sentence. In keeping with the approach of this book, assignments often ask that you develop a research question from which the thesis emerges. As one put it, "[The] introduction should make three points: It should briefly introduce your question and its significance, state your answer, and orient the reader regarding your way of proceeding. This is the place to say, 'I'm going to argue. . . .'"

Also pay close attention to what context the assignment asks you to establish for your research question—course discussion, literature review, or both. Some instructors are keen on having you write a paper that somehow extends the course's readings or discussion points. Others want you to become familiar with the scholarly conversation that might extend beyond the class. Here's a question to ask about this:

- What is the more important context for establishing the significance of my research question or thesis—what we talked about in class or what I discover when I review the relevant literature?

The logical structure of an argumentative research paper doesn't vary much (see the discussion about this in Chapter 4), although in some disciplines you will be instructed to use the organizational conventions of the field; for example, scientific papers might require an abstract, introduction, methods, results, discussion, and conclusion, in that order. Generally, the body of your paper must draw on evidence from your research to support your thesis, though frequently your assignment requires that you also consider opposing points of view. How are they misguided? In what ways do they fail to address your research question? Also pay attention to whether your assignment asks you to tightly tether each paragraph to the thesis using topic sentences that address how that paragraph supports it.* Outlining the topic sentences before you draft your essay can help you with this.

Since one of the aims of teaching research writing is to help you understand its conventions, assignments almost always discuss the need for proper citation, correct format, a required number of scholarly sources, attention to grammar and mechanics, and so on. You need to determine the relative importance of this. Some research paper assignments, for example, devote much more ink to describing the required format—location of page numbers, font, margins—and the need for "perfect" grammar than they do a discussion of the research process, formulating a thesis, or the larger goals of the assignment. In this case, you might give these conventions more attention. If you're not sure about this, ask this question:

- When you evaluate the paper, what is the relative importance of getting the format right? Do you give that concern as much weight as the quality of your thesis or the soundness of your thinking?

As you know, *The Curious Researcher* encourages essays in which writers have a strong presence. The easiest way to do this is to enter the text directly by using the first person, though in an

---

*Some teachers heavily stress the use of topic sentences in paragraph writing, though there is considerable evidence that much writing, including academic prose, doesn't consistently feature topic sentences.

earlier chapter we explored other ways to do this. Research paper assignments rarely mention whether you can use "I." Silence on this question usually means that you should not. One of the conventions of much academic writing is a more formal register, the sense that the paper speaks rather than the writer. Yet a considerable number of the assignments I reviewed encouraged students to write with "voice" and lively, vigorous prose. The most effective way to inject voice into your research writing is to find your own way of saying things, something that "writing in the middle"—the note taking strategies encouraged in this book—should help you with. Assignments that say nothing about voice or style probably expect what one assignment described as writing that is "formal in tone, working to establish an authoritative, critical and analytical voice." If you're unsure about this, consider asking your instructor the following question:

- Should the voice in my paper mimic the scholarly sources I'm reading, or can it be somewhat less formal, perhaps sounding a bit more like me?

Types of Evidence: Primary or Secondary

You might remember a figure earlier in *The Curious Researcher* that illustrates how some of the key elements of a paper—tone, structure, and writerly presence—shift as the audience becomes more scholarly. One of the most important of these elements is the type of evidence. In popular writing—say, articles in *Wired* or *Discover* or op-ed pieces in the newspaper—the types of evidence that writers use to convince readers are quite varied. Personal experience and observation, for instance, are often excellent ways to support a point. But as you begin writing research papers in academic disciplines, you need to pay attention to what your instructor considers *appropriate* evidence in that field and for that particular assignment. Scientific papers, for example, often rely on experimental data. Literature papers lean most heavily on evidence culled from the literary text you're writing about. Papers in anthropology might rely on field observations.

Sometimes assignments explicitly talk about appropriate evidence for your paper. More often they do not. Generally speaking, research papers that are assigned in lower-division courses won't require you to conduct experiments or generate field notes. They will likely ask you to draw evidence from already published, or secondary sources, on your topic. But this isn't always the case. A history paper, for example, might require that you study a primary text, perhaps letters by historical figures, political documents, or archived newspapers. This is something you need to know. If the types of evidence you should use in your paper aren't clear, ask this question:

- What types of evidence should I rely on for this paper? Primary or secondary sources? And is personal experience and observation, if relevant, appropriate to use?

In the spirit of writing a conventional conclusion, let me restate what might be apparent by now: The most important thing you must do when you get a research assignment is read the handout carefully, considering what you've already learned in the class about writing in that discipline. I read a lot of research paper assignments, and they usually provide very good guidance. But if they don't, that's never an excuse for floundering. Ask, ask, ask. Your instructor wants you to.

Index